LOUIS ARMSTRONG

LOUIS ARMSTRONG

The Life, Music and Screen Career

Scott Allen Nollen

McFarland & Company, Inc., Publishers
Jefferson, North Carolina, and London

ALSO BY SCOTT ALLEN NOLLEN AND FROM MCFARLAND: *Paul Robeson: Film Pioneer* (2010); *Abbott and Costello on the Home Front: A Critical Study of the Wartime Films* (2009); *Warners Wiseguys: All 112 Films That Robinson, Cagney and Bogart Made for the Studio* (2008); *Jethro Tull: A History of the Band, 1968–2001* (2002); *Robin Hood: A Cinematic History of the English Outlaw and His Scottish Counterparts* (1999; paperback 2008); *Sir Arthur Conan Doyle at the Cinema: A Critical Study of the Film Adaptations* (1996; paperback 2005); *Robert Louis Stevenson: Life, Literature and the Silver Screen* (1994); *Boris Karloff: A Critical Account of His Screen, Stage, Radio, Television and Recording Work* (1991; paperback 2008); *The Boys: The Cinematic World of Laurel and Hardy* (1989; paperback 2001)

Frontispiece: Louis Armstrong displaying his trumpet.

The present work is a reprint of the illustrated case bound edition of Louis Armstrong : The Life, Music, and Screen Career, *first published in 2004 by McFarland.*

LIBRARY OF CONGRESS CATALOGUING-IN-PUBLICATION DATA

Nollen, Scott Allen.
Louis Armstrong : the life, music, and screen career /
Scott Allen Nollen.
p.   cm.
Includes discography (p.   ), filmography (p.   ),
bibliographical references (p.   ), and index.

ISBN 978-0-7864-4918-7
softcover : 50# alkaline paper ∞

1. Armstrong, Louis, 1901–1971.
2. Jazz musicians— United States— Biography. I. Title.
ML419.A75N65   2010   781.65'092 — dc22   2004009589

British Library cataloguing data are available

Cover image ©2010 Comstock

Manufactured in the United States of America

McFarland & Company, Inc., Publishers
Box 611, Jefferson, North Carolina 28640
www.mcfarlandpub.com

For

every cat and chick who digs Pops:
I hope this book brings you a fraction of the joy
that Louis Armstrong gives me every time I *dig* him

In memory of my heroes

Louis Armstrong,
Lillian Hardin Armstrong, Count Basie,
Barney Bigard, Clifford Brown, Sidney Catlett
Nat Cole, Johnny Dodds, Roy Eldridge
Duke Ellington, Ella Fitzgerald, W. C. Handy
Coleman Hawkins, Earl Hines, Johnny Hodges
Billie Holiday, Mahalia Jackson, Billy Kyle
Thelonious Monk, Arvell Shaw, Bessie Smith
Billy Strayhorn, Fats Waller, Ethel Waters
Ben Webster, Lester Young, Trummy Young

Contents

Preface:
The Most Righteous Cat

I'm not looking for to be on no high pedestal. I'm just appreciating what I'm doing, you know. Yeah, I'm happy. Doing the right thing, playing for the highest people to the lowest. That's the way it's supposed to be. And I don't expect nothing but applause. That's all that's necessary. 'Cause I got my life. They got their categories.... I listen to the other fellow ... but they don't move me to want to be like them or play like them. I don't listen to all them different styles as far as trying to prove anything.... Just don't impress me. I think all I can do is play the way I feel.
— Louis Armstrong[1]

While we were vacationing on Mobile Bay, a family friend asked how I choose my literary subjects.

"I don't," I told her. "*They* choose me. I need three components: passion, significance, and a nearly insurmountable challenge. That's all."

I mentioned that I might "retire" for a while. Later, as I walked from the beach house into the humid Alabama air, I considered writing *one more* book. A few days earlier, I had been in New Orleans, where Louis Armstrong made his first sound — which I assume resembled scat.

How many dilettantes believe Elvis Presley revolutionized music? Yes, 1956 was a point of revolution, when Elvis' "Negro music" shocked the American public, rolling a rock that has yet to stop.

Well, "Satchmo"—the most significant musician of the 20th century—ignited the *original* revolution, proliferating a force that would shape all future music, including "the King's" rock 'n' roll. Louis was supremely *bad* more than a decade before Elvis even opened his eyes in Mississippi.

I am not a "Louis Armstrong scholar" nor a "Louis Armstrong historian." As Pops himself might call me, I *am* a "half fast" musician. I'm definitely a Louis Armstrong *fan*. To me, he's the *most righteous cat*.

As Columbia University professor Robert O'Meally pointed out, writing about

1

Armstrong presents a double danger. Don't get hagiographical about Pops, but don't underestimate him either.[2] O'Meally has written a most eloquent description of the man: "Louis Armstrong is always above us, maintaining a celestial relationship of heat and illumination or moving the tides and sending down the snow ... he is the sky of modern American music at its most original. No matter where you turn, there he is."[3]

My birth just prefaced the era of assassination. The day after I arrived, Dr. Martin Luther King, Jr., began a crucial civil rights demonstration in Birmingham, Alabama. Two months later, Medgar Evars, leader of the Mississippi NAACP, was shot — in the back — and killed in Jackson. I was seven months old when JFK was assassinated, quickly followed by Malcolm X, King and Robert Kennedy, all of them connected to the civil rights movement. One of my most vivid recollections is of Dr. King, gunned down on the balcony of the Lorraine Motel in Memphis two days after my fifth birthday.

Before I started to play jazz, I knew that Louis Armstrong was special. I had no technical grasp of how great, profoundly innovative and wonderfully human he was, but I had instantly *felt* it in the music flowing from my parents' console stereo.

For years I had no idea what was so appealing about the music I loved, but it was only the most profound feeling in the world — *soul*. And that spirit came from ethnically-based music, regardless of genre — "Beyond category," in the words of Duke Ellington. I experienced it most in Celtic, European and Indian folk music, and, profoundly, in African American jazz and blues.

My parents loved New Orleans, and Louis Armstrong was part of it. That's how I was introduced to him. They enjoyed good music and wanted me to play it in some form. I learned to play the drums, but I really learned to swing just a few years ago — by listening to Louis Armstrong.

At 16, I spent a day with the great Louis Bellson, who, among other jazz triumphs (including being cool enough to marry Pearl Bailey and driving the bands of Benny Goodman, Tommy Dorsey, Harry James and Duke Ellington), played drums on the magnificent 1957 Verve albums *Louis Armstrong Meets Oscar Peterson* and *Ella and Louis Again*, Satchmo's second, superlative collaboration with Ms. Fitzgerald and the Peterson trio.

While studying African American history as a graduate student, I was part of a hip group of aspiring historians who hung out at a local café. There were a half dozen of us, so it was a cozy, friendly bunch. One of the cats actually marched with Dr. King in Chicago, so he obviously was the coolest. On one memorable afternoon, my companions all had been served, while I sat, increasingly impatient, sipping a glass of water.

After 15 minutes passed, I asked what had become of my minestrone soup. The waitress returned with a piping hot bowl and dumped the pungent contents into my lap!

Dead silence reigned in the restaurant, until my friend Paul proudly announced, "Well, whitey got his soup!"

"Ignored *and* abused," another cat remarked. Following more colorful comments from around the table, I was dubbed "the Honorary Negro."

Many years later, after reading "Mezz" Mezzrow's excellent book *Really the Blues*, I realized I was a latter-day Mezz, though I've never played the clarinet nor sold marijuana! But I share the deep love of African American expression in general, and Louis Armstrong in particular, that this "ofay" Chicago jazzman always dug. My companions and I often talked about jazz, and whenever Armstrong was mentioned, it was always with affection and a positive vibe. None of us considered him in the negative light that became prevalent during the 1960s.

During the summer of 1988 I had the privilege of spending an evening with actor Ernest Morrison, who achieved fame as "Sunshine Sammy" in the early 1920s. While chugging from St. Paul down the Mississippi on a riverboat (like the ones favored by Armstrong while little Ernie was making his first Hollywood films), he and I discussed what it was like for African Americans during the early days of film. Like Armstrong, Ernie was born in New Orleans, and, though saddled with stereotypes, was a pioneer who opened doors for black performers who followed in his wake.

Ernie's father worked for the Hollywood-connected family of child star Baby Marie Osbourne; and after the three-year-old Ernie filled in for another infant actor who failed his test as a "real black child" in *The Soul of a Child* (1916), he appeared alongside silent greats Harold Lloyd and Snub Pollard. In 1921 he became the first African American actor offered a Hollywood contract (by the legendary Hal Roach, who placed Ernie in his own "Sunshine Sammy" series and the first of the "Our Gang" shorts). "At first, Roach didn't know what to do with me," Ernie said.[4] He was the first black child star.

Sure, he was expected to adhere to a rigid cinematic category born of bigotry. But when I asked him how he felt about it, he answered, "I did the very best I could with the opportunities I was given."[5] A diminutive man, he also did his best in vaudeville, in Europe during World War II, while touring with George Burns, Gracie Allen and Jack Benny, and in the aircraft industry for 30 years. Ernie passed away one year after our meeting, but his recollections continued to have a major influence on me, especially his admiration for a hometown cat called Satchmo.

Though the Armstrong idea had been brewing for a while, I made the decision while visiting the National Civil Rights Museum, formerly the Lorraine Motel, in Memphis. As I stood next to Dr. King's former room and the balcony where he was shot—just a few feet from where he fell dead—I thought of many things, including Armstrong and the myths about him that needed to be addressed.

Armstrong was not only a virtuoso musician, singer, composer and actor, but also a dedicated writer who typed hundreds of letters and reminiscences, carrying a typewriter with him on his constant travels around the globe. The man never stopped creating, and constantly communicated with friends and acquaintances. When quoting his letters and autobiographical writings, I have done very little "tidying up," instead retaining the creative spellings of words and odd punctuation choices he used for effect—a form of improvisation not unlike his singing, playing and jive talk.

Everything Pops did was jazz. *He was jazz*—so I've tried to invest these pages with that personality, and how his unique verbal, musical and visual content and style permeated everything he touched. Included are the major events of his life, his artistic innovations and cultural achievements, a detailed survey of his recordings and live performances, and in-depth discussions of his screen performances—not only his Hollywood feature film appearances, but his performances in short films, European concert films, and dozens of television shows broadcast from Hollywood, New York and Europe.

Pops was a dependable presence on the small screen from its inception until his death more than two decades later. Television often gave him a larger, and less racist, spotlight than the movies. From 1937, his screen activities were supported by the Negro Actors Guild of America, of which he was a vice president.

An author could spend a lifetime writing about what Louis Armstrong *did* and have no inkling of his significance until he or she really *digs* his music. After all, in the words of Robert O'Meally, Louis was "the Prometheus who stole the molten fire of improvised soloing from the gods and delivered it to the mortals."[6]

I would like to thank the Schomburg Center for Research in Black Culture, a branch of the New York Public Library, located on Malcolm X Boulevard (formerly Lenox Avenue) in Harlem. During a day of research into the records of the Negro

The lucky author at Birdland with trumpeter extraordinaire Clark Terry, a good friend of Armstrong's and a session player on several Satchmo sides, including the "What a Wonderful World" session and the *Disney Songs the Satchmo Way* album, New York City, April 2003.

Actors Guild, I was assisted by very helpful professionals. It was a pleasure perusing these materials in the environment where Armstrong, Ellington and so many other heroes used to swing.

A special thanks is due the staff of the Louis Armstrong House and Archives at Queens College, the City University of New York. Director Michael Cogswell, curator Peggy Alexander and registrar Baltsar Beckeld provided terrific information and access to Pops' letters, manuscripts, contracts, scrapbooks, photographs, and audio tapes that he recorded and carefully preserved in his personal collection. Fortunately, CUNY's Center of the Humanities presented a conference, "Writing Lives: The Past and Future of Biography," while I was in New York. Charles Darwin, Sappho and Satchmo were the three figures discussed during the conference; the highlight for me being the Armstrong material, including presentations by Robert O'Meally and Gary Giddins, one of my jazz-literature influences and a true pleasure to witness at work. It was also a major kick sitting next to David Ostwald, Armstrong aficionado and leader of the Gully Low Jazz Band.

Another major thank you goes to Dave Brubeck and his wife, Iola, for chatting about working with Armstrong on the concept album *The Real Ambassadors* and the subsequent live performance at the 1962 Monterey Jazz Festival. Two great talents and terrific human beings, the Brubecks have consistently produced significant jazz projects. The indefatigable 83-year-old composer chatted about their current ambitious project with the Baltimore Symphony, *The Gates of Justice*, a tribute to Martin Luther King and the prophet Isaiah. Hearing him warmly recite Louis' closing lines from *The Real Ambassadors* is an experience I'll never forget.

The following individuals also contributed to this book: J. B. Dyas, Executive Director of the Brubeck Institute at the University of the Pacific in Stockton, California; Thomas Fortunato and Diane Kelley, my superb hosts in Washington, D.C.; Susan Gordon, the little girl who sang with Pops in *The Five Pennies*; Chuck Granata, for encouraging comments; John ("Jimmy Said") Jensen, for his computer expertise, home theater (and ofay rap); George Moore, Dave Brubeck's assistant; Harold and Shirley Nollen, my parents; Dr. Oscar Peterson, one of the all-time great jazz pianists; Lauren, Reese and Ellen Porter, for a great New York meal in great New Jersey company; Douglas Siegal, my singular friend in New York; Clark Terry, trumpeter extraordinaire, Louis' friend, and a session player on several Satchmo sides; Valerie Yaros, historian at the Screen Actors Guild in Los Angeles; and all the truly cool cats and chicks I've met over time and space — especially Matthew Johnson, Rudy Pearson and Paul Young, wherever you are!

Most of all, my undying gratitude goes to the Daddy of 'Em All, who gave this world Louis Armstrong for an all-too-brief 69 years. I wouldn't want to imagine what this place would be like without Pops.

Scott Allen Nollen

Introduction:
You've Got to *Dig* Pops

*Before black ballplayers and political activists became household names,
musicians were the only blacks able to attract white America's attention,
and Satchmo was the first to make it big. He was the first black man to
be featured in Hollywood movies made for white audiences, as well as
the first to serve as host on a sponsored network radio show. The power
of his genius, combined with his loving manner, forced whites to rethink
their racism, whether they knew it or not.*

— David H. Ostwald[1]

Louis Armstrong. Louis. Little Louis. Louie. Our Louie. Laughin' Louie. King
Louie I. King of Jazz. Sun King of Jazz. Satchmo. Satch. Satchelmouth. Ambassador
Satch. Satchmo the Great. Reverend Satchelmouth. The Reverend Elder Eatmore.
Gatemouth. Gate. Gabriel. Slow Foot. Boat Nose. Hammock Face. Rhythm Jaws.
Face. Sacraface. Ol' Sackreface. Dippermouth. Dipper. Dip. Papa Dip. Poppa Satch.
Daddy. Pops.

There are as many different Louis Armstrongs as there are names for him. And
then there are the vocations and achievements: heavenly musician; revolutionary
vocalist; prolific composer; prodigious autobiographer; creator of jive talk; irre-
pressible humorist; America's Ambassador; motion picture and television actor.

A controversial figure since the 1930s, he has been perceived in three basic ways.
To the public at large, he is the unique, irreplaceable, beloved entertainer Lou*ie*
"Satchmo" Armstrong, always pleasing his audience, blasting out incomparable
trumpet solos, swinging lyrics and scat with his warm voice of gravel, smiling from
ear to ear and wiping away the sweat and saliva with a white handkerchief.

To the sophisticated, scholarly "intelligentsia," he has been the subject of myr-
iad debates: a towering musical pioneer, a genius who perhaps sacrificed his art to
become something less, an *entertainer* who pandered to the masses; or perhaps not,
actually always an artist whose later playing became richer and more personal, particularly in the face of new revolutions such as bebop.

To some African Americans during the 1960s, Armstrong was a "sell-out." Was he an "Uncle Tom" who turned away from the great revolutionary musical form of jazz to become a servant to the creations of mainstream white America — Tin Pan Alley popular music and Hollywood cinema?

Armstrong never thought of himself as an "Uncle Tom," an "artist" or a "genius." He knew he had pioneered a new style of playing and singing. He realized how influential he had been — how he had affected untold musicians and all forms of American music that followed in the wake of his cascading, high register, melodic majesty.

Had Armstrong remained focused only on "pure jazz," he still would have been one of the most important musicians in American history, but he never would have reached out to, and brought countless hours of pleasure to, millions of people world-wide. That achievement was made possible by his infectious stage persona during grueling tours across the globe, his hundreds of popular recordings with many different musical aggregations, and his appearances in nearly 40 feature films, shorts and documentaries, and dozens of television programs.

Armstrong *loved* being an entertainer. Regardless of the social circumstances surrounding a job, he used his multifaceted talent to rise above the material he was saddled with — whether dictated by contemporary realities of economics, popular tastes and trends, social attitudes or bald-faced bigotry.

In the fields of music, broadcasting, cinema, and even international relations, Armstrong was able to use the power of his artistry and his personality — which were inseparable — to open doors that few, if any, African American performers had been able to walk through. Many people of later generations, black and white, who first viewed him as an "Uncle Tom" embracing tenets of minstrelsy, came to realize that what he actually did was, while surrounded by the effects of many decades of racial inequality, work within that system to prove that strides could be made by standing above it all — by creating positive outcomes from whatever opportunities came his way, and by swinging in the face of forces designed to keep him "in his place."

He was the living embodiment of the notes he played and sang. He *was* music — and music, particularly jazz, at its best is true democracy in action. With his music, acting and attitude, Armstrong brought legions of people together all over the world. To be sure, he was well aware of the divisions and divisiveness that exist everywhere, but did he project bitterness over it and therefore propagate it? No. He attempted to — and, more importantly, did — transcend it.

Blues music is the sound of surviving slavery. The blues are among the most profound expressions of spirituality ever developed by the human race. More than any other individual, Louis Armstrong was responsible for synthesizing and trans-porting the blues from the Mississippi Delta to the streets of Chicago, New York and beyond, unleashing a creative force that proliferated and transformed every form of American music: jazz, big band, pop-jazz, bluegrass, country, rhythm-and-blues, soul, rock 'n' roll, fusion, rap, even orchestral. The African American cultural influence is immeasurable, perhaps infinite — with Armstrong at the summit as the nation's equivalent of Bach or Beethoven.

Actor Ossie Davis said that the power of Armstrong's trumpet could *kill*; but, of course, Louis only really did that in the musical sense. However, when the going got truly tough, so did he. From its inception in 1937, he was a member, and then vice president, of the Negro Actors Guild of America. In 1957, after bayonets were flashed in the faces of little African American schoolchildren in Little Rock, he stood up to segregationist Arkansas governor Orval Faubus and president Dwight D. Eisenhower, and cancelled a State Department–sponsored tour of the Soviet Union. And he stood alone. Many whites criticized him — and so did a number of blacks, including Sammy Davis, Jr.

Nearly 30 years earlier, on July 19 and 22,

Louis Armstrong

1929, Armstrong had recorded versions of "Fats" Waller, Andy Razaf and Harry Brooks' "(What Did I Do to Be So) Black and Blue?" originally a song about a dark-skinned African American woman who loses her man to a lighter-skinned woman. When Pops performed the number, he transformed it into a poignant portrait of a man persecuted by racism.

Gary Giddins wrote:

> He is the only major figure in Western culture who influenced the music of his time equally as an instrumentalist and singer. His popularity enabled him to shatter countless racial obstacles, while his manner undermined Europhile assumptions about the way an artist was supposed to present himself. He advocated and perfected purity of tone and obeisance to melody; patented the rhythmic gait known as swing; transformed a polyphonic folk music into a soloist's art; established the expressive weight of blues tonality; proved the durability of harmonic improvisation. But he also relished the tradition of humor that had grown out of the black archetype in minstrel shows that had become a mainstay of black entertainment throughout the first two decades of his life.[2]

When Pops dug deep into some gut-bucket blues, he still produced a joyous sound. And whether on the silver screen or the small, mired in trappings often corny and sometimes appalling, he left a visual and aural impression that has the power to delight us today. Although the powers-that-were tried to depict him as a stereotypical black character, he was no shuffling, dimwitted do-little like the characters played by Lincoln Perry ("Stepin Fetchit") and Willie Best ("Sleep 'n' Eat"). He had something else in mind.

Nonetheless, African American historian Donald Bogle referred to Armstrong as an "important Fetchit imitator."[3] On the contrary, one viewing of *any* of Pops' cinematic scenes proves that his performance style had almost nothing in common with that of Fetchit, who moved and spoke so slowly that he often seemed near death's door.

Bogle ranks Louis with the performer he calls "the greatest coon of all time"; yet, in his introduction, noting the scarcity of previous histories of blacks in the cinema, Bogle wrote:

> For me, it was not enough to dismiss Hattie McDaniel and Butterfly McQueen as mere mammy and pickaninny. Anyone who had seen *Gone with the Wind* and left the theater with no more than that impression really missed or ignored the strength of the performances, and at the same time denied black America a certain cultural heritage…. From my point of view, the history of blacks in American films is one in which actors have elevated *kitsch* or trash and brought to it arty qualities, if not pure art itself…. [M]any black actors—from Stepin Fetchit to Louise Beavers to Sidney Poitier to Jim Brown and Whoopi Goldberg—have played—at some time or another—stereotyped roles. But the essence of black history is not to be found in the stereotyped role but in what certain talented actors have done with the stereotype.[4]

Bogle defines a "coon" as a black buffoon, and a "tom" as a kind, submissive black. Though he refers to Louis as a "musician par excellence," he also claims that, in performances devoid of his music, "here was a coon and a tom all rolled into one." Bogle accuses him of "often [selling] himself down the river," and calls his style "high-flung mugging madness."[5] In his section on Stepin Fetchit, he lists the "coon" qualities as being "lazy, no-account, good-for-nothing, forever-in-hot water [and] natural-born comedian."[6] These traits certainly apply to the characters played by Fetchit, Best, Mantan Moreland and other black actors of the period, but only the last one *really* applies to Armstrong. Bogle's book is an important and often spot-on interpretation of its subject; but, in "evaluating" Armstrong, does he offer the same consideration he gives to McDaniel and McQueen?

Referring to Bogle in his 1996 essay "Actor and Musician: Louis Armstrong and His Films," Krin Gabbard notes, "These kinds of judgments tell us more about the critics than they do about Armstrong himself."[7] In subsequent chapters, Bogle convincingly points out how lauded actors Sidney Poitier, Ossie Davis and Roscoe Lee Browne were 1950s and '60s updated versions of the classic "tom" and why later stars such as Richard Pryor and Eddie Murphy harked back to the "old-style coon." One of Bogle's most perceptive statements, referring to Poitier, can also be applied to Armstrong: "In the early days, Poitier no more molded his image than did Stepin Fetchit; he lived out Hollywood's fantasies of the American black man."[8]

Perhaps the most far-fetched analysis of Armstrong, neglecting the reality of an era prior to the modern civil rights movement, is that of jazz historian Rudi Blesh, who wrote:

> Had Armstrong understood his responsibility as clearly as he perceived his own growing artistic power — had his individual genius been deeply integrated with that of the music, and thus ultimately with the destiny of his race — designated leadership would have been just.... Around Louis clustered growing public cognizance of hot music and those commercial forces, equally strong and more persistent, which utilize the musical communications system of the phonograph record, the then new radio and talking motion picture, and the printed sheets of Tin Pan Alley tunesmiths. And behind this new symbolic figure was aligned the overwhelming and immemorial need of his own race to find a Moses to lead it out of Egypt.[9]

Here the critic believes that Louis Armstrong — a black musician who hit the American scene during the 1920s — somehow had the "responsibility" to be a modern-day Moses.

To play off the Exodus metaphor, and without exaggerating — Louis *was* a musical Moses, a visionary who led his followers away from the confines of written arrangements (artistic "bondage") toward improvisation (the spiritual plane of individual, creative expression, or *soul*). This African American prophet, definitely possessing a preternatural gift, freed the soul of the musician, but also taught him how to use that freedom for the common good, the jazz ensemble. He was responsible for innovating a rare example of true democracy.

Armstrong didn't care to act like a prophet. He didn't have to *act* like anything. Everything he did flowed from the same natural source — his spiritual gift. How could a man who loved to perform for audiences, to make them happy with his amazing musical ability, assume the persona of a civil rights activist, particularly in an era when such a thing was almost unheard of? Without inciting turmoil and martyring himself, Louis Armstrong became a true revolutionary while living an immensely productive, useful and joyful life.

It has been said that a true revolutionary isn't the obvious one, out in streets rousing the rabble, but rather subtly working within the system peacefully to initiate change. Louis Armstrong accomplished this feat time and again, sometimes when he played the trumpet, but more often with his verbal innovations as a singer and an actor. While performing Tin Pan Alley standards, or even earlier minstrel-show standbys, he would sing the original lyric, but subtly, naturally slip in distinctly African American innovations, namely scat and jive — a "Yeah, man," a "Dig it, Daddy" or a "Swing it, Gate" — delivered with that wondrous *rhythm* that only he possessed. Regardless of the material — whether innovative jazz or mediocre pop — the end result was the same: pure Louis Armstrong.

And Armstrong brought that same transforming quality to his screen characterizations. Placed in their proper historical context, and alongside the performances of his black contemporaries, his film and television roles can be viewed for what they really are.

In his 1979 autobiography, *To Be or Not to Bop*, Dizzy Gillespie wrote:

> If anybody asked me about a certain public image of him, handkerchief over his head, grinning in the face of white racism, I never hesitated to say I didn't like it. I didn't want the white man to expect me to allow the same things Louis did. Hell, I had my own way of "Tomming."... Later on I began to recognize what I had considered Pops' grinning in the face of racism as his absolute refusal to let anything, even anger about racism, steal the joy from his life and erase his fantastic smile. Coming from a younger generation, I misjudged him.[10]

Other Armstrong detractors have blamed his high-power manager, Joe Glaser, for his continual acceptance of demeaning cinematic roles. Yet, through Glaser, Louis never turned down paying work that gained him wider exposure.

Like Dizzy Gillespie, Duke Ellington was an acquaintance of Armstrong's. In his 1973 autobiography *Music Is My Mistress*, Ellington wrote (in a realistic and common-sense manner) about the Armstrong-Glaser relationship:

> [I]n spite of how well Joe Glaser did for himself, Louis still ended up a very rich man.... This is not a fact to be ignored, for what more can one man do for another: Joe Glaser watched over Louis like the treasure he was, and saw to it that his partner was well fixed for the rest of his life.
>
> Louis Armstrong was the epitome of jazz and always will be. He was also a living monument to the magnificent career of Joe Glaser.... Joe paid the sidemen in Louis' band the kind of money musicians would like to be making today. And Joe had his own personal physician travel with Louis all over the world.... So you see Joe used money generously to protect his partner, and Louis was more partner than most people expect.
>
> I loved and respected Louis Armstrong. He was born poor, died rich, and never hurt anyone on the way.[11]

Arguably the greatest composer in American history, Ellington consistently transcended the stereotypes of his day in an elegant manner born of his upbringing and education in Washington, D.C., an environment quite different than the one in which Louis Armstrong was raised. Knowing better than anyone else the musician's lifestyle that Louis led, who was more qualified to "judge" the merits of the man?

While many different interpretations of Louis Armstrong's legacy will remain, all interested parties can agree on one fact beyond his stature as the individual who changed popular music forever: the often confounding complexity of his artistry. Simplistic labels rarely do justice to anyone, and are particularly useless—not to mention destructive—when leveled at the sometimes unexplainable phenomenon known as "Satchmo."

1

Big Easy to Big Apple

A creative musician is an anarchist with a horn, and you can't put any shackles on him. Written music is like handcuffs; and so is the pendulum in white-tie-and-tails up on the conductor's stand. Symphony means slavery in any jazzman's dictionary. Jazz and freedom are synonyms.
— Milton ("Mezz") Mezzrow[1]

"My whole life has been happiness," Louis Armstrong said. The grandson of slaves, he was born into an environment of poverty, unstable parenting, prostitution and violence known as "the Battleground," yet outwardly took it in stride. By using his unique combination of gifts as artist and entertainer, he rose above it all to become a recognized musical genius, movie star and globetrotting ambassador — a staggering achievement. Against formidable odds, he transformed the family from slavery to celebrity in only two generations.

In 1875, Tennessee had enacted the first segregationist "Jim Crow" law, inducing other Southern states to follow suit. Ten years later, most states had separate schools for whites and blacks, and wrote new constitutions supporting a strict color line. In 1896, just five years before Louis was born in New Orleans, the U.S. Supreme Court, ruling on the *Plessy vs. Ferguson* case, set a precedent by upholding a Louisiana statute legalizing "separate but equal" railroad carriages. Soon after, this segregationist practice affected every kind of public arena on a statewide, then national, basis.

Following the Civil War, freed slaves had settled in a poor area of New Orleans called "Back o' Town," which was shunned by lighter-skinned Creoles, many of whom had been free prior to the conflict and now saw their rights disappear in the wake of Jim Crow. Louis' grandparents were Back o' Towners, and it was at 723 Jane Alley that the little "nigger, illegitimus" was born to Mary Ann ("Mayann") Armstrong on August 4, 1901. (Louis claimed he was born on July 4, 1900, which made a stunning story.) Shortly after his birth, his father, William ("Willie") Armstrong, separated from Mayann.

Mayann was forced to leave Louis with her mother, Josephine, while she hit the streets, searching for work. She may have resorted to prostitution while living in a shanty on the corner of Liberty and Perdido streets, the rock bottom of town. She would have been operating in conditions far worse than in Storyville, the city's red-light district.

Louis' father had moved in with another woman, and occasionally the boy would stay with Willie's brother, Isaac ("Uncle Ike"), where he usually fended for himself. He recalled, "I did not see my father again until I had grown to a pretty good size, and I did not see Mayann for a long time either."[2] He dearly loved his grandmother, who "spent the best of her days raising me, and teaching me right from wrong."[3]

Josephine worked as a domestic for whites and imparted a strong work ethic to the boy. When she thought he had erred in his ways, she'd make him fetch a switch from a Chinaball tree for a furious whipping. She described slave life, taught him about voodoo, and took him to Baptist and Catholic churches, where he developed his vocal abilities while singing in choirs. He also accompanied her to work, where he had his first experiences with white children (trying to fool them at hide-and-seek).

When Louis was five, a family friend took him back to Mayann, who had tried to reconcile with Willie, but now was ill and unable to care for his little sister, Beatrice ("Mama Lucy"). Louis was heartbroken over having to leave his beloved grandmother, and had a startling experience on the way to Mayann's shack when he unknowingly sat in the "whites only" seats on the Tulane Avenue Trolley. Thinking the protestations of a white passenger were a joke, he remained seated until he was manhandled to the back of the car. "It was my first experience with Jim Crow," he later wrote.[4]

When Mayann recovered, Louis shared the one-room dwelling with several relatives. Willie was living nearby at 611 South Roman Street with his wife, Gertrude, and young son, Willie, Jr. Louis felt bitter about the man who abandoned him, but conditions improved when Mayann took a domestic job with a nice white family, and he again was happy to play with other children.

A carry-over from the days of slavery when blacks were forced to eat spoiled food, Mayann's obsession with "physic," or purging the body of toxins, was strongly instilled in Louis and Mama Lucy. Armstrong wrote, "We both gave May Ann our word that we will stay Purge minded for the rest of our lives. May Ann would take a *purge* right along with the rest of us, every night before going to bed."[5] Until the end of his life, Louis kept his promise.

He also learned a lot more about slavery, a subject he bitterly addressed in a 1970 memoir:

> May Ann and Uncle Ike had a little touch of Slavery. Because their relatives right before them came up right in it. They said the Slaves, Acted *Dumb* and Ignorant, kept Malice and Hate among themselves so the Whites took Advantage of it…. They would make plans among themselves and *one* Negro would cross them by sneaking back and tell the white man everything they had planned to do. Quite naturally that would make him the Head Nigger. At least for the time being anyway…. *Slavery* was just like anything else. B. S…. *Dirty* White Folks … got full of their *Mint Julep* or that *bad* whisky, the poor white Trash were Guzzling down, like water, then when they get so *Damn* Drunk until they'd go out of their minds—then it's Nigger Hunting time. *Any* Nigger.
>
> They wouldn't give up until they would find one. From then on, Lord have

mercy on the poor *Darkie*. Then they would Torture the poor Darkie, as innocent as he may be. They would get their usual Ignorant *Chess Cat* laughs before they would shoot him down — like a Dog. *My my my*, those were the days.[6]

Other than his beloved red beans and rice, the music that permeated New Orleans was the joy of Louis' life, and he could remember the sights and sounds of Mardi Gras from the age of five. He and his friends would risk a head whipping from "Captain Joe" to fetch oil lamps from freight sheds on Calliope Street, hoping to earn tips while lighting the way for nighttime revelers.

The brass-band music blown by uniformed black and Creole musicians for local funerals — a West African custom — fascinated him. He enjoyed marching alongside the drummer Henry Zeno during processions to the cemetery. Finally, there were the endless tunes pouring from the Battlefield honky-tonks, where the musicians, on Saturday nights, would venture into the streets to lure in dancers. Since 1899, the music had been called "ragtime" because of its irregular rhythms.

Louis knew about the legendary cornetist Buddy Bolden, whose powerful, high-register playing, people swore, could be heard over the span of a mile. While the "Uptown" black folks listened to the Bolden Band, the more sophisticated Creoles "Downtown" appreciated the suave John Robichaux Orchestra, though some of them liked Buddy, too. Sometimes both outfits had a musical battle, allowing the audience to choose the winner.

Though Louis never saw Bolden, he may have heard his music flowing from a honky-tonk. Unfortunately, the cornetist had mental problems (possibly bipolar disorder, complicated by syphilis), went berserk during the 1906 Labor Day parade, and was institutionalized the following year. He remained confined for 24 years, until his death in 1931.

One of Louis' concerns was contributing to the meager family finances. For a time he peddled the New Orleans *Item* in the streets and to streetcar passengers, and buckets of red-brick dust to prostitutes, who ritualistically dumped it on the sidewalks in front of their cribs. Finally, at age seven, he was able to land a decent job with the Karnofskys, a Lithuanian family of junk dealers who had a profound influence on his personal development. In particular, the positive reinforcement he received from the family — the first he experienced from whites — gave him a lifelong appreciation for the Jewish faith.

Louis got his first chance to play an instrument while riding on the Karnofsky junk wagon, tooting on an old tin horn "as a call for old rags, bones, bottles or anything that the people and the kids had to sell."[7] In the evenings, whenever they would arrive home late, Louis would enjoy a Jewish meal, especially matzos, which he continued to eat all his life. He also recalled singing with the family, particularly "Russian Lullaby,"

> when mother Karnoffsky would have her little baby boy in her arms, rocking him to sleep. We all sang together until the little baby would doze off.
> The Jewish people have such wonderful souls. I always enjoyed everything they sang…. Of course I sang the lullaby song with the family. I did not go through every song they sang. But I was a good listener.[8]

His blowing on the tin horn inspired him to consider a real instrument: a dirty, five-dollar cornet he spied in a pawn shop window. When the Karnofskys loaned him money against his future salary, he managed to save 50 cents a week. After buying the old horn, he shined it constantly, until "it was ... pretty to me."[9]

In 1912, Louis' work responsibilities forced him to drop out of the Fisk School. At 11, he enjoyed school, but had been attending irregularly, often going with little sleep after working for the Karnofskys at night. One of his additional money-raising efforts was busking near Maylie's Restaurant on Poydras Street. He sang tenor in a quartet with three other young dropouts, often adding a bit of Terpsichore to his performance. When the boys began performing on a regular basis, often wandering through the streets passing a hat, they were noticed by trumpeter Bunk Johnson, who, along with Buddy Bolden, had been one of the first New Orleanians to play jazz during the mid–1890s. Johnson mentioned the quartet to clarinetist Sidney Bechet, then 17 but already a remarkable and innovative musician. Bechet enjoyed the boys' harmonies and asked them to dinner at his home, but later was disappointed that Louis, after accepting 50 cents to get his shoes repaired, failed to show up.

On New Year's Eve that year, Louis carried off a celebratory prank that quickly brought his busking for coins to a halt, but indirectly led to his learning to play the cornet. After finding his stepfather's .38 revolver stashed in his mother's cedar chest, he tried to impress his fellow singers by blasting it off while walking down Rampart Street. When he was pinched by a white policeman, his friends split the scene, leaving "Dipper" to fend for himself. Though he pleaded with the policeman, young Louis was carted off to Juvenile Hall, where he was locked up and "slept on a hard bed until the next morning."[10]

On New Year's Day 1913, a frightened Louis was taken to Judge Andrew Wilson, who, after a 15-minute trial, sentenced him to the Colored Waifs' Home, a reform school located on the outskirts of town since 1870. Wilson ordered Louis to serve time for an "indefinite" period — which, Louis wrote, "meant until he set me free or until some important white person vouched for me and for my mother and father."[11]

Forced to endure strict military-style discipline, he discovered the brass band led by Peter Davis, who initially labeled Louis a "tough" kid from a bad neighborhood. Inspired by memories of Bolden, Johnson and Joe Oliver, Louis wanted to learn to play the cornet. During supper one evening, Davis surprised him with an invitation to join the band.

Offered tambourine, drums, and alto saxophone, Louis finally was given a bugle when its former player was released from the home. Proving his prowess on the instrument, he graduated to the cornet and was promoted to band leader, performing in parades and at New Orleans picnics — gigs that gave him his first taste of "stardom." Scores of people from the old neighborhood turned out to cheer on their home boy. After serving 18 months, Louis was released into the custody of his father and stepmother on June 16, 1914.

Willie Armstrong, who now worked stoking a furnace at a local turpentine factory, had asked his boss to help get Louis released, but he again had very little to do with his son. In fact, returning to an environment of poverty, vice and crime made

Louis wish he was back at the home with his mentor. After living with Willie and his wife for several months, he was glad to move back in with Mayann.

Soon Louis ran into an old acquaintance, "Cocaine" Buddy Martin, an employee at Joe Segretta's honky-tonk, who told him about an opening for a cornetist at Henry Ponce's joint across the street. Interestingly, Segretta and Ponce, both local Mafiosi, were bitter enemies. Fifteen-year-old Louis landed the gig and, from the time of his first paying job as a musician, began working for tough guys tied to organized crime. He played into the early morning, slept a few hours and then went to his day job at the C. A. Andrews Coal Company, located two blocks from Ponce's. For 10 hours each day he shoveled and hauled hard coal for 15 cents a load. When the tonks were temporarily closed down during a local election campaign, he labored to keep money coming in. He wrote:

> Every time things went bad with me I had the coal cart to fall back on, thanks to my good stepfather Gabe. I sure did like him, and I used to tease Mayann about it.
> "Mama, you know one thing?" I would say. Papa Gabe is the best step-pa I've ever had. He is the best out of the whole lot of them."
> Mayann would kind of chuckle and say: "Aw, go on, you Fatty O'Butler."
> That was the time when the moving picture actor Fatty Arbuckle was in his prime and very popular in New Orleans. Mayann never did get his name right. It sounded so good to me when she called me Fatty O'Butler that I never told her different.[12]

Louis didn't have time or money for movies, but his awareness of Arbuckle suggests that he knew about popular film stars.

Ponce had abandoned his tonk for a more legitimate business, and Louis and his friends began hitting other joints, looking for gigs. Constantly exposed to the activities of drunks, pimps, whores, and other unsophisticated and violent characters, Louis met the likes of "Black Benny," "Nicodemus," "Slippers," "George Bo'hog" and "Mary Jack the Bear," whom he saw get fatally carved in a bloody knife fight with another woman. "They were as tough as they come," he wrote.[13]

Black Benny was a coal hauler for the Andrews Company, a gambler, a bouncer and a boxer, but also an accomplished drummer. He eventually began looking after little Louis, and the two played in New Orleans funerals together. "Benny was the musician's friend," Louis wrote. "Whenever one of us was in hard luck Benny would help him out, and he was always ready to come to the aid of the underdog."[14]

On November 12, 1917, New Orleans mayor Martin Behrman, under pressure from the U.S. Navy and Department of War, declared prostitution illegal. When the whores and their dependants moved out, the red-light district—Storyville—basically ceased to exist. Mayann wanted Louis to concentrate on his coal-hauling job, and didn't encourage his musical aspirations, though he briefly joined a funeral band in Houma, Louisiana, where an undertaker called Mr. Bonds gave him room, board and a weekly salary.

After returning to his job on the coal cart—aided by "Slippers," the bouncer—he landed a job as cornetist at Henry Matranga's tonk, a real Mafia joint, and was back in the thick of it, surrounded by "illegal" prostitutes, pimps and killers, hauling in

$1.25 each night. He also sat in for Joe Oliver during a two-night gig at Pete Lala's tonk, where he earned $3.00.

One day, while having a beer at Matranga's, he was arrested during a raid by police looking for "a black man" who had committed a robbery. Tossed into Parish Prison, not far from Mayann's, he was insulted by prisoners and guards, including a yard captain called "Sore Dick." A few days later, Matranga got him released, marking the first of many times Louis would be aided by a white man with strong mob connections.

Louis worked a number of odd jobs to aid his family during the influenza epidemic of 1918, and began to think he'd never break out of the endless cycle of poverty. Fortunately, Black Benny introduced him to trombonist Edward ("Kid") Ory, who had seen him in one of the Waifs' Home parades. Ory asked Louis to sit in with his band on several occasions, and soon was hiring him on a regular basis. The prodigious young man was grateful to spend some time with Joe Oliver — a major influence in matters of music and life in general. When Oliver's departure left the cornetist's chair open, Louis grabbed it, enjoying gigs at the New Orleans Country Club and Tulane University. Oliver had become part of the "jazz diaspora," musicians seeking employment outside New Orleans.

Louis recalled how he began developing his stage persona:

> About that time, I worked up a little "jive" routine, which was a little tap dancing and a little fooling around between numbers to get laughs. That routine came in handy later on in my first year in Chicago.[15]

Armistice Day, November 11, 1918, brought an end to rationing and blackouts in New Orleans, allowing many of the tonks and dance halls to reopen. Overjoyed that the war was over, Louis quit hauling coal and devoted himself to a full-time musical career. He continued playing with Ory, and on Saturday nights at the Brick House in Gretna, a joint favored by levee workers and prostitutes.

"Bottles would come flying over the bandstand like crazy," Louis recalled, "and there was just lots of just plain common shooting and cutting. But somehow all of that jive didn't faze me at all, I was so happy to have some place to blow my horn."[16]

While blowing at the Brick, he spied a 21-year-old Creole chick — "one ... looking at me with the stuff in her eyes" — Daisy Parker.[17] Though Daisy had an "old man," Louis fell in love with her and, following a dangerous affair, impulsively married her at New Orleans City Hall in January 1919. The marriage was rocky from the start, and when she found him talking to a former sweetheart, she chased him with a razor and slashed his hat to ribbons. Later she tossed a stack of bricks at him and was thrown in jail. Louis wrote:

> Daisy did not have any education. If a person is real ignorant and does not have any learning at all that person is always going to be jealous, evil and hateful. There are always two sides to every story, but an ignorant person just won't cope with either side.[18]

On a Sunday afternoon in November 1919, Louis and Kid Ory's band were playing on the back of a truck to advertise a concert at New Orleans' Economy Hall. At the intersection of Rampart and Perdido Streets—the very spot where Louis had been pinched for firing the .38—they furiously dueled with another mobile band. Fortunately for Louis, Mississippi riverboat bandleader Fate Marable was listening, impressed by the young man who "almost blew [his] brains through [his] trumpet."[19]

Marable, a "hot" pianist who switched to calliope while steaming on the Mississippi, had a widely known reputation as a serious musician. Unlike the men in Ory's outfit, his band members were music *readers*—a requirement insuring a suitable musical education for Louis, who was impressed that Fate's jazz cats could improvise *and* sight read the latest popular tunes. Marable led his "Colored Orchestra" in performances for white patrons on boats owned by the Streckfus Lines.

"I lost no time in joining the orchestra," wrote Louis, who began his Marable experience aboard the *Dixie Belle*.[20] During the summer of 1920 he went on excursions to St. Louis, Missouri; Quincy, Illinois; Davenport, Iowa; and St. Paul, Minnesota, their northernmost port. In Davenport, aboard the *Sidney*, his innovative sound impressed a local 17-year-old cornetist named Leon ("Bix") Beiderbecke, whose parents expected their son to play "proper" music. However, the brilliant, ultimately tragic Bix loved jazz and became the first white musician to be influenced by Louis' style.

In 1921 the great vocalist Ethel Waters toured the South. During a stay in New Orleans, her pianist, Fletcher Henderson, heard Louis blow and asked him to help form a band in New York. Louis declined, instead joining the Marable orchestra for another summer on the Mississippi.

"Daisy and I couldn't get along any better than before," he wrote. "We were running into our fourth year of marriage, so we decided to get a divorce."[21] He was ready to move on with his life—and his music—when, in July 1922, he received a telegram from King Oliver asking him "to come at once to Chicago."[22] A few days after hearing from "Papa Joe," he said goodbye to Mayann, Mama Lucy and his friends at the train station.

Louis arrived at Chicago's Illinois Central Station at 12th and Michigan Avenues at 11 P.M. on August 8, 1922. He rushed to the Lincoln Gardens at 31st and Gordon Streets, heard Oliver's band wailing away inside, and was scared to enter. Finally, the King himself went outside to get him, calling him a "little dumb sumbitch" and "Slow Foot." On the bandstand, Louis was impressed by his mentor, "standing out there in front of his orchestra, swinging away."[23] In the band were Johnny Dodds on clarinet, his brother Warren ("Baby") Dodds on drums, and Honore Dutrey on trombone.

Oliver took his apprentice home, offering a "fattening up" at the hands of his wife Stella. Intimidated by the unfamiliar environment, Slow Foot felt more at home when "Mama Stella" prepared his beloved red beans and rice. Oliver then took him to a boardinghouse at 3412 South Wabash.

The following week Louis began rehearsing with the band. Mindful of Oliver's position as *first* cornetist, he played in between the King's licks. "I was so wrapped up in him and lived his music that I could take second to his lead in a split second," he recalled.[24] Oliver also took him to the Dreamland Cafe on State Street, where he was introduced to pianist Lillian Hardin. Lil was a classy, sophisticated, accomplished musician, and her first impression of Louis was that of an overweight, rather shabbily dressed Southern hick. Born in Memphis, she had been a musically prodigious child, and after studying at Nashville's Fisk University for about a year, moved with her mother to Chicago, where she became immersed in jazz and blues. When she joined the New Orleans Creole Jazz Band, she did so in secret, due to her mother's disdain for popular music.

Louis referred to Lil as "an attractive-looking brown-skinned girl" and "one of the best woman jazz pianists in the country."[25] At the time of their first brief meeting, she "was already married, to a Singer named Jimmy. They were on the Outs."[26] He didn't see her again until she signed with Oliver a couple months later, and they soon became constant companions. After his experience with Daisy Parker — an almost exclusively sexual relationship culminating in abuse and violence — his attitude toward women had matured; and Lil's intelligence, ambition and worldliness (she was three years older than he) appealed to him. When Lil signed with Oliver, she was paid $100 per week, more than Louis was earning.

Almost from the start, Lil told Louis that he was a better musician than the King, whose chops were beginning to fade. Louis recalled:

> We used to practice together, "woodshed" as we say.... I had learned to transpose from a piano part. We used to play classical music together sometimes.... Through this, later on, we played in churches once in a while. All of this was giving me more knowledge of my music.[27]

Lil encouraged him to develop his own style, to break away from Oliver's overriding influence. While rehearsing a piece that became a namesake, "Dipper Mouth Blues" (which he cowrote with Oliver), Louis pioneered a muted "wah-wah" sound that resembles human conversation — a technique sometimes attributed to Bunk Johnson.

Years later, after Johnson claimed to be his mentor, Louis said, "Bunk didn't actually teach me anything; he didn't *show* me one thing.... So you don't need to give the credit to Bunk, other than the tone. I mean, there could be similarity of tone, but that's all."[28]

Lil spirited Louis about town in her car, exposing him to singers currently performing in Chicago's clubs. At the Erlanger Theatre during the autumn of 1922 he was particularly impressed by the style of Bill ("Mr. Bojangles") Robinson, and began to incorporate the dancer's combination of elegance and outright showmanship into his own act.

During the ensuing months, as Louis continued to pioneer a new style of improvisation, he became a star of the regional music scene, impressing his peers, both black and white. Among the "ofay" musicians who frequented the Lincoln Gardens to hear him blow were Bix Beiderbecke, Hoagy Carmichael and Paul Whiteman. Louis also remembered "a professor of music in one of the big Chicago colleges who used to...sit there night after night, taking notes. The waiters didn't like him much because he never ordered a drink and never brought anybody with him, but just sat there and listened."[29]

During after-work jam sessions that raged into the wee hours, he proliferated his jive talk:

> "Swing it, Gate," one of them will sing out and that will be a "sender" to them and they'll all go into their music, swinging hot, only because they love it. That "sender," "Swing it, Gate," by the way, came from me. When I was a kid, you remember, they started calling me "Gate-mouth," and then "Satchel-mouth." Well, I started calling the other boys "Gate," too, to sort of throw it back at them, so it wouldn't stick too close to me, I guess. Then I got used to saying it and when I got into Kid Ory's band when the boys were all swinging good and hot, I would sing out, "Swing it, Gate." That has stuck to me ever since … and now "Gate" is a word swing players use when they call out to one another in their own language, but most of them, I guess, don't know how it started.[30]

Milton ("Mezz") Mezzrow, a white, Illinois-born clarinetist who became obsessed with black culture, developed a close relationship with Louis. Regarding jive, he explained:

> White America perpetrated a new and foreign language on the Africans it enslaved. Slowly, over the generations, Negro America, living by and large in its own segregated world … found its own way of handling English, as it had to find its own way in handling many other aspects of a white, hostile world. Jive is one of the end results. Jive talk may have been originally a kind of "pig Latin" that the slaves talked with each other, a code — when they were in the presence of whites…. *Ofay*, of course, is pig Latin for *foe*.[31]

Like many other musicians who feared their material would be exploited or that people would stop attending live gigs, Joe Oliver had shied away from making recordings. But after he cut a deal with Gennett, a small record label, the Creole Jazz Band finally went into a studio in Richmond, Indiana, on April 5 and 6, 1923. Though recording in Richmond required a five-hour train ride, Beiderbecke, Carmichael and Jelly Roll Morton already had made the trip.

Ironically, no one in Oliver's outfit realized that Indiana boasted the largest Ku Klux Klan membership in the United States, or that Gennett was the KKK's "unofficial" recording company. Richmond alone was home to several thousand Klansmen, some of whom were Gennett employees. Fortunately, the studio's engineer, Ezra Wickemeyer, a Catholic who loathed the KKK records, concentrated on producing the best possible takes from the current acoustic recording system, which used a large, five-foot megaphone to transmit the sound to a steel needle that cut grooves into a spinning wax disc.

The musicians, including Oliver, Dutrey, Lil, the Dodds brothers and Bill Johnson (banjo), were nervous, but Louis considered the sessions just another gig, playing brief solo spots on "Just Gone," "Canal Street Blues" (cowritten by Oliver and Louis), "Mandy Lee Blues," "I'm Going to Wear You Off My Mind" and "Chimes Blues." During the initial take of the first number, Wickemeyer stopped the band and had Louis, whose powerhouse playing was twice as loud as the others', move to a far corner about 12 feet away.

After the first day, which yielded 27 takes (only five were saved), the black musicians left Richmond to stay overnight in a somewhat safer environment. The next morning they returned to wax "Weather Bird Rag," "Dipper Mouth Blues," "Froggie Moore" and "Snake Rag." Marketed as "Snappy Dance Hits on Gennett Records by Exclusive Gennett Colored Artists," these sides were available primarily in black neighborhood shops. A small number of white-owned stores carried them, but kept the discs behind the counter, where customers could request them discreetly.

The true alpha of jazz recordings, the Gennett discs—and particularly Louis' playing—began to influence countless musicians in Chicago and beyond. Only weeks after they were released, Okeh Records sent scouts to the band's Music Trades Convention gig at the Drake Hotel, where they were signed to wax some sides at the company's Chicago studio located at 227 West Washington Street. They recorded some of the same tunes, including "Dipper Mouth Blues" and "Snake Rag"; and, as their reputation grew, the band returned to Richmond for another record date on October 5, waxing "Alligator Hop," "Zulu's Ball," "Working Man Blues" and "Krooked Blues." They also recorded sides for Paramount (including "Mabel's Dream," "The Southern Stomp" and "Riverside Blues") and Columbia.

The popularity of the Creole Jazz Band was accompanied by the musicians' need to stretch out, both musically and financially. Lil, who wasn't fond of the way Oliver treated Louis, kept pushing him toward a solo career. The King had kept a portion of his salary, telling him it was being saved for his own good, but Lil insisted that he use his hard-earned pay to buy some clothes befitting his status. She didn't want Oliver to hold him back any longer, and said she'd "take care" of him.

Dutrey, Johnson, and the Dodds brothers also became suspicious of Oliver, who never let the band members see the royalty checks. Eventually they discovered that their $75-per-week salaries actually had been $95, and that the King was pocketing an additional $20 per man each payday. They threatened violence, and Oliver began carrying a pistol to the gigs.

On December 23, 1923, Louis was granted a divorce from Daisy Parker. Free from Oliver's financial grasp, he now wed his new mentor on February 5, 1924, and moved with her and her mother, Dempsey, into a new home at 421 East 44th Street in Chicago. He also sent for his eight-year-old cousin, Flora Myles' illegitimate son Clarence, whom he had cared for in New Orleans. Now the boy became his adopted son, known as "Little Louis Armstrong." Louis and Lil encouraged his education at a school for "backwards boys" and, over the years, saw that he was in good company when they were away from home.

Mayann, worried by rumors about her son, also was living in Chicago. Expecting to find him sick and starving, she was overjoyed to see him robust and healthy, blowing with Oliver at the Lincoln Gardens. Convincing her that he was fine, he bought her some nice gifts and showed her the town before she returned to New Orleans.

Daisy, too, was in Chicago looking for Louis, and, for a time, made things rather difficult—until she got into a knife fight with a drunken man, which sent her to the hospital. When she recovered, she returned to New Orleans, and—much to his relief—never again caused trouble.

After the Lincoln Gardens engagement ended, Louis and Lil agreed to tour with Oliver, but the rest of the band walked out. When they returned to Chicago, Lil finally persuaded her husband to go solo. At first he found it difficult to get gigs. When he asked bandleader Sammy Stewart, who hired only light-skinned Creoles, for a job, he was told that no one was needed. Finally he landed the first-trumpet position with Ollie Powers, who was forming a new band to play at the Dreamland.

In October 1924 he received another offer from Fletcher Henderson, to play first trumpet with his 12-man orchestra at New York's famed Roseland, located at Broadway and 51st. Lil originally went with him, but returned to Chicago to care for her ailing mother — a wise economic move, considering that Louis' pay was only $55 per week.

Louis' arrival coincided with the flowering of the Harlem Renaissance. This borough of New York, situated between the northern boundary of Central Park and 168th Street, became a great center of African American culture, and also attracted important white artists, writers and musicians. Whites flocked to Harlem, particularly to enjoy the refreshing absence of Prohibition enforcement and the stunning black talent on the stages of the Cotton Club and Connie's Inn.

Black boxer Jack Jackson had owned the Cotton Club when it was known as the Club DeLuxe, but, after falling on hard times, partnered with gangster Owney Madden. And Connie's Inn, though run by Connie and George Immerman, actually was a front for the illegal activities of the heinous Arthur Flegenheimer, aka "Dutch Schultz."

When Louis wrote of the Harlem Renaissance, he revealed his admiration of acting by mentioning several African American stage performers:

> [T]he most brilliant and talented musicians and actors and poets and artists of our race ... had come from everywhere to Harlem.... There was Charles Gilpin, the great actor in *The Emperor Jones*, and Florence Mills ... and Paul Robeson and Ethel Waters and Bill Robinson and Duke Ellington and Cab Calloway and Chick Webb and James Weldon Johnson, our great poet, and those fine people who later went into the cast of *The Green Pastures* and carried that beautiful play all over the United States for five years, and many others whom I should mention.[32]

He immediately began rehearsing with Henderson, and was intimidated by the presence of the superb saxophonists Coleman Hawkins and Don Redman, whose written arrangements gave the orchestra a sound later made famous by the big bands. But Louis' passionate improvisational style quickly knocked the other players for a loop, and actually stopped dancers who stared in amazement as they *listened* to him.

Believing that his singing was as important as his playing, Louis wanted to flex his vocal muscles, but instrumentalists weren't usually given that opportunity. One Thursday night, when a vocal competition was held, he joined in just to see the reaction of the audience. He sang "Everybody Loves My Baby, but My Baby Don't Love Nobody but Me," and when he was asked to line up with the other contestants, the applause was deafening when the money was held over his head. He also ventured over to the Savoy Ballroom and jammed with the band. When Duke Ellington heard of Louis' formidable talent, he took his band over to Roseland.

Between October 1924 and August 1925, Louis recorded with Henderson, for Regal, Columbia, Pathé, Banner and Vocalion. Though he only received brief solo spots on tunes such as "Shanghai Shuffle," "Copenhagen" and "Sugar Foot Stomp," his impassioned improvisations threatened to break free from Redman's arrangements. His melodic variations and harmonic explorations, together with his rhythmic inventions—stretching the beat into a groove subsequently called *swing*—set in motion the shape of jazz to come. Pops actually *swung* around the continuum of time.

Coleman Hawkins recalled, "He was only with us a short time, but he completely changed the character of the band. If you listen to our recordings before he joined the band, and the ones we made after he left, you can tell the difference. He had an impact on all of us. He taught us how to swing."[33] In November, Henderson allowed Louis to cut his first vocal take, on "Everybody Loves My Baby," but—just to be safe—an instrumental version also was waxed. On "Naughty Man" Louis followed Hawkins and trombonist Charlie Green's rather perfunctory breaks with a swinging solo that proved superior in every respect.

Louis also recorded with singer Alberta Hunter (who used the name "Josephine Beatty") and the Red Onion Jazz Babies. On November 8, 1924, Hunter sang "Texas Moaner Blues" as Louis, Lil, Buster Bailey (clarinet), Aaron Thompson (trombone) and Buddy Christian (banjo) played from strategic points around the small New York studio. An instrumental, "Of All the Wrongs You've Done to Me," closed the sessions, but the band returned on the 26th to cut "Terrible Blues" and "Santa Claus Blues," on which Pops' cornet glided effortlessly above the pulsing rhythm of Lil's piano. Three days before Christmas, Louis and Lil joined another Red Onion session, with Hunter, Sidney Bechet (clarinet and soprano sax) and Charlie Irvis (trombone). Hunter sang "Nobody Knows the Way I Feel This Morning" and "Early Every Morn" as the blues literally oozed from Bechet, who dominated the solo spots. Pops grabbed a little space at the conclusion of the latter, playing a few notes resembling his later "West End Blues" introduction. Vocalist Clarence Todd joined Hunter on "Cake Walking Babies from Home," on which Louis and Bechet exchanged swinging obbligati.

Others who hired Pops included singers Maggie Jones, Ma Rainey, Margaret Johnson and Clara Smith, and pianist-composer-publisher Clarence Williams, whose Blue Five featured his wife, singer Eva Taylor, Sidney Bechet, Don Redman, Coleman Hawkins, Buster Bailey and Buddy Christian. Louis and Bechet traded superb solos on "Texas Moaner Blues," and he added a driving cornet break after Taylor's vocal on "Everybody Loves My Baby." On January 8, 1925, Louis again dueled with Bechet on "Cake Walking Babies from Home."

On January 14, Louis played on sessions with "The Empress of the Blues," Bessie Smith, at Columbia's studio in Columbus Circle. He knew she was "the Greatest and Highest Salaried Race Star in the World," and added the perfect instrumental accompaniment to her transcendent vocals and Fred Longshaw's piano and reed organ on "St. Louis Blues," "Reckless Blues," "Sobbin' Hearted Blues," "Cold in Hand Blues" and "You've Been a Good Ole Wagon."

In April, Henderson took his band on a tour of New England and into Pennsylvania. Louis recalled:

One night we happened to be playing for a big dance in Lawrence, Massachusetts, given by the local Elks Lodge. They had had a beauty contest and that night the winner of it was there. She had won a free trip to Hollywood and a chance to try out for the movies. The girl was Miss Thelma Todd who later came to a tragic death in Hollywood…. All show-people have lots of troubles in their lives, I think.[34]

On May 26 and 27 he waxed four more sides with Bessie Smith, who was recovering from a recent "accident" (actually a deliberate stair tumble fueled by alcohol and a turbulent relationship). Fred Longshaw was back at the piano, joined by Charlie Green on trombone. "Nashville Woman's Blues" was followed by the classic "Careless Love Blues," "J. C. Holmes Blues" and "I Ain't Gonna Play Second Fiddle."

After spending a year with "Smack" Henderson, Louis was tired of elegant arrangements that reigned in his desire to experiment. Smack wanted a trumpeter who played Redman's charts, not a jazz pioneer. Urged by Lil, who objected to the bandleader's refusal to give her husband "proper" billing, Louis returned to Chicago, where Lil was now pianist and bandleader at Dreamland.

At Lil's insistence, he was billed as "Louis Armstrong, the World's Greatest Trumpet Player." He wasn't fond of such pretension, nor the reality of working for Lil, who made more money than he did. But, together, the couple raised enough dough to purchase a new car and a lot at the Idlewild summer resort, where he liked to go swimming, canoeing and horseback riding.

Ironically, Joe Oliver was playing at the Plantation Club, just across the street from Dreamland. The King not only avoided a reunion with his former protégé, but sent a message, ordering, "Close those windows or I'll blow you off 35th Street." But Pops blew a powerful wind of his own, both at live gigs and in the studio. In November he recorded with Bertha ("Chippie") Hill, and joined Johnny Dodds and Johnny St. Cyr to accompany blueswoman Sippie Wallace's nephew and niece — pianist Hersal Thomas and his sister, Hociel, who sang on six Okeh sides, including "Gambler's Dream" and "Adam and Eve Had the Blues."

In his "off" hours, Pops had begun working on arrangements for a new recording outfit of his own, Louis Armstrong's Hot Five. The day after the Thomas assignment, he returned to Okeh to inaugurate what became a truly historic series of sessions:

I don't know how I stood it. I never had any time to be at home, except for just a few hours' sleep. I met myself coming and going. I guess it was about that time, and because of that, that Lil and I first started to drift apart, although we didn't see it then…[35]

"The Hot Five" was the result of Okeh's decision to put together a studio group of New Orleans musicians to record authentic jazz. For a fee of $50 each, cats could walk into Okeh and, without rehearsing, wax some numbers together. A scout, Richard M. Jones, booked the talent, and a man named E. A. Fern managed the Chicago office, but it is unclear who actually formed the band. Beginning on November 12, Okeh personnel told Louis how many sides to record; then he and his cohorts—Lil, Kid Ory, Johnny Dodds and Johnny St. Cyr — would choose the tunes and do some brief run-throughs before cutting the actual takes, still using the acoustic process. If one of the musicians wanted another take, Pops simply would tell the engineer to try it again.

The Hot Five recordings are the bedrock of jazz. The November 12 sessions yielded Louis' "Gut Bucket Blues" and "Yes! I'm in the Barrel," and Lil's "My Heart." During "Gut Bucket," which features spoken introductions of each soloist, Louis shouts, "Ah, whip that thing, Miss Lil. Whip it, kid!" and Kid Ory exclaims, "Blow that thing, Papa Dip!" as Pops solos. Robert O'Meally cited this number's ensemble playing as an example "of jazz as a music of superior democratic action, one where you can have your say but where you also pay close enough attention to the voices around you to make a statement that coheres as an aesthetic whole."[36]

In early 1926 Louis accepted a position with Professor Erskine Tate's "little symphony orchestra" at the Vendome Theatre, where his workday began at 7 P.M. After finishing a full show, he'd join after-hours jam sessions that ended around 4 A.M. His Vendome responsibilities included playing, singing and, occasionally, acting. One number he sang was "Heebie Jeebies," which paired his own improvised lyrics with the original tune by Boyd Atkins. During the second chorus, he substituted nonsense syllables for the actual words while maintaining an incredible, swinging rhythm. The audience thought he had invented a new style of singing, but "scat" had been an enjoyable way of vocalizing between cats in New Orleans. His innovative use of the technique, in a professional context, startled and thrilled listeners—particularly after he recorded the song with the Hot Five on February 26, 1926.

The apocryphal story originated by Johnny St. Cyr and subsequently confirmed by Louis—that, during the recording, he began scatting after accidentally dropping the jotted-down lyrics—is belied by his endless flow of vocal improvisation, from actual words to scat and back again. The genesis of modern singing can be heard in every swinging syllable of "Heebie Jeebies," a rare historic record of pure human creativity that sets your foot tapping and your spirit soaring. This memorable Okeh session also yielded six more numbers, including "Muskrat Ramble," a tune written by Pops but credited to Kid Ory and R. Gilbert, "Georgia Grind," featuring vocals by Louis and Lil, and "Cornet Chop Suey," Louis' swinging tribute to Chinese food, his second favorite cuisine.

After Mezz Mezzrow played a copy of "Heebie Jeebies" at the Chicago musicians' union office, Okeh was cleaned out of records in a week. The disc eventually sold 40,000 copies, and Louis' rhythmic gibberish began to influence singers everywhere as they incorporated it into their performances and public conversations, scatting in each other's faces on the street. Though Louis didn't originate scat, his use of it profoundly altered vocal jazz, inspiring singers to consider the voice an actual musical instrument that could produce infinite improvisations.

Admirers flocked to the Vendome just to see him, then left before the movie began. A few detractors called his exaggerated performance style "tomming," but his joyous, humorous, unrestrained delivery was a natural extension of his personality. One of his fervent fans was an attractive 18-year-old girl named Alpha Smith who worked for a white family in Hyde Park. Believing that Lil was involved with "a Chicago pimp," Louis went for Alpha, who became a backstage fixture. Soon he was spending afternoons in Hyde Park, enjoying her "deelicious meals" while her employers were out shopping, and visiting her at a dingy apartment she shared with her mother at 33rd Street and Cottage Grove Avenue.[37]

Louis often took his adopted son to see Alpha. Clarence loved the kind treatment and good food. Eventually Louis left Lil, and he and the boy moved in with the Smiths. Leaving his wife also meant quitting her band to concentrate on his Vendome gig, as well as a reunion with King Oliver, whose chops were literally wearing out. At the Musicians' Local 208, at State and 39th Streets, he met a handsome young pianist named Earl ("Fatha") Hines, who, after jamming, convinced him to forego Oliver for a spot in Carroll Dickerson's orchestra at the Sunset Café, where he blew for the first time on April 10, 1926.

On May 28 Louis and the Vendome band recorded "Stomp Off, Let's Go," a hot Tate arrangement during which he burns through some incendiary stop-time breaks. That same day, the Hot Five waxed two numbers, "Georgia Bo Bo" and Louis' "Drop That Sack," under the band name Lil's Hot Shots. Though Louis had signed an exclusive contract with Okeh, Vocalion Records persuaded him to hand the reins to his wife for a rival session.

On June 16 the band reassembled at Okeh to record four sides, including Louis and Paul Barbarin's furiously swinging "Don't Forget to Mess Around," and Lil's "I'm Gonna Gitcha." Louis and Richard Jones (piano) also played on "The Bridwell Blues" with country-blues singer Nolan Welsh. Two days later the Hot Five returned to the studio to back Joe ("Butterbeans") and Susie Edwards on the suggestive "He Likes It Slow."

The following week they waxed Lil's "King of the Zulus," which features Clarence Babcock interjecting some humorous Jamaican dialogue, and "Big Fat Ma and Skinny Pa." That evening the band played their sole live gig, a promotional concert staged at the Coliseum by Richard Jones, who also booked King Oliver and Erskine Tate. Louis, billed as the "king of them all ... world's hottest jazz cornetist," gave a stunning performance. Still married to his pianist, Louis left Alpha's apartment in August to accompany Lil on a three-week vacation at the Idlewild summer cottage.

After playing at the Sunset for several months, Pops became the bandleader when club manager Joe Glaser fired the perpetually drunk Dickerson. Louis admired Glaser, who "seemed to understand colored people so much" and revived the billing "Louis Armstrong—The World's Greatest Trumpet Player."[38] Glaser was connected to the Capone syndicate, which provided greater benefits to musicians than any legal authority. Louis remembered Capone as "a nice little cute fat boy—young—like some professor who had just come out of college to teach or something."[39]

Pops also benefited from his nightly interaction with Earl Hines' fluid playing, a far cry from Lil's somewhat stilted technique. Hines further developed a "trumpet style" melodic method, helping to spread Louis' influence to every other instrument in jazz.

Louis' acting abilities really developed at this point, whenever he'd take the stage as "the Reverend Satchelmouth" and deliver a sermon while dressed in an old black deacon's coat. The integrated audience (often up to 90 percent white) included Illinois' own "Austin High Gang," Eddie Condon, Mezz Mezzrow, and members of Paul

Whiteman's orchestra, particularly Bing Crosby, who was profoundly influenced by Pops.*

Mezzrow's capable clarinet playing was mainly a cover for his real job as a drug peddler. The son of a pharmacist, he first sold bootleg hooch and then began smuggling marijuana into the States from Mexico. His "golden leaf" was very popular with Chicago jazz musicians, and "mezz" became one of Louis' favorite terms for reefer, which he would roll into large, well-packed cigarettes referred to as "mezzrolls." (His other pet names were "gage" and "shuzzit," which meant "good shit.") Louis first tried marijuana when a white musician passed around "a new cigarette" backstage at the Chicago Savoy. Enjoying the effect, he used it regularly, considering it much safer than the poison sold by bootleggers, and narcotics (or "ungodly shit")[40] which he didn't use. He seriously believed that smoking gage enhanced his musical abilities.

Bix Beiderbecke, whose classically influenced, "spectral" style differed from Louis' head-on melodic majesty, was now a member of Whiteman's orchestra, and sometimes stayed long after the last show at the Sunset to play in locked-door jam sessions that soared into the wee hours.

On November 16 the Hot Five cut "Big Butter and Egg Man," on which Louis sings a duet with May Alix (who had been performing the song with him as part of the floor show at the Sunset), and several other numbers, including Lil and Louis' "Jazz Lips" and a scat exercise of Lil's called "Skid-Dat-de-Dat." Pops cowrote "Big Butter" and "Sunset Café Stomp" (another duet with Alix), with Percy Venable, the floor-show manager at the club. His collaborations with Alix provide a stark contrast between his modern rhythmic singing and the more conventional, stilted pop style of the 1920s. Two more Armstrong-Venable collaborations, "You Made Me Love You" and "Irish Black Bottom," both featuring Henry ("Hy") Clark on trombone, were waxed at a November 27 session.

Louis recorded six more sides for Vocalion, again by ceding leadership to a band member (this time his superb clarinetist), for an April 22, 1927, session as Johnny Dodds' Black Bottom Stompers, a lineup also featuring Earl Hines, Roy Palmer (trombone), Barney Bigard (tenor sax), Bud Scott (banjo) and Baby Dodds (drums). The most memorable number, "Wild Man Blues," was repeated two weeks later when Louis and Johnny rejoined their usual bandmates at Okeh for the first Louis Armstrong and His Hot Seven session, adding Baby Dodds and Peter Briggs (tuba). The studio recently had upgraded to the new electrical recording technology, which created much more realistic-sounding platters.

"Willie the Weeper" became the first number waxed by the Hot Seven on May 7, followed by Louis' miraculous, fat-toned cornet on "Wild Man Blues," though he claimed a preference for the Dodds Vocalion take. Following a May 9 recording of "Chicago Breakdown" with his former "boss," Carroll Dickerson, whose lineup included Earl Hines, Peter Briggs and his old King Oliver crony Honore Dutrey, Pops was back with the Hot Seven the following day, cutting "Alligator Crawl" and one of

*Though Whiteman's title as "King of Jazz" is understandably frowned upon, this white man tried to hire black musicians, but was discouraged by his management. He did, however, succeed in using African American arrangers and writers, including Fletcher Henderson and William Grant Still.

his most brilliant compositions, "Potato Head Blues," featuring a climactic 55-second solo that is one of the superlative performances in recorded music.

May 11 yielded three more excellent sides, "Melancholy," "Weary Blues" and the rhythmically wondrous "Twelfth Street Rag," followed by another pair, "Keyhole Blues," featuring some fiery trumpet-like scat, and Louis' "S.O.L. Blues," on the 13th. The original title of "S.O.L."—quite unreleasable—was "If You Don't Like This Song, You Can Kiss My Fucking Ass." Though the finished version included nothing profane, Okeh had Pops record an alternate version, retitled "Gully Low Blues," the next day, when they also waxed "That's When I'll Come Back to You," featuring a rap duet between Louis and Lil.

Louis' Vendome gig had ended the previous month, and now he augmented his regular appearances at the Sunset with a position in the Clarence Jones Orchestra at the Metropolitan Theater, jazzing selections from classical and operatic works, including Puccini's *Madame Butterfly*. In July he also accepted a two-week engagement at Blackhawk's, a whites-only restaurant, in the Loop.

The original Hot Five reconvened at Okeh on September 2, 1927, to cut "Put 'Em Down Blues" and "Ory's Creole Trombone." One number, "The Last Time," was recorded during a session four days later. Saddened by the death of his mother, who had been suffering from arteriosclerosis, Louis was suddenly unemployed when both of his regular gigs ended in November. Returning to Okeh on December 9–10 and 13, he waxed six more tracks with the band. Though Louis wrote the great dance tune "Struttin' with Some Barbecue," he credited Lil for a title referring to the swagger of a man who's out on the town with his lady, and also for "Got No Blues" and "Hotter Than That" (featuring furious scatting and beautifully integrated soloing by Pops and Johnny Dodds), and as his cowriter on "I'm Not Rough" (the latter two and a third number, Kid Ory's "Savoy Blues," augmented by the guitar work of Lonnie Johnson).

Louis also decided to open his own club, at Warwick Hall, off Forrestville Avenue. Choosing not to spend money promoting the "Hot Six," which included Lil, Earl Hines, and his old New Orleans pal Zutty Singleton on drums, Louis realized he'd made a mistake and closed the joint after a few evenings. When he failed to pay the rent, the owners of the building sued him.

Pooling their meager resources, Louis, Earl and Zutty opened a smaller club on Chicago's West Side, but, after a promising start, this venture also ended abruptly when a drunken killer ran in, waving a pistol. The band managed to escape unscathed, but the offender eventually was chased down and shot to death by police. Following this escapade, Louis rejoined Clarence Jones at the Metropolitan, and then Carroll Dickerson at the new Savoy Ballroom, where he also landed the drum seat for Zutty.

At Okeh (now owned by Columbia) on June 26, 1928, Pops, Earl, Jimmie Noone (clarinet) and Mancy Carr (guitar) somehow managed to work through four songs with stiff, off-key songbird Lillie Delk Christian. The next day Louis assembled a new Hot Five lineup (actually featuring six musicians): Earl, Mancy, Zutty, Fred Robinson (trombone) and Jimmy Strong (clarinet). For three days Louis recorded some of his most sublime sides, establishing a smooth groove with his cohorts, all of whom were encouraged to share his good shuzzit beforehand. The first day yielded "Fireworks,"

"Skip the Gutter" and Hines' "A Monday Date" (during which Louis refers to Earl *and* Zutty as "Pops"), while the 28th became one of the most important dates in the history of American music.

After cutting Lil's "Don't Jive Me," Pops turned to a Clarence Williams tune previously waxed by King Oliver — "West End Blues" — and created a rarefied performance marking the apex of his small-group recordings. As he opens the number with a blazing nine-measure cadenza, melding rhythmic velocity, melodic beauty and capacious tone, he reaches a spiritual plane achieved only by the truly blessed. Seventy-six years after the session, his introduction, sensuous scat vocal (itself a trumpet solo) floating above Strong's low-register clarinet, and concluding solo that digs deep into the blues to glide them effortlessly into the musical ether (he sustains one note perfectly, with a hint of vibrato, for 12 seconds) remain unsurpassed by any other recording. And all of Pops' magnificence dances over the supreme, woozy blues groove of the band, highlighted by Hines' insouciant piano and Singleton's rompy cymbal-crown work. As Gary Giddins has inquired, "How can one explain the large number of violinists who can play Bach's D-minor Chaconne when no trumpeter, in or out of jazz, has convincingly replicated Armstrong's ... intro?"[41]

Louis followed "West End" with "Sugar Foot Strut" (interestingly playing a solo written for the arrangement rather than improvising), then returned to the studio the following day to cut "Two Deuces" and "Squeeze Me," on which he sings a vocal duet with (reportedly) Fred Robinson. One additional number, the bouncy "Knee Drops," was recorded on July 2.

Louis' performances with the Dickerson orchestra now were broadcast from the Savoy Ballroom, giving most listeners their first exposure to his music. On July 5 the "Savoyagers" waxed "Symphonic Raps," featuring solo breaks by Hines and a ride by Pops that is leagues ahead of his bandmates' blowing. When he accepted an offer to play the *St. Paul* riverboat in St. Louis, he received $100 per day, plus expenses, but was nearly drowned when thousands of excited passengers piled aboard to hear him and the Floyd Campbell band battle it out with the Alphonso Trent band. Back in Chicago, he vowed never to blow aboard a boat again.

On September 21, Louis and Zutty spent an evening with Guy Lombardo at the whites-only Granada Cafe. He and Lombardo admired each other's styles, and, while the bandleader picked up instrumental ideas from the trumpeter, Pops, always open to new ways of arranging, became interested in the big-band sound. When Fletcher Henderson, during a visit to Chicago, asked Louis to rejoin his orchestra, Pops turned him down, using the offer to persuade the Savoy management to increase his salary to $200 per week.

On December 4–5 and 12, the Hot Five created more musical masterpieces, with Don Redman filling the clarinet chair on "No One Else But You," the hard-swinging "Beau Koo Jack" (translation: a lot of bread) and "Save It, Pretty Mama." Benefiting from the wider dynamic range allowed by electrical recording, Zutty now was able to play the bass drum in his kit, giving the band a more driving pulse. Hines split his talent between piano and celeste on "Basin Street Blues," and Zutty used brushes to contribute some precision snare work to Louis' "Muggles" (named after one of his slang terms for marijuana), on which he played some exquisite low-down blues. Two other Armstrong original instrumentals, "Hear Me Talkin' to Ya" and "Weather Bird," were waxed, the latter an impressive duet he and Hines had been honing during live gigs. The New Orleans classic "St. James Infirmary" also went down, featuring Pops' vocals, Robinson's trombone, Redman's clarinet and alto sax, and more of Zutty's brush work. Pops, Zutty and Hines all engaged in comic banter on "Tight Like This," a laid-back swinger combining playful naughtiness with virtuoso high-register soloing.

By spring 1929, Louis' finances were again at low ebb. He had paid off the Warwick Hall debt, but bad business at the Savoy threatened his regular gig. When Okeh turned over his contract to Tommy Rockwell in New York, he immediately was summoned back to the Big Apple to wax some tracks. A tough promoter, Rockwell had no knowledge of music, but knew exactly where the bread was. Intending to refashion his client as a powerhouse solo act, he steered Louis away from "race" material and toward popular Tin Pan Alley songs.

On March 5, Pops teamed with bandleader-pianist Luis Russell and eight other musicians to record "I Can't Give You Anything but Love" (lending his scat to a big-band arrangement) and "Mahogany Hall Stomp" (during one solo spot, sustaining a note for 10 measures). This integrated session included guitarist Eddie Condon, who joined Louis to write "Knockin' a Jug," which became the first of many Armstrong collaborations with "ofay" trombonist Jack Teagarden.

Having created musical transcendence with the Hot Fives and Sevens, Louis moved from being the ultimate soloist with a jazz ensemble to a star entertainer, blowing and singing at center stage. Though Louis had driven to New York with his bandmates, Rockwell had no intention of using the other musicians. Told to report to Philadelphia to rehearse for the Broadway show *Great Day*, Louis was soon out of a job when producer Vincent Youmans cut the trumpeter role from the cast.

Bunking in with Duke Ellington bassist Wellman Braud in Harlem, he accepted some dough for his boys, and they began to look for local club gigs. After filling in for Ellington's orchestra at the Audubon Theatre in the Bronx, they played the Savoy on June 1 and 2, landing an audition with Florenz Ziegfeld for his new production, *Show Girl*, with music by George Gershwin, and starring Ruby Keeler and Jimmy Durante. Unfortunately, they lost out to Ellington, who achieved a modest success with the show.

On June 4, Louis joined Tommy and Jimmy Dorsey, violinist Harry Hoffman and a rhythm section to back singer Seger Ellis on two Okeh sides. Though significant as an integrated session, the results were less than impressive, thanks to the lifeless, pedantic vocals intended for a white audience. When Pops plays a brief solo on "S'posin'," it literally sounds like he is attempting, unsuccessfully, to raise the dead. Jimmy Dorsey's clarinet opens "To Be in Love," during which Louis again mercifully provides a rhythmic contrast to Ellis' moribund warbling.

On June 24, Louis and his cats opened at Connie's Inn, playing for the white elite — Wall Street financiers, actors and actresses, publishers and authors. Connie Immerman had promoted the previous band, led by Leroy Smith, to play in his successful Broadway show *Hot Chocolates*, which depicted various aspects of Harlem street life. The show, with music by Fats Waller and lyrics by Andy Razaff, had opened at the Hudson Theatre on June 10, 1920. Now Immerman added Louis, to play trumpet numbers during the entr'acte, before joining his band for the nightly club gig. Pops recalled:

> It was in *Hot Chocolates* that I introduced the song, "Ain't Misbehavin'," playing a trumpet solo in the high register. From the first time I heard it, that song used to "send" me. I wood-shedded it until I could play all around it…. When we opened, I was all ready with it and it would bring down the house, believe me! I believe that great song, and the chance I got to play it, did a lot to make me better known all over the country.[42]

Louis, Zutty, Fred Robinson, Mancy Carr, Jimmy Strong and Gene Anderson (piano) waxed two humorous Okeh sides, "Funny Feathers" and "How Do You Do It That Way?" with Dallas singer Victoria Spivey on July 10. Nine days later, Pops, backed by his entire orchestra, recorded his own vocal version of "Ain't Misbehavin'," setting a precedent of creating jazz interpretations of popular songs. Having transformed the music of his fellow blacks, he now brought his innovations to the white domain of Tin Pan Alley, planting the seeds of a jazz revolution that finally would gain wide appeal nearly a decade later, after Benny Goodman spread the sound of swing to whites across America, culminating in the historic Carnegie Hall concert on January 16, 1938.

After opening "Ain't Misbehavin'" on trumpet, Pops allows Carroll Dickerson a brief violin solo before singing, blending Andy Razaf's lyrics with some ebullient scat. He closes with a powerful solo, swingingly ascending the high register on the ending. On July 22 he and the band cut the remaining Waller and Razaf numbers from *Hot Chocolates*. After playing an introductory solo on "(What Did I Do to Be So) Black and Blue?" Pops—while recording the *second* "pop" song of his career—made his first public statement about discrimination, transmuting a lyric about a downtrodden dark-skinned woman into a significant statement about racism. (The allegation that his move into Tin Pan Alley made him an "Uncle Tom" falls on its face here.) He followed it with the driving swing of "That Rhythm Man" and laid-back bounce of "Sweet Savannah Sue."

Pops waxed another version of "Ain't Misbehavin'" on August 23, this time a draggy, whites-friendly version featuring the Dorseys, Eddie Lang (guitar), Joe Venuti (violin) and a frosted vocal by none other than Seger Ellis. Louis and his orchestra returned to the studio on September 10 to record—at the "suggestion" of Tommy Rockwell, who was uncertain about the popular appeal of his client's singing—vocal and instrumental versions of "Some of These Days," a process they repeated the following day for "When You're Smiling," and on the 26th for "After You've Gone." Though the band sounds lackluster on these sides, Pops' singing and playing, particularly on "After You've Gone," is as energetic and moving as ever.

One night at Connie's Inn, Dutch Schultz introduced Louis to Harry Gibson, a white pianist who worshipped Pops' playing. Schultz and Gibson were often in the audience, and the latter was soon taken backstage to share one of Louis' cigar-sized reefers. The good times came to an end, however, when *Hot Chocolates* closed its Broadway run, and (due to the tardiness of several musicians) Immerman, expecting the return of Leroy Smith's band, gave Louis and his boys two weeks' notice.

On his own again, Louis had to part ways with his old pal Zutty, whom he felt was taking advantage of his generosity. The October 29 stock market crash was beginning to affect every aspect of life in Harlem, and most of the musicians were facing hard times. Now the "Reefer King" of Harlem, Mezz Mezzrow, was responsible for the emerging success of Pops' records on the city's juke boxes, which previously had been ruled by the sound of Guy Lombardo. Soon the boxes "blared out Louis, Louis and more Louis. The Armstrong craze spilled over from Harlem right after that, and before long there wasn't a juke box in the country that Louis wasn't scatting on."[43]

On December 10 and 13, Louis cut vocal and instrumental versions of four popular songs with the Luis Russell gang, including Henry ("Red") Allen (trumpet), J. C. Higginbotham (trombone), Albert Nicholas (clarinet), George ("Pops") Foster (bass) and Paul Barbarin (drums). The band swung hard as Louis blew and sang splendidly on Spencer Williams' "I Ain't Got Nobody," "Dallas Blues," Hoagy Carmichael's "Rockin' Chair" (featuring a vocal duet with the composer), and his first solo recording of W. C. Handy's "St. Louis Blues," a driving arrangement including some Latin percussion rhythms by Barbarin and hot solos by Allen and Higginbotham. Interestingly, Pops closed out the "roaring" decade with an integrated set, waxing masterworks by Memphian Handy, the "Father of the Blues," and Indianan Carmichael, a titan of Tin Pan Alley.

2

Jim Crow and
the Jazz Man

"I'm proud to acknowledge my debt to the Reverend Satchelmouth. He is the beginning and the end of music in America. And long may he reign."

— Bing Crosby[1]

Two vocal jazz pioneers made their Hollywood debuts during 1929, in an industry still depicting the racist stereotypes established in D.W. Griffith's *Birth of a Nation*, released 14 years earlier, and the somewhat more "modern" characterization of the black jester, recently popularized by the "lovable pickaninny" characters in Hal Roach's *Our Gang* comedy series. The first of Roach's wide-eyed, soul-food eatin' tots, Ernie ("Sunshine Sammy") Morrison, was followed by the more familiar Allen Clayton ("Farina") Hoskins, who landed his role after demonstrating his prodigious ability to burst into tears.

Two major features released in 1929 purported to depict the "black cultural experience": *Hearts in Dixie*, which introduced Stepin Fetchit to audiences, and *Hallelujah*, shot on location in Tennessee and Arkansas by director King Vidor. While the former typically depicts an idealized portrait of plantation life, where contented darkies serve their white masters; the latter, in its dramatization of a gentle rural family's tribulations with a "son gone bad," proved a watershed in presenting some degree of authentic "Negro" emotion and experience. Because of its use of black actors in lead roles, *Hallelujah* was banned by the Southern Theatre Foundation.

In the jazz-oriented releases, the incomparable Bessie Smith sang W. C. Handy's "St. Louis Blues" in director Dudley Murphy's short of the same name, and Ethel Waters played herself in Warner Bros.' *On with the Show*, directed by Alan Crosland. In the former, Smith portrays a blues singer done wrong by Jimmy the Pimp, creating a characterization Donald Bogle called "the most sensual black woman ever to have been turned loose in an American movie."[2]

The all-white *King of Jazz* also went into production in 1929. After firing two directors—Wesley Ruggles and Paul Fejos—Universal finally entrusted this "super-special 100 percent talker" to John Murray Anderson, and guaranteed star Paul Whiteman 40 percent of the net proceeds. Also appearing in the film were "The Rhythm Boys": Bing Crosby, Al Rinker and Harry Barris.

The following year, Duke Ellington and his band made the trip to tinsel town to provide music for *Check and Double Check* (1930), and became the first African American outfit to land such a gig. This RKO-Radio release was the talkie feature-film debut of "Amos 'n' Andy" (white actors Freeman Gosden and Charles Correll in blackface). Incredibly, black musicians Juan Tizol and Barney Bigard also had to black up after the producers labeled them too light-skinned.

Tommy Rockwell had been pursuing Hollywood opportunities while Louis recorded more Okeh sides with Luis Russell. On January 24, 1930, the valet who worked for the orchestra took over the drum seat from Paul Barbarin, who played vibraphone on "Song of the Islands," which includes such exotic elements as a violin trio and a chorus backing Pops' scat vocal. Two more numbers, "Bessie Couldn't Help It" and "Blue, Turning Grey Over You," were waxed on February 1.

On April 5, Louis recorded a graceful duet of "Dear Old Southland" with pianist Ford Washington Lee (later known as "Buck," of the team "Buck and Bubbles," with John W. Sublett as "Bubbles"), during which he refers to Buck as "Pops" and "Satchelmouth" before blowing some beautifully sustained notes on the ending. Washington Lee also played with the Mills Blue Rhythm Band (here billed as the Cocoanut Grove Orchestra) on Hoagy Carmichael's "My Sweet," but sat out on "I Can't Believe That You're in Love with Me" and four more songs cut May 4: "Indian Cradle Song," "Exactly Like You," "Dinah" and "Tiger Rag." Louis blows and sings joyously on all of them, using his trumpet and voice like two aspects of the same improvisational instrument, particularly on "Indian Cradle Song," which he had used to crowd the dance floor at Connie's Inn. "Dinah" cooks along at a good clip, with Pops' airy voice providing a contrast to his brightly melodic, then bluesy, solo; while the flagwaver "Tiger Rag" swings with a vengeance as Pops burns through an incendiary trumpet ride.

Though Rockwell hadn't booked any gigs in California, Louis boarded a Los Angeles–bound train in May 1930, intending to escape the hard times in New York and Chicago. While staying at the Dunbar Hotel, he met a young man named Luther ("Soldier Boy") Gafford, who introduced him to Frank Sebastian, manager of the New Cotton Club, located next to MGM Studios in Culver City. Sebastian hired him to front the house band, led by Leon Elkins, and soon the outfit was promoted as Louis Armstrong and His Sebastian New Cotton Club Orchestra. Among the musicians were Lawrence Brown (trombone) and Lionel Hampton (drums).

Though Lil arrived in Los Angeles, planning to reclaim her husband, Louis was enjoying his tinsel town gig and had no intention of reconciling, especially after he discovered that she had a "boyfriend" in tow. Alpha, who had been writing regularly, also turned up, waiting for him in his dressing room after a set.

Louis made his Hollywood recording debut on July 16, playing on "Blue Yodel No. 9" with country pioneer Jimmie Rodgers, who liked recording with African American musicians. "The Singing Brakeman" quoted Nolan Welsh's "Bridwell Blues" in his vocal, Lil accompanied him on piano, and Pops played his first straight blues solo in five years. Five days later he settled in for a session with the Sebastian boys. Lawrence Brown opened "I'm a Ding Dong Daddy (from Dumas)," during which Louis began to sing the lyrics, then interjected "I done forgot the words" and launched into some scat before playing a cheery solo. After waxing "I'm in the Market for You" (a song written for the 1930 Janet Gaynor–Charles Farrell film *High Society Blues*), for the B-side, the band returned on August 19 to record "I'm Confessin'" and "If I Could Be with You One Hour Tonight." Following an argument with Tommy Rockwell, 22-year-old Lawrence Brown left the group to sign with Duke Ellington.

On October 9, Louis and Lionel Hampton formed a new lineup with bandleader Les Hite. Written by Johnny Green earlier that year, "Body and Soul" was chosen as their first recording, with Pops indicating his respect for the material by sticking to the lyrics, while still becoming adventurous with the phrasing and melody. One week later the Hite aggregation returned to cut two Eubie Blake–Andy Razaf songs— "Memories of You" (opened and closed by Hampton's vibes) and "You're Lucky to Me."

The New Cotton Club's prime location attracted a galaxy of Hollywood stars— directors, too, including D. W. Griffith on at least one occasion. Bing Crosby was singing with Gus Arnheim's Orchestra at the Cocoanut Grove Hotel and filming *King of Jazz* with Whiteman at Universal City, and often spent his evenings watching Pops perform. Louis recalled, "After Bing — the band — Mr. Arnheim and boys would finish work at the Grove they would haul ashes over to the Cotton Club where we were playing and swing with us, until 'Home Sweet Home' was played."[3]

That December, when Bing's bride, Dixie, was scheduled to arrive in Los Angeles, Crosby asked Pops to attend her reception at the train station: "Oh — Daddy Bing — Harry Barris and Al Rinker — they gave me all sorts in inducements, etc., to just go down to the station and sorta toot a few hot ones as she hit the ground from the train."[4] But Pops had other plans that evening.

The New Cotton Club Orchestra's sets were broadcast on a regular basis, reaching listeners who couldn't make the trip to Culver City. The band's radio exposure led to an offer from Tiffany Productions to appear as the "colored orchestra" in *Ex-Flame* (1930), George Draney and Herbert Farjeon's film adaptation of Mrs. Henry Wood's hoary stage play *East Lynne*— an incongruous pairing, considering that this stilted melodrama depicts the marital and parental problems experienced by English aristocrats. *Variety's* "Sime" wrote:

> This week "East Lynne" at Warners' Beacon. That's where it belongs, and at other neighborhooders where perhaps the women may go for this near-sobber called "Ex-Flame" and billed as a "modernized version of 'East Lynne'." ... And with a colored jazz orchestra.[5]

The film received a limited commercial release and was quickly forgotten. (No prints are known to exist.)

One evening, between sets, Louis and Vic Berton, a white drummer who had recorded with Red Nichols' Five Pennies, were sharing a joint in the parking lot when two detectives arrived. Confiscating the reefer, one of the "dicks" allowed Pops to play his final set before arresting him. During the ride to the station, he discovered that the detective was a fan and had no intention of "busting his chops." In fact, he told Louis that he had been arrested due to the informing of a rival bandleader at a local club. With no bail set, he was tossed into a cell at the Los Angeles City Jail to await trial for possession of marijuana. Offering no help, Frank Sebastian merely replaced him with another trumpeter who attempted to ape his vocal style.

Nine days later, Louis was taken to court, where quite a scene was developing. Attorneys, journalists from Chicago, and even strangers claiming to manage him crowded into the room. Much to Louis' relief, Tommy Rockwell had sent one of his "associates," Johnny Collins, who persuaded the judge to give his client a suspended sentence. That night Pops was back blowing at the Cotton Club, more popular than ever. Even the detectives who had busted him came to some of the gigs. However, Collins stayed on, demanding a cut from members of the band.

Louis recorded five more numbers with the Cotton Club Orchestra: "Sweethearts on Parade," "You're Driving Me Crazy" (complete with introductory shtick by Pops and Hampton, whom he calls "Satchelmouth," "Gate" and "Gatemouth") and "The Peanut Vendor" on December 23; and "Just a Gigolo" and "Shine" on March 9, 1931. When the Cotton Club engagement ended that month, Louis returned to Chicago. Though he stayed with Lil, he made his intentions very clear. He was biding his time until he could get a divorce and marry Alpha.

After Collins booked a brief run at the Regal Theater, Pops began fronting a new orchestra, supplementing the rhythm section of piano, banjo, bass and drums with a second trumpet (Zilner Randolph), trombone, tenor saxophone and two alto saxes. On April 20 all the musicians gathered to wax three sides for Okeh: "Walkin' My Baby Back Home," "I Surrender Dear" and "When It's Sleepy Time Down South," which Louis would incorporate as his official theme song, using it to warm up audiences at his live gigs. This seminal recording of the song includes an introductory rap by Pops and pianist Charlie Alexander, who calls Louis "Dipper."

Fans of the Hot Fives and Sevens disliked the new band, which, due to the influence of Guy Lombardo, played "sweet" rather than "hot." Instead of dazzling listeners with virtuoso trumpet solos, Louis often relied on strange, improvised lyrics, scat and his own brand of jive — lending a unique texture to familiar songs. In particular, "Sleepy Time" came under criticism for being a nod to minstrelsy. Depicting an idealized South, the song — to Pops — seemed like solace for hard times. The "death" of traditional New Orleans jazz came at the hands of practicality, as explained by Mezz Mezzrow:

> Storyville was fast becoming just another chapter in the jazzman's storybook, a fable about some mythical land-of-dreams. Tin Pan Alley was soon to be the main stem in the music world, and Basin Street just a one-way road to the poorhouse. ... Of all the great delta-bred musicmakers, it wasn't but a few ... who were still beating it out around Chicago, and not all of them were playing their original ad-lib style with small musical units. The wind was being sucked out of the Windy City. ... We were the keepers of the faith, the purists, the cats who stayed with it. The others were out to make money, not music.[6]

The band hit two more Okeh sessions in April, recording "Blue Again" (with Pops quoting "West End Blues" during the opening solo), "Little Joe" and the delightful "I'll Be Glad When You're Dead, You Rascal You" ("Oh, you dog — you *dog*") on the 28th; and "Them There Eyes" (with woozy trombone by Preston Jackson) and "When Your Lover Has Gone" the following day. Collins booked a regular Loop gig at the Showboat cabaret, a joint that served as a front for the mob. After ignoring threats of extortion from Joe Fiore and Emmet Ryan, two local wiseguys, Louis was relieved when they were arrested and charged with blackmail. However, he still had to deal with Tommy Rockwell, who had learned of Collins' attempts to grab a piece of the action. Louis had not known of the enmity between the two "managers," and was not about to return to New York, where he had been fired by Connie Immerman.

One night, while on the bandstand, Louis was startled by a thug who told him a visitor was waiting in his dressing room. After the set he hurried backstage, thinking "one of the cats" would be there, but instead discovered a bearded white man who called himself Frankie Foster. Louis quickly learned the purpose of the "visit" when Foster pulled a pistol on him, ordering him to catch a New York–bound train the next morning. Louis then was escorted to a telephone, where he heard a "familiar voice"— reportedly that of a Dutch Schultz associate — asking when he was going to play Connie's Inn.

"Tomorrow," replied Pops.

Johnny Collins immediately canceled the contract with the Showboat and sent the band on the road. After Louis and Alpha joined them, they played more than 50 cities in the Midwest and South, including New Orleans— his first visit in nine years— in mid–June. When they pulled into the train station, eight different bands were swinging away, and a huge crowd welcomed Pops, carrying him down Canal Street.

Spotting his old Waifs' Home instructors, Captain Jones and Peter Davis, in the crowd, he promised to visit the following day. Dapperly dressed, he fouled up the elaborate celebration plans by ducking into the kitchen with Louis Duplan, an old pal from the home, and happily devouring a plate of red beans and rice. Satisfied by his favorite meal, he clambered up to the dormitory and found his old bed, where he dozed off, much to the amazement of the current "waifs."

Booked into the Suburban Gardens for a three-month engagement, Louis thought he was out of harm's way. However, the American Federation of Musicians— informed (by Tommy Rockwell) of his "not fulfilling a contract with a New York nightclub"— expelled the members of the Armstrong orchestra. Then announcements of "niggers comin' down to New Orleans and taking the white musicians' jobs" were broadcast on the radio.

With Collins by his side, Louis defiantly appeared on stage at the whites-only venue. With 5,000 white folks packed inside — and 10,000 blacks lining the levee outside — the radio emcee looked at Pops and said, "I can't announce that nigger man."

Ordering the band to blast out a chord, Louis announced himself and then led his musicians in a swinging set. His courage in the face of racism and mob threats made him a hero to the blacks— and many whites, to boot — in his hometown, where he continued to play each evening. He also sponsored a local baseball team, naming it "Armstrong's Secret Nine," and donated radios to the Waifs' Home.

Following a visit by Lil, who ended her stay by stealing his car and driving back to Chicago with a hotel bellboy, and a close call at the Gardens when a drunken white woman stumbled onto the stage and grabbed Zilner Randolph's hand, Louis gleefully planned a free concert for his black admirers, to be held at a local Army base. After a huge crowd arrived, Louis and the band found the gate locked. Told that dancing was forbidden at U.S. Army bases, the congregation finally was driven out by bayonet-wielding National Guardsmen.

In September, Collins took the band on a bus tour of the South. When they arrived in Memphis, the bus driver, thinking the band would be white, refused to let them board. Soon the police arrived and, spying Louis sitting beside Collins' white wife, arrested them all. At the station they were told, "You ain't gonna come down to Memphis and try to run the city. We'll kill all you niggers."

In his cell, Louis responded by lighting up the joint his valet, Sherman Cook, had in his pocket. Cook had been worried that the reefer would be found on him, so Pops "destroyed the evidence." The following day the manager of the Palace Theater posted bail, in exchange for Louis' agreement to do a radio broadcast. Mezz Mezzrow recalled:

> When that bus pulled into Memphis the pecks all crowded around goggle-eyed, staring at the well-dressed colored boys in this streamlined buggy, and especially at the one colored boy up front, God forbid, sitting there actually talking to a white woman cool as pie, just like he was human. … When they hit the air, Louis started off with some doubletalk…. Halfway through the broadcast he announced that he wanted to dedicate his next number to the Chief of Police of Memphis, Tennessee. "Dig this, Mezzerola," he warbled while the band played his intro. Then he started to sing "I'll Be Glad When You're Dead, You Rascal You."[7]

Expecting a harsh response, the musicians were amazed when some cops thanked them for the honor.

For six months the band stayed on the road, heading back to the Midwest and East. While in Chicago on November 3–6, they waxed "Chinatown, My Chinatown," "Wrap Your Troubles in Dreams," "You Can Depend on Me," "The Lonesome Road," "I Got Rhythm" and Hoagy Carmichael's "(Up the) Lazy River," "Stardust" and "Georgia on My Mind" for Okeh. Louis vocally riffed up a storm on "Chinatown," "mug[ging] lightly, slightly and politely" before blowing a superior solo, smoothly gliding high-register notes over the band's driving pulse. Two takes of "Stardust" were cut, the unissued version (preferred by Carmichael) featuring an ultra-swinging vocal (nearly everything Pops does was appropriated by Bing Crosby) and a spectacular concluding solo.

At a gig in Philadelphia, Mezz Mezzrow and Zutty Singleton were in the audience. When Collins booked a gig at the Broadway Paramount-Publix Theatre in New York, Rockwell and Immerman sued for breach of contract. After losing the Broadway engagement, Louis filmed the title song for the Betty Boop cartoon *I'll Be Glad When You're Dead, You Rascal You* (1932) in a small studio in Fort Lee, New Jersey. First appearing in a live-action sequence with his band, he then is depicted in cartoon form as an African cannibal chasing the profusely sweating Bimbo and Koko

I'll Be Glad When You're Dead, You Rascal You (1932). In this Betty Boop cartoon, an African cannibal transforms into a swinging Louis as Bimbo and Koko run for their lives.

as they run for their lives. Finally, Pops transforms into "himself" as his own face is superimposed over the animation.

His second film of 1932, the nine-minute Paramount musical short *A Rhapsody in Black and Blue,* was directed by Aubrey Scotto from a story by Phil Cohan. A trumpet solo from "I'll Be Glad When You're Dead, You Rascal You" opens the film, as Louis receives above-the-title billing. The first scene fades in on the record spinning on a phonograph. The camera tracks back to show a black man enthusiastically (and badly) banging on pots and pans with large wooden spoons as he listens to the swinging tune. Soon his ogre of a wife appears, yelling that he should be mopping the floor.

Claiming to be a music lover, he wants "to listen to Louis Armstrong!" As soon as she leaves the room, he returns to slacking, commenting, "These mail-order wives don't work out."

She quickly returns to pummel him over the head with the mop, knocking him cold. While unconscious, he dreams that he is the King of "Jazzmania"—literally jazz heaven—where Louis is the official entertainer. Wading in soap bubbles and garbed in leopard skins, Louis improvises to the hilt on "I'll Be Glad When You're Dead," bracketing his ultra-bizarre gibberish lyrics with a few trumpet blasts. Ordered by the King to "blow 'Shine'," Pops does so, tearing into a wicked solo while completely ignoring the racist tableau surrounding him.

A Rhapsody in Black and Blue (1932). As the official entertainer of "Jazzmania," Louis, wading in soap bubbles and garbed in leopard skins, sings "Shine."

When the lazy husband recovers consciousness, he tells his wife, "I'll be glad when *I'm* dead, you rascal you," before getting the record smashed over his head.

Discussing this film, Gary Giddins wrote of Louis' "unequivocal self-confidence, bordering on macho arrogance ... a personal magnetism that transcended every trace of racial inferiority. ... He transcends the racist trappings by his indifference to every sling and arrow."[8] Donald Bogle noted:

> [T]he 1930s was for individual black performers a Golden Age. Admittedly, the black servants were repeatedly exploited and mistreated.... But through their black characters, the actors accomplished the almost impossible: they proved single-handedly that the mythic types could be individualized and made, if not things of beauty, then at least into things of joy. Almost every black actor of the period approached his role with a *joie de vivre* the movies were never to see again. ... With their own brand of outrageousness, the blacks created comic worlds all their own in which the servant often outshone the master.[9]

Hanging out in Harlem's theaters, Mezz Mezzrow observed:

> The most interesting part of the show was the race's reaction to the movies that filled in between stage shows. The pretentious acting in those beat-up Hollywood epics,

A Rhapsody in Black and Blue (1932). **Ignoring the racist tableau surrounding him, Louis tears into a wicked solo on "Shine."**

which had always kept me away from the movies (to me the flickers were just a mild Minsky's on celluloid), was the ridicule of all Harlem. ... The audience would roar so loud the picture was all forgotten for a few minutes.[10]

Back in Chicago the band played a few gigs, but called it quits in March 1932 when Louis decided to return to California. After a brief engagement with Les Hite's Band at the New Cotton Club, Louis and Collins made plans for an entirely different kind of tour — in a locale free of mobsters.

Collins had booked some gigs in England, where the press had been running articles about Louis, speculating about the possibility of his playing London. Jazz first reached Britain, courtesy of Sidney Bechet, in 1919; and now an Armstrong imitator, Nat Gonella, was performing for a loyal group of fans who happily bought any of Louis' recordings released by the Parlophone company.

On July 9, 1932, Louis and Alpha, joined by Collins and his wife, sailed from New York aboard the S.S. *Majestic.* Arriving in Plymouth five days later, Pops was greeted by *Melody Maker* reporter Dan Ingman. Learning that Collins had neglected to reserve lodgings, Ingman called several hotels, only to be turned down when the managements discovered that Louis was black. Finally, rooms were booked at the Howard Hotel on Norfolk Street, where journalist Percy Brooks assailed him with, "Hello, *Satchmo*."

Shaking the Englishman's hand, Louis asked, "Whatcha say, Gate?" Later, he wrote:

> *Man* I flipped. That was my *first* time hearing this name. ... And the first time I had a chance to talk to my trombone player who came from Paris to join my Band in England—I said to him, "The Editor of the Melody Maker Magazine just Shook my hand and called me *Satchmo* when my name was *Satchelmouth* before I came over here, why?" ... He said to me, "Because the man *thinks* you've got *Mo Mouth*." Hmm. So *that's* how it happened. And I've been *Satchmo* ever since.[11]

Posters advertising his two-week engagement at the London Palladium were plastered across the city. The billing "Louis Armstrong and His New Rhythm Band, Presented by Johnny Collins" was acceptable, but the caricature of Pops—a tuxedo-clad monkey blowing a horn—was outrageous. Louis had to speak to his Parisian musicians through an interpreter during rehearsals and the opening gig on July 18. He recalled:

> I was mighty glad to see Peter Du Conge from New Orleans among them! We had a nice talk about home. Also my friend Charley Johnson was along. There were several colored French musicians ... but ... all swing men can talk together and understand each other through their music, so we got along fine.[12]

On opening night—and at every gig after that—half the patrons walked out, utterly shocked at the manic display on stage. Many of them had loved Louis' sublime Hot Five and Seven recordings, but actually seeing him dance and mug his way through "Them There Eyes," "When You're Smiling," "Chinatown, My Chinatown" and "I'll Be Glad When You're Dead, You Rascal You" was too much to assimilate. Pops, however, remembered the gig as a rousing success:

> Well, we broke the all-time record at the Palladium for a band! We were at the top of the bill and out in big lights. We played at the Palladium for two weeks to standing room only. ... The management ... presented me with a beautiful gold French Selmer trumpet with my name engraved on it.[13]

Indeed, *Melody Maker* was effusive in praising his talents, but more conservative publications like the *Daily Herald* focused on his physical characteristics, especially his color. In his review, the racist Hannen Swaffer, noting that only "pale aesthetes" and "the young Jewish element" cared for the music, personally attacked Pops:

> Armstrong is the ugliest man I have seen on the music-hall stage. He looks, and behaves, like an untrained gorilla. He might have come straight from some African jungle and thereafter to a slop tailor's for a ready-made dress suit, been put on the stage and been told to sing.[14]

Louis saved all the reviews, paying little attention to the bad ones, in a scrapbook documenting the trip.

After closing at the Palladium, he hit the road with a 10-piece band of white English musicians—the first time he fronted an "ofay" ensemble—playing Nottingham, Liverpool and Glasgow. Though a few diatribes hit the newspapers, and some patrons continued to walk out, he wasn't publicly molested with the hateful remarks he often heard at home.

In late October, Louis and Alpha spent a week in Paris before sailing for New York. Arriving home on November 2, 1932—the day Franklin D. Roosevelt defeated Herbert Hoover for the presidency—Pops began a series of Eastern dates, opening at the Lafayette in Harlem. Ignoring an option that Okeh still held on Louis' services, Collins accepted an offer from the Victor Recording Company; and Louis, accompanied by the Chick Webb Orchestra—and nursing an extremely sore lip—waxed four numbers, including "That's My Home," "Hobo, You Can't Ride This Train" (on which Mezz Mezzrow sat in on bells as Pops laid down an enthusiastic vocal and fiery solo) and "You'll Wish You'd Never Been Born" at a church in Camden, New Jersey, on December 8. Two weeks later, a different group of musicians congregated in Camden to cut two medleys of "Armstrong Hits": the first, "I'll Be Glad When You're Dead," "When It's Sleepy Time" and "Nobody's Sweetheart"; the second, "When You're Smiling," "St. James Infirmary" and "Dinah." On these tracks Louis sounds as joyous as ever, bridging the numbers with stop-time solos, and laugh-scatting through the lyrics.

Mezzrow also joined Louis at a Baltimore gig on New Year's Eve 1932, witnessing the ritual of tending to his sore lip with a needle, removing the small pieces of dead skin so they wouldn't clog his mouthpiece. Following a grueling tour of one-nighters, Louis returned to Chicago in late January 1933 and cut more sides for Victor. Leading a 10-piece band that included Zilner Randolph and Teddy Wilson (piano), Pops completed 12 usable songs, including "I've Got the World on a String," "I've Got a Right to Sing the Blues" (which he opens with, "What's the matter wit'chu, boy?"), the foot-tappin' "Some Sweet Day," "Basin Street Blues," "Mahogany Hall Stomp" and a Randolph original, "Swing, You Cats." On April 24 and 26, they waxed 11 more numbers, including the frantic, shuzzit-fueled "Laughin' Louie" and "St. Louis Blues." A Midwestern tour followed, including dates in Indianapolis, Omaha and St. Louis.

In Philadelphia in early July, Louis was confronted by mobsters at a local vaudeville house. After playing his set, he hurried to the police station, placing himself in protective custody. Picked up by Collins, he then was whisked away to the London-bound S.S. *Homeric*.

While sailing to England, the often-inebriated Collins' shabby treatment of Louis worsened. Jazz patron John Hammond, who also was on board, became tired of hearing Collins call his client a nigger, and punched him out. After reaching London, Collins again got roaring drunk and finally left the country, taking Pops' passport with him. Though Louis now had to deal with another red-tape issue, he was glad to be rid of the obnoxious gangster. Considering a lengthy "jazz exile" to escape the mobs and racism back home, he temporarily hired English bandleader Jack Hylton as his manager.

Though the *Daily Express* had reported his death the previous winter, Pops quickly convinced the British that he was alive and swinging. Lodging at the Astoria Hotel, he played local clubs and enjoyed Chinese cuisine before he opened at the Holborn Empire on August 5.

In October he and his "Harlem Hot Band" embarked on a tour of Scandinavia. When he reached Denmark — where "Hot Clubs" of fervent jazz fans were common — he nearly was trampled when 10,000 admirers broke through a police barricade at the Copenhagen train station. In the midst of eight gigs at the city's Lyric Park, the band also performed for the camera on October 21. This 70-minute film, released as *København Kalundborg Og?*, includes a framing story featuring two "comic talents" at a radio station, and brilliant performances of "I Cover the Waterfront," "Dinah" and "Tiger Rag" by a supercharged, obviously high, Louis.

To start each of the numbers, Pops announces the title twice, lopes toward the band, and thrusts his trumpet to establish the tempo. During "Dinah," a cut-away shot shows the audience thrilling to his manic "choreography" just before he launches into a soaring solo. Then he spurs on the band to play a ferociously driving "Tiger Rag." The footage, directed by Holger Madsen, and photographed by Ludvig Branstrup and Flemming Geil, also includes the orchestras of Erik Tuxen, Roy Fox and Lili Gynes. Josephine Baker, who also performed in Copenhagen in early November 1933, was publicized as a member of the cast, but doesn't appear in the film.

Throughout the tour, Louis referred to Alpha as his spouse. In Stockholm, when

København Kalundborg Og? (1934). Louis sings a hard-swinging "Dinah" with his "Harlem Hot Band" at Copenhagen's Lyric Park on October 21, 1933.

København Kalundborg Og? (1934). Louis hits his climactic high note at the conclusion of the furious "Tiger Rag."

a reporter asked him if he liked Swedish women, he sent him packing with the reply, "Man, my wife has the best smorgasbord in the world."[15]

The following month he was back in London, entertaining the Prince of Wales. During one gig at the Holborn, he split his lip so badly, soaking his shirt with blood, that he was forced to take an extended rest. He resisted playing for the next four months, the first time he did so in 15 years of constant blowing. Though he received a telegram from Collins, who claimed he'd booked some major New York gigs, he threw it away.

The real proof of his determination not to play came in April 1934 when he refused to join "the Hawk"—tenor sax ace Coleman Hawkins—for a duet concert at the London Hippodrome. In fact, neither musician wanted to appear at such a concert, and this "bullshit" induced Louis to abandon Jack Hylton for another manager, Audrey Thacker.

Louis spent the late spring and summer of 1934 in Paris, sharing a flat on the rue de la Tour Auvergne with Alpha, who put him on a strict diet that dropped him to a slim 165 pounds. Free of the pressures of concerts and touring, he rested his lip, picking up the trumpet only when he wanted to jam with some fellow cats. He dug the scene with other American expatriates, including an ailing Josephine Baker, and enjoyed being respected as an artist for the first time. He was (at worst) a "nigger" and (at best) a "colored entertainer" in the States; in Europe he was followed by jazz critics who hailed him a genius, *le Roi du Jazz* and the personification of the *art negre* movement.

In October he formed a group — including musicians from his first stay in London — to record some numbers at Brunswick's Paris studio. Two versions of "On the Sunny Side of the Street" were waxed, as well as Louis' tribute to reefer, "Song of the Vipers," one of his finest recorded performances. At this point in his career he further refined his style, tempering his flights of vocal and instrumental improvisation with fewer, more carefully chosen notes, while still demonstrating formidable melodic and rhythmic abilities. "Vipers" was released in the United States, but when Brunswick wised up, they recalled it from record shops.

On November 9 and 10, 1934, Pops and his band played Paris' Salle Rameau, where the enthusiastic French audience demanded an exhausting number of curtain calls. A local promoter, N. J. Canetti, then booked them for a winter tour of Belgium, France, Italy and Switzerland, where they played a New Year's Eve gig at Lausanne. But when Louis' lip again became raw, an extension of the tour into North Africa had to be canceled. Threatened with a lawsuit by Canetti, Louis and Alpha sailed for New York on January 24, 1935.

As soon as Pops landed on American soil he was beset with lawsuits—from Canetti in France, Thacker in England, and Collins in New York. Joining forces with Mezz Mezzrow, who wanted to stop dealing drugs but (unbeknownst to Louis) was unable to kick a heroin addiction, Louis entered into unsuccessful negotiations with a Broadway producer. Before leaving for Chicago, Louis left $500 with Mezzrow, his "new manager."

Louis visited Lil at the 44th Street house, but rather than giving him the divorce he wanted, she sued him for $6,000 in maintenance. While waiting for Mezzrow to complete new arrangements in New York, Louis made the rounds of Chi town, blowing with old pals in familiar nightspots— until Joe Glaser, former proprietor of the Sunset Cafe, signed on as his *sole* manager.

Born in Chicago, Joseph G. Glaser had worked as a bootlegger and fight promoter connected to the Capone syndicate, and recently had been involved in prostitution and other illegal activities. While most people who knew Glaser held a low opinion of his talents, he became a father figure to Louis. Achieving true financial stability for his client — whom he molded into an entertainment superstar — Glaser went on to manage other African American jazz and blues giants, including Duke Ellington, Billie Holiday, Lionel Hampton, Dizzy Gillespie and B. B. King (while pocketing 50 percent of the take). Louis viewed him as a logical successor to his early New Orleans "protectors" like Black Benny, and overlooked his sordid past.

Glaser immediately set to work creating a clean slate for Louis, taking over management of the band from Zilner Randolph and crafting an "interview" piece for *Down Beat* magazine, announcing his management of "the king of the trumpet" and blaming his client's recent problems on Johnny Collins. He paid off Collins and Rockwell, and told Louis to forget about the lawsuits in Europe and Lil's insistence on alimony payments.

On July 1, 1935, Glaser hit the road with Louis and the band. Three weeks later they were in New Orleans, playing a six-night stand at the Golden Dragon, a club favored by blacks. A one-dollar fee was charged the first three nights, but Pops honored the promise he made four years earlier, blowing free for his black admirers during the second half of the engagement.

In September they headed north to play the Apollo Theater in Harlem, but the New York union wouldn't allow the musicians to perform. Wasting no time, Glaser replaced them with an orchestra led by Luis Russell. Though some of the players were below his usual standard, Louis enjoyed leading them. Glaser also landed a new record deal, with Decca's Jack Kapp, who recently had signed Bing Crosby and the Mills Brothers. The first session, on October 3, yielded four sides, including "I'm in the Mood for Love."

Now that Glaser was running the show, mobsters let up on Louis. On October 29 the band opened a four-month engagement at Connie's Inn. Connie Immerman had met his maker, and the club was under new management. Louis and the boys also waxed 10 more sides for Decca before the year ended. Louis' polished vocal on "I've Got My Fingers Crossed" is a prototype for all the big-band singing that followed over the ensuing decade, and his trumpet solo a prime example of his ever-evolving balanced blend of attack, volume, clarity and phrasing — a fully developed, beautifully melodic composition improvised on the spot.

Louis and Zilner Randolph's "Old Man Mose" features delightful vocal interplay between Pops (enthusiastically singing, "Mose kicked the bucket!") and his musicians. Other songs from the sessions include "Red Sails in the Sunset," "On Treasure Island," and "Solitude." During "I Hope Gabriel Likes My Music," Louis instructs each soloist to "swing one for Gabe" before blowing one himself.

"By the looks of Gabriel, he didn't think so much of that one," he says. "Well, I tell you one thing, Gabe! Me and Little Satchmo are going to go up there and hit you some high ones. I know you're going to like this. Look out, son, let's swing one!" Growling into his mouthpiece, he rhythmically climbs into the high register, then asks, "How's that, Gabe?"

After turning a tidy profit in Harlem, Louis and the band hit the road, playing Chicago, Detroit, Kansas City and St. Louis, often facing segregationist policies that forced them to eat and sleep in the bus. Glaser did what he could to overcome such discrimination, both on tour and in another arena he wanted to open up for his client: Hollywood motion pictures.

During the summer of 1935, Bing Crosby had planned to produce an independent feature film. Paramount had agreed to let its star undertake the venture, and the studio's former chief of production, Manny Cohen, partnered with Crosby, Bing's brother Everett and John O'Melveny to form Major Pictures Corporation. While at Paramount — a studio hit hard by the Depression — Cohen had incurred the wrath of the moneymen when he signed Bing, Mae West and Gary Cooper to personal contracts.

The first Major Pictures production — a musical, of course — would not be distributed by Paramount. Columbia's Harry Cohn won the bidding war, and expected one-third of the take — the other two-thirds to be split between Bing Crosby, Inc., and Cohen.

Working from the novel *The Peacock's Feather* by Katherine Leslie Moore, Jo

Swerling wrote the screenplay *Pennies from Heaven*, in which Crosby was cast as Larry Poole, an unjustly jailed stowaway on a "smuggling ship" who is asked by a death-row murderer to deliver a letter to the family of the people he accidentally killed. Eager to repay his vocal mentor in some professional way, Bing insisted that Pops be cast in a conspicuous role — one that eventually had him working for director Norman Z. McLeod during July and August 1936.

In the meantime, he cut 13 more Decca sides in New York, including Irving Berlin's "I'm Putting All My Eggs in One Basket" and Hoagy Carmichael's "Ev'ntide," and the originals "If We Never Meet Again" and "Swing That Music," which he coauthored with pianist-writer Horace Gerlach. On the latter, a furiously driving song, he blows a brilliant solo, hitting 50 continuous high Cs before climbing even higher on the ending.

Although his screen time in *Pennies from Heaven* is brief, Louis is listed fourth on the same credits panel as Crosby — the first time an African American received "star" billing in a mainstream Hollywood feature. If the film had been a studio production, he would have rated just another name in the cast listing. When Manny Cohen — who didn't want to deal with Joe Glaser — claimed that Louis would prove too expensive, Bing ignored him.

On August 7, Pops joined Jimmy Dorsey and His Orchestra to record five bigband arrangements, including "Skeleton in the Closet" from *Pennies from Heaven*, the novelty song "When Ruben Swings the Cuban," "Hurdy Gurdy Man" and "Swing That Music," driven home by an incendiary solo. Marking Louis' first collaboration with an established Hollywood band of white musicians, Dorsey dug into a New Orleans groove for a version of "Dipper Mouth Blues."

Ten days later Pops joined Bing, Frances Langford and the Dorsey Orchestra to record a *Pennies from Heaven* medley and an arrangement of the title song. The medley opens with Langford singing "Let's Call a Heart a Heart" and "So Do I," which Crosby opens, then segues into Pops swinging "Skeleton in the Closet," while "Pennies from Heaven" features vocals by all three.

On August 18, Pops returned to the studio for a session only possible in tinsel town, singing and blowing on two numbers with a "Hawaiian" combo, the Polynesians, including Lionel Hampton on vibes. Though he sounds decidedly out of place vocalizing a romantic ballad like "To You, Sweetheart, Aloha," his solo and Hampton's riffs get the band swinging for the length of a verse. "On a Cocoanut Island" became his first medium-tempo pop song, replete with a chorus of Caucasian crooners, but his trumpet playing again injects a slight groove.

The opening of *Pennies from Heaven* is quite grim for a Bing Crosby musical, as a newspaper headline announces, "Hart Dies Tonight." Following Hart's plea to "the fellow with the guitar" ("It's a lute," Larry advises, "a 13th-century lute" — a running gag in the film), he then begins walking "the last mile" as the scene fades out. The doomed Hart (John Gallaudet) bequeathed all his worldly belongings — including an old house in New Jersey — to "the Smiths," whom Larry sets out to find. Three weeks and 165 Smiths later, he tracks down Patricia ("Patsy") Smith (Edith Fellows) at a carnival.

While Larry and Patsy are busking on a street corner (he plays the lute, as she

Pennies from Heaven (1936). Larry Poole (Bing Crosby) discusses the "chicken situation" with Henry (Louis) in the first Hollywood feature film to award "star" status to an African American performer.

dances), a note requesting "Please come up to apartment 2B" hits the sidewalk. Soon Larry is face to face with Susan Sprague (Madge Evans), a Union County Welfare Board social worker assigned to commit Patsy to an orphanage. Discovering that the girl and her "Gramps" (Donald Meek) have been squatting in abandoned dwellings, Larry accompanies them to the "haunted house" left by the executed Hart. Agreeing to help Gramps create some "gainful employment," they transform the joint into "The Haunted House Café," where Larry will sing and they'll serve chicken dinners produced by their livestock: one rooster and one hen.

Larry then pounds the pavement, selling percentages to bankers, costumers, restaurant suppliers, even the musicians hired to back him up during the floor show. When Henry (Louis) is told that he and his band will receive a 10-percent cut, the trumpeter requests that seven percent would be easier to divide among the seven musicians.

"I told them cats you'd do the right thing!" Henry replies joyously. Informing Larry that both chickens are hens, he proposes that he and his cats heist 50 fowl from a local farmer. If they can each lift seven hens, Larry replies, he'll give them 14 percent.

More than 30 years after he worked on the film, Louis recalled:

Those scenes I had with Bing in that picture were Classics. Especially the scene where he wanted to open this Big Time Haunted House Night Club. But he didn't have enough loot to open this joint. And he liked our little seven piece band. So ... He said Henry (that was my name in the film), I would like to hire your band and I will give you and your boys "TEN" percent of the business, so you go and talk it over with your Musicians. Come back tomorrow and let me know as to what conclusion your boys came to. The next day I was right on time. And — Mr. Poole (Bing's name) met me halfway in the back yard, saying Henry, have your boys decided yet? And I said, Mr. Poole, I talked it over with my boys and told them you are willing to give them ten percent of the business. And my boys said they cannot figure out ten percent as we're only seven men. So if you will be so kind as to give us seven percent. We'll — Just then Mr. Poole said, OK Henry, it's a deal. And I smiled as I walked away saying Mr. Poole, *thank* you *very* much. — I told those guys that you would do the right thing. — "GASSUH" personified.[16]

The following scene features Louis' alternately chilling and electrifying performance of "Skeleton in the Closet," as he regales the patrons who enjoy being scared as they eat the stolen chickens. A visual highlight, the sequence includes a striking montage of medium close-ups featuring silhouettes of the pianist, bass player, drummer and Pops playing his trumpet.

Sixty years after the film's release, Krin Gabbard noted:

> When a dancer in a skeleton costume appears on stage, Armstrong's eyes bulge as he strikes a pose of trepidation. Those critics looking for signifying in this scene might note that Armstrong's reaction seems underplayed in comparison to the usual medley of exaggerated expressions that cross his face. They might also observe that his reactions have an aura of parody, perhaps allowing him some distance from the racist material. This first major appearance in a Hollywood film shows that Armstrong's mannerisms were already suited to anyone wishing to argue that he was working against the grain. It is possible that Bing Crosby, with whom Armstrong had already established a relationship, may have encouraged or at least tolerated the trumpeter's attempts to take liberties with the scripted material.[17]

Louis' "eye bulging" facial expressions are not much different from those he regularly did on stage while emphasizing particular syllables during a vocal performance, especially while scatting. (Any television performance from his later career proves that he did it until the end of his days.) And the white performers respond with exactly the same frightened gestures during this scene, as well as in an earlier sequence in which a local yokel transports Larry, Patsy and Gramps in his haycart. Observing the "haunted" house, the hick does the familiar "wide eyes and lump in the throat" bit.

The high point of Pops' performance is his demonstration of sheer musical power — as he had done in *A Rhapsody in Black and Blue* four years earlier — when he literally blows the skeleton off the stage with his climactic sustained high note. "That cat don't want no more of me," he tells the customers. (Here Ossie Davis' assertion that Louis' trumpet could kill is turned on its head when Pops uses it to vanquish the *undead*.)

The scene at the Haunted House Café contains familiar black stereotypes, but

Pennies from Heaven (1936). Henry prepares to vanquish the undead during "Skeleton in the Closet."

also includes an integrated performance of "Let's Call a Heart a Heart," during which Louis, standing beside Crosby, conducts the African American band—though at a physical distance (not to mention a cinematic separation created by careful editing). When the sheriff arrives with the chicken-deprived farmer, Pops and the rest of the musicians dive out the open windows.

In an attempt to raise money for the restaurant permit, Larry attempts to perform a "death-defying" act at the local carnival, but ends up in the hospital. After Patsy is committed to the orphanage and Susan loses her job for standing up to her boss, Larry (in an absurd, classic Hollywood sequence) searches New York for his "love," who agrees to marry him and adopt the girl, saving her from the horrendous institution! (Pops is never seen again after he flees through the window.)

Larry Poole is one of Crosby's most likeable characters, and he benefits from an excellent Arthur Johnston score, with unforgettable lyrics by Johnny Burke, who became his personal songwriter. Burke not only penned the words for "Pennies from Heaven," but later wrote "Moonlight Becomes You," "What's New?," "Swinging on a Star," "But Beautiful," "Like Someone in Love" and "It Could Happen to You"— songs that became standards—for Bing.

The film received poor reviews from Frank S. Nugent in the *New York Times* and "Land" in *Variety*, who wrote, "Best impression is by Louis Armstrong, Negro cornetist and hi-de-ho expert. Not as an eccentric musician but as a Negro comedian he suggests possibilities."[18]

On Sunday, September 27, 1936, a small group of African American performers gathered at New York's 135th Street YMCA to discuss forming a Negro Actors Guild. The project was the brainchild of bandleader Noble Sissle, who had been attempting to rally support for a black actors' union for several years. Chairing the meeting, he told the group that, "the present time was opportune because of the large number of celebrated colored artists appearing in and around the vicinity of New York."[19] Using the charitable work of the Catholic and Jewish actors guilds as a guide, they discussed the formation of their own organization with Allen Corelli of the New York Theatre Authority. Other speakers included Rex Ingram, Leigh Whipper, Ham Tree Harrington and Bill Robinson, who promised to donate $2,500 "if the guild confined its efforts mainly to welfare and charitable work."[20] Before adjourning, Sissle announced another meeting, to be held in his office at 1560 Broadway the following Thursday.

On October 1, seven performers—Sissle, Ingram, Harrington, Whipper, Muriel Rahn, Ada Brown and W. C. Handy—filed a certificate of incorporation for the Negro Actors Guild of America, Inc., with New York Supreme Court Justice William T. Collins. Identifying themselves as "Negroes of the Amusement Art," these founders set down a list of 10 objectives, including "upholding the honorable and sacred traditions of the Race," "to foster and promote the spiritual welfare of the Negro Actors and Actresses" and "to offer ... whenever possible voluntary financial assistance to its members."[21] Initially, the founders planned to hold an annual meeting on the first Monday of October, and additional gatherings "for discussions tending to promote Americanism, American ideals, good citizenship, good fellowship, and for the good and welfare of the theatrical profession."[22]

Active members of NAG could choose one of four membership levels: Active ($2 per year); Patron, "interested in the welfare of the Negro in the theater" ($5); Sustaining, "those who desire to help support the charities" ($10); and Life, "those who pledge their life-long support" ($50).[23] Naming Bill Robinson as "President-in-Memoriam," the constitution identified the titles of 22 officers, including 13 vice-presidents, to be elected at the annual membership meeting. While the first three vice-presidents had to be "members of the theatrical profession," the remaining 10 could be "laymen." Louis was among the musician-actors who joined early on, remaining a member until his death.

Louis' first memoir, *Swing That Music*, was published on November 7, 1936. As part of a major publicity campaign, Glaser thought the book would further his client's reputation with white Americans. Though Pops had been typing letters and stories since the early 1920s, he used Horace Gerlach as an amanuensis on portions of this project. Though the ghostwriter diluted some of Louis' language and added his own embellishments, this first published biography of an improvisational musician has been called "one of the earliest American attempts to trace the development of jazz."[24]

Another aspect of "remolding" Louis' image was Glaser's attempt to break him of his marijuana habit. Fearing that Pops and the musicians would be arrested, he forbade him to smoke his good shuzzit—an ultimatum that sparked heated arguments, usually resulting in Louis shouting, "Fuck you!" and leaving the room. Eventually—much to Glaser's relief—he confined his use to the dressing room.

Back in New York on March 24, 1937, Pops laid down some more exotic pop tracks with his "Polynesian" compatriots—now called Andy Iona and His Islanders—injecting one of his trademark licks at the beginning of his "On a Little Bamboo Bridge" solo, then scatting the same melody after blowing the final note. This performance is another example of his innovative technique of blending clever jazz improvisation with written pop arrangements. Rather than allowing the format to limit his expression, he subtly and naturally expanded the boundaries of popular song.

On April 7, Louis joined the Mills Brothers—Harry (another influence on Bing Crosby), Herbert, Donald and John—to wax two songs, "Carry Me Back to Old Virginny" and "My Darling Nelly Gray," adding lead vocals, smooth scat and gently swinging trumpet to their four-part harmonies and guitar accompaniment. The meeting of Pops and the fraternity proved so satisfying that they reassembled two months later for another pair of folksy numbers, "In the Shade of the Old Apple Tree" and Stephen Foster's "The Old Folks at Home (Swanee River)." Opening the Foster ode to antebellum life by playing a slight variation on the original melody, Pops then subtly undermines the antiquated references to "darkies" and "longing for the old plantation" with a liberating "yeah, man" and a little scat.

Regardless of its content, *Pennies from Heaven* marked a motion-picture milestone for African Americans. On April 9, 1937, Louis matched the feat, on radio, when he became the first black to host a network program, sponsored by Fleischmann's Yeast. Rudy Vallee—who had praised Pops' "most extraordinary style of singing ... [his] subtle musical understanding and keen mind"[25]—persuaded CBS to hire him, but *Variety* criticized his singing and band, calling the music "noise" that "sounded like a boiler factory in swingtime."[26]

In July, Louis gathered the Luis Russell boys for two New York recording sessions. Eight master takes were released by Decca, including Ted Koehler and Harold Arlen's "Public Melody Number One," in which Pops claims that "Frankenstein" would be "a bundle of joy ... compared to notes shot from a hot cornet."

Following a scale-climbing cadenza, he pauses as the chorus shouts, "Look out, Jack!"

"Well, all right, then," he mumbles into his mouthpiece. "You know I'm gonna make that note, ummm." Sliding up to an even higher note, he inspires a concluding chord from the band.

During a hard-driving arrangement of Irving Berlin's "Alexander's Ragtime Band," Pops advises, "Now listen, Gate; I want you to meet the leader of the band," before blowing a solo that merges with the trumpet section. The session also yielded an arrangement of "I've Got a Heart Full of Rhythm," cowritten by Louis and his *Swing That Music* collaborator, Horace Gerlach.

Though he didn't participate in the productions, Louis was represented in three 1937 cartoons: *Old Mill Pond*, *Clean Pastures* and *Swing Wedding*. Produced by Hugh Harman and Rudolph Ising for MGM, *Swing Wedding* affectionately animates several African American performers as frogs who participate in the nuptials of Minnie the Moocher and Smokey Joe (characters drawn from Cab Calloway's 1931 song "Minnie the Moocher").

Due to the tardiness of Smokey Joe (based on Stepin Fetchit), Minnie is swept off her legs by a romantic Calloway frog. The Satchmo frog first plays a trumpet and then sings "Sweethearts on Parade" before hopping into Joe, whom he informs of his sweetheart's decision to wed Calloway. Inspired to dance for Minnie, Joe sends his rival fleeing across the pond to join the orchestra in "Running Wild." Amidst the madness, Fats Waller and Bill Robinson frogs also appear. During the soiree, the Satchmo frog blows again, but breathes in so much air that he balloons out into the water, where he enthuses, "Ah, swing," as he floats away. As Krin Gabbard points out, "Although this cartoon feature is unquestionably dominated by racist stereotypes, the black entertainers are in some ways honored by the attention that has been lavished upon reproducing their images and habits of movement."[27]

During a September 1937 tour of the South, while shopping for food in Savannah, Georgia, Louis was shocked when he recognized a potato peddler as Joe Oliver, whose career had been derailed by Depression economics and worn-out chops. Giving the erstwhile King all the cash he had, Pops told him to buy some decent clothes. Before the gig that evening, he collected more dough from the musicians, who were pleased when Oliver, dressed to kill, appeared in the wings.

During October 1937 Louis was back in Hollywood, filming scenes for three major Paramount films: *Artists and Models*, *Doctor Rhythm* and *Every Day's a Holiday*. Jack Benny made his starring feature-film debut in *Artists and Models*, for the formidable Raoul Walsh, dead-panning alongside Ida Lupino, Richard Arlen, Gail Patrick, Ben Blue, Judy Canova and Hedda Hopper. Dressed as a menacing mobster, Louis "blasts" effectively in a Vincente Minnelli–directed sequence highlighting "Public Melody Number One," a performance that *Variety*'s "Abel" feared might prove a setback for up-and-coming mouther Martha Raye, who appears in blackface:

> There are a couple of misguided sequences, one of which may react negatively to the future of Martha Raye whom the studio has developed into sizeable b.o. It's that "Public Enemy Number One" sequence, done in a frankly Harlem setting, with Louis Armstrong tooting his trumpet against a pseudo-musical gangster idea. While Miss Raye is under cork, this intermingling of the races isn't wise, especially as she lets herself go into the extremist manifestations of Harlemania torso-twisting and gyrations. It may hurt her personally.[28]

Southern exhibitors agreed, sending complaints to Joseph Breen at the Production Code Administration. While community leaders in Atlanta referred to Raye's appearance with Louis as an "obscene" act that "would offend taste anywhere," *Shreveport Journal* editor Dolph Frantz wrote (to Paramount's Adolph Zukor), "For negroes and whites to be shown in social equality is offensive in this part of the country, where the races have nothing socially in common."[29]

While working on *Artists and Models*, Louis ran into his old pal, songwriter Ted Koehler, who years earlier had been shown quite a time on Chicago's South Side by Pops and Zutty Singleton, and now had given him the "Public Enemy Number One" persona. He wrote of Koehler, "He's a fine cat. I hope he writes a hit every time he breathes."[30]

On November 15 Pops led an octet, including Luis Russell (piano), Red Cal-

Artists and Models (1937). The controversial "Public Melody Number One" scene, pairing a black-faced Martha Raye with Pops.

lender (bass) and Paul Barbarin (drums), during an L. A. session that produced two Decca sides. "Once in a While" was followed by "On the Sunny Side of the Street," during which Louis lays down some gut-bucket scat, then sings, "I'll be rich as Rockiefeller —*no, suh!*" Russell and Barbarin returned for a larger-group session on January 12, 1938, to cut eight numbers, including "Satchelmouth Swing," featuring Louis' timebending lyric, "Rhythm don't mean a thing, when Satchelmouth begins to swing!"

Hoagy Carmichael and Stanley Adams' "Jubilee" was recorded for the soundtrack of *Every Day's a Holiday* (1938), featuring Louis as a bandleader in a street parade. Having enjoyed some degree of creative license at Paramount, Mae West now was making her final appearance for the studio. Following a recent "objectionable" radio performance with Edgar Bergen and Charlie McCarthy on *The Chase and Sanborn Hour*, front-office suits feared that West would quickly become box-office poison. Though she had toned down the suggestive content of her screenplay depicting the escapades of Peaches O'Day, a con woman who masquerades as French singeractress "Mademoiselle Fifi," "decent-minded" patrons spent their scarce Depression dollars on other cinematic fare. *Variety*'s "Flin," however, pointed out:

> By whatever standard posterity judges the acting career of Mae West, it never shall be said that she was ever dull. And her new film ... is a lively, innocuously bawdy

and rowdy entertainment, more typical of the star of "She Done Him Wrong" than her other recent vehicles. At the present moment Miss West's public relations are somewhat entangled by criticisms.... Such protests are likely to have a commercial influence, for good or ill.... It is certain she will not attract the morally conservative — but then, she never did.[31]

The *Every Day's* trailer features Pops, with the ballyhoo "A jubilee of music and laughter with Louis Armstrong, blowin' sweet and sassy," and he receives special billing in the film's opening credits, though his screen time is brief. His first appearance depicts him sweeping the street before pulling a trumpet from under his uniform to blast a few licks. A later, more substantial sequence shows him leading a band of black city employees as they jive down the street, playing "Jubilee," which he closes with one of his sustained high notes. At one point West plays a drum kit while riding on a wagon. Though Louis sings, he has no dialogue and is shown accompanied only by the other African American performers. Aside from his societal station as a street sweeper, his material is relatively free of harsh stereotypes. Thirty years after filming his scenes, Louis recalled, "I think [Mae's] name was Fifi in the picture, and I knowed her so well that every time I go up there I blow that line — still say, 'Miss Fifi, look me up, Mae West.' It could ruin a hundred dollars worth of takes."[32]

Every Day's a Holiday (1938). Louis as the bandleader in Mae West's final film for Paramount.

After incurring the wrath of Inspector "Honest" John Quade (Lloyd Nolan) for selling the Brooklyn Bridge to Fritz Krauftmeyer (Herman Bing), a bizarre "R"-rolling Teuton, Peaches falls in with Police Captain Jim McCarey (Edmund Lowe) and runs his mayoral campaign. The majority of the screenplay showcases West's famous witticisms ("Oh, there you are, boys. I was just beginning to crave a little action" and "With one more brain, you'd be a genius"); and her question, "How are you gonna sell a copper to the voter?" is answered by the huge political rally capped off by Louis' swinging march. Much of the film's comedy is provided by the insane antics of society swell Van Reighle Van Pelter Van Doon III (Charles Winninger) and his butler, Larmadou Graves (Charles Butterworth), who nearly trash an entire nightclub after the former preaches that anyone who goes out on New Years' Eve is "an idiot."

Pops was back with Bing, supposedly contributing "Specialty Numbers" to *Doctor Rhythm* (1938), directed by Frank Tuttle. Crosby's second independent feature for Major Pictures, it would be released by Paramount as "Adolph Zukor's presentation of an Emanuel Cohen production." Bing approached the film as a romp with his friends, including Beatrice Lillie, Mary Carlisle and Louis, who was scheduled to enjoy two production numbers and several dialogue scenes.

Following a month of rewriting, Tuttle began shooting in October 1937, but only one sequence featuring Louis— a musical number — remained in the script, and all of his dialogue had been eliminated. Paramount's pressbook, printed prior to the distribution of the final cut, described Pops' performance in less-than-flattering terms:

> [A]s the light comes up we see that the musicians aren't a symphony orchestra at all, but a hot Negro dance band, and the leader no Toscanini in black full dress, but a chubby darkie in a dress suit of silver cloth. He stands there dreamily until someone toots an impatient note at him from the rear, then he bestirs himself to reality, sighs, raises his trumpet and goes into "The Trumpet Player's Lament," which begins, "I wish that I could play like Jose Iturbi, Instead of tootin' notes into a derby..." The disconsolate one is Louis Armstrong.[33]

By the time the studio released the film in early 1938, Louis' scene had hit the cutting-room floor, a victim of Southern exhibitors who objected to his appearance with an integrated orchestra. (Tuttle, however, had been careful to distribute publicity stills showing Louis with black musicians only.) Crosby wanted his friend in the film, but, due to a series of problems (one involving his relationship with shady golfing pal "Mysterious" John Montague), his hands were tied. Pops recorded "The Trumpet Player's Lament" during the January 12, 1938, session with Luis Russell.

Based loosely on O. Henry's short story "The Badge of Policeman O'Roon," the finished film stars Crosby as Bill Remson, a successful physician, and the wildly hammy Beatrice Lillie as Mrs. Lorelei Dodge-Blodgett. While attending an annual reunion at the Central Park Zoo with three fellow alumni of Brooklyn's P. S. 43, Remson poses as his pal, Patrolman O'Roone (Andy Devine), in an attempt to woo lovely Judy (Mary Carlisle). In his *New York Times* review, Frank S. Nugent wrote:

Bing Crosby, Bea Lillie & Co. are wooing the comic muse as though they had a $5 bet on its surrender. Maybe a $3 bet. Nothing quite so grim as their pursuit of the elfin guffaw has been seen in these parts since Martha Raye fell down the incinerator chute.[34]

The first official meeting of the Negro Actors Guild had been held at 1560 Broadway in New York on Saturday, December 4, 1937. Noble Sissle was unanimously elected President by a small group of members, who also chose Bill Robinson as Honorary Vice President, the Rev. Adam Clayton Powell as Chaplain, Fredi Washington as Executive Director, W. C. Handy as Treasurer, Muriel Rahn as Recording Secretary, J. Rosamond Johnson as Chairman of By-Laws, Cab Calloway as Chairman of the Executive Board, Elmer Carter as First Vice Chairman, Leigh Whipper as Second Vice Chairman, and Simon S. Feinstein as Counsel.

Louis was elected Seventh Vice President among a group of 10, including Ethel Waters (First), Duke Ellington (Fourth), Marion Anderson (Eighth) and Paul Robeson (Ninth). All members suggested names of African American performers who should be asked to join the Guild, and another meeting was scheduled for 11:30 P.M. on Tuesday, December 7. The energetic Fredi Washington, who had come to prominence as "Peola" in Universal's *Imitation of Life* (1934), spoke to the gathering, informing them of an *Amsterdam News*–sponsored benefit to be held at the Apollo Theatre at midnight on December 17.

At a NAG Executive Board meeting on February 7, 1938, a presentation included several communications from Guild supporters, including Louis, W. C. Handy, Countee Cullen and New York Mayor Fiorello LaGuardia. Following the death of King Oliver, who suffered a cerebral hemorrhage in his New York room on April 10, the Executive Board met again on May 6. Fourteen members, including Handy and James Weldon Johnson, discussed paying for Oliver's funeral, at which Adam Clayton Powell had officiated. Louis, who played during the service, had disliked Powell's moralistic sermon, which focused on Oliver's philandering ways, but — as reported by Fredi Washington — contributed $28 toward the $190 funeral expense. $100 had come from the NAG Actors Fund, and another $10 had been chipped in by Duke Ellington, leaving the remaining $52 to be picked up by the Guild.

Back in New York, Pops and the Russell cats waxed eight Decca sides during two May sessions. "As Long as You Live (You'll Be Dead If You Die)," featuring a distinctive melody and lyrics, swings hard with a fine solo; and "Reverend Satchmo … beat[s] out a mellow sermon" on his first recorded arrangement of "When the Saints Go Marching In." A highlight of the second session, the Gershwin's "Love Walked In" swings along nicely, with Louis laying some smooth scat over a stop-time bridge.

The following month Pops cut three more songs with the Mills Brothers. "The Flat Foot Floogie" is the standout, combining Louis' trumpet and scat with the *harmony* scat of the brothers. The song ends with Pops rapping, "Flat foot, slew foot, sugar foot, cush foot, wing foot, big foot, and *satchel* foot."

On June 14 he was backed by the Decca Mixed Chorus on four gospel numbers, including his first recordings of "Shadrack" and "Nobody Knows the Trouble I've Seen," a respectful spiritual arrangement with a calming, straightforward lead vocal.

Ten days later, fronting a group of musicians featuring guitarist Dave Barbour, Louis tore it up on "I Can't Give You Anything but Love" and his first recording of "Ain't Misbehavin'" in a decade.

Two of Pops' "Reverend Elder Eatmore" performances, supported by Harry Mills and a mixed chorus, were recorded on August 11. Entertaining examples of his dramatic and comic abilities, the con man–preacher's "Sermon on Throwing Stones" and "Sermon on Generosity" provide a glimpse of the actor he could have been.

He made another film appearance in late 1938, for Warner Bros. producer Hal B. Wallis in the Dick Powell–Anita Louise musical *Going Places*. The third cinematic adaptation of the Victor Mapes–William Collier play *The Hottentot*, this version did little to boost the faltering career of Powell, whose previous two films, *Hard to Get* (1938) and *Cowboy from Brooklyn* (1938), fared poorly at the box office. As ambitious sporting goods salesman Peter Mason in *Going Places*, Powell impersonates a famous jockey, falls in love with Ellen Parker (Louise), and reluctantly rides her wealthy uncle's horse "Jeepers Creepers" in a major race. As Jack Withering, the rich man's playboy son, Ronald Reagan contributes an entertaining performance, but Louis steals the show as "Gabe, the Black Hostler." Pops performs Harry Warren and Johnny Mercer's "Jeepers Creepers," first using it to tame the savage beast of a horse, and then to spur the steed on during the climactic steeplechase.

Though the screenplay is awash in stereotypes, Louis (who earned $5,000 for the role) was able to develop a characterization that rises above the other black bit parts, including the typical servant types and a fellow stable worker who does nothing but lie around all day. Gabe is introduced from behind as he grapples with the raging horse. Unable to subdue the animal, he fetches his trumpet and begins to blow "Jeepers Creepers" just as Maxie (Harold Huber) and Droopy (Allen Jenkins), two mob-connected racetrack touts, arrive at the corral.

Observing his serenade, Maxie remarks, "What kind of place is this? An insane asylum for horses?" and suggests that he stop loafing and do some real work.

After Droopy calls him "Uncle Tom"—a comment he ignores—Gabe informs them that he named the song after Jeepers Creepers in an effort to control the horse. Maxie then repeats the Uncle Tom remark, and Gabe trots into the corral to blow the animal into submission as the two touts argue about the possibility of getting it into the upcoming steeplechase.

As the horse hides out in some bushes, Gabe sings the opening verse of "Jeepers Creepers." When he hits the chorus, the horse, utterly enchanted, runs over to him. "Where'd you get those eyes—*Gate*? Where'd you get those eyes—*Satch*?" he sings to the animal. The situation is utterly absurd, but Pops' transcendent performance and the clever editing create a charming scene. *Variety*'s "Char" noted, "Armstrong sells [the song] effectively, apart from doubling for comedy relief, which makes him a wholly interesting and amusing character."[35]

Louis again appears at the stables when Ellen takes Peter to see Jeepers Creepers. After the horse breaks out of its stall and chases Peter around the building and onto the roof, the terrified "jockey" falls onto its back and is taken for a furious ride through the countryside. When the girl makes a remark about Peter's "strategy," Gabe replies, "You can call it strategy, Miss Ellen, but I call it immediate murder,"

Going Places (1938). "Where'd you get those eyes — *Gate*?" Gabe, the Black Hostler (Louis), sings "Jeepers Creepers" to the song's racehorse namesake.

and rides off on a scooter in hot pursuit! Catching up to horse and rider, he again blows "Jeepers Creepers" on the trumpet and saves Peter from a potentially fatal accident. (This cinematic maneuver is perhaps the strangest ever enacted by one of the world's great musicians.)

Pops' third scene is a lengthy production number during which he performs Warren and Mercer's "Mutiny in the Nursery," a song about children's rhymes, accompanied by "specialty" vocalist Maxine Sullivan (who is dressed as the Withering family maid) and a gang of dancers and backing singers. The lavish number also involves Powell and Louise, who join in on vocals but remain cinematically segregated throughout. The romantic pair are never included in any of the shots featuring the black performers — and actually only appear in one shot with the other white actors (seen in the background). The scene culminates with Louis climbing up to a high note that he holds for 14 seconds, just before the "Black Groom" (Eddie "Rochester" Anderson) runs in to inform the Witherings that their mare, "Lady Ellen," is missing. (She has been horse-napped by the two touts.)

Pops next appears, dressed in a nice three-piece suit, at the local hotel to visit Peter, who is about to ride Jeepers Creepers in the steeplechase. Approached by Droopy, who tells him of his bet on the horse, Louis engages in some well-played, Oliver Hardy–type verbal humor as he expresses his disapproval. In the hotel room, he tells the terrified would-be jockey about the previous tenant of the room, who

Going Places (1938). Enjoying a rare character part, Louis valiantly ignores the insensitive shtick of racetrack tout "Droopy" (Allen Jenkins).

was just as healthy as Peter but, two hours later, was "on the ground, dead" after an equine ride. The scene fades out as Peter whispers some instructions into Gabe's ear.

The final scene opens with Gabe again tussling with the horse, now attempting to entice him behind the starting line at the track. Hopping aboard his scooter, he drives over to a flatbed truck, were his fellow musicians await. They then speed along the outside of the fence, playing a big-band arrangement of "Jeepers Creepers" to encourage the horse. At one point the truck cannot follow the course, and Jeepers Creepers runs amok — through a family picnic, washlines (a black laundress watching the white-sheet clad Peter on horseback suggests a frightening, perhaps unintentional, connotation), and trenches where men are working. Finally, the truck pulls back close to the track, Jeepers Creepers wins the steeplechase, and Peter and Ellen engage in a golden-age Hollywood embrace. Learning that his partner placed their $10,000 on another horse, Maxie chases Droopy onto the course and falls into a water pit as the film fades out.

Though the early scenes contain the expected racial stereotypes, the character depictions are well balanced. Gabe is twice referred to as "Uncle Tom" by the touts, but these moronic criminals (depicted as far less intelligent than the "Black Hostler") also call the white characters sarcastic, demeaning names, mocking both appearance and mental capacity. In one scene, Maxie and Droopy (called "Dopey" by his colleague) refer to Peter's balding, eccentric supervisor, Franklin Dexter (Walter

Catlett)—who is posing as his valet—as "Fancy Pants," "Eight Ball" and "Gabby Puss." The film is populated with buffoonish characters, including Ellen's uncle, Colonel Withering (Thurston Hall), who cheats on his wife with a young woman who calls him "Poopsie," and uses the money given to him for "expeditions" to buy stuffed big-game animals to prove that he went on African safaris. The most absurd character is an obese customer (Ferdinand Munier) at the sporting goods store who comes in to ride the mechanical horse. All told, *Going Places* is representative of late 1930s Hollywood cinema, rife with content now considered politically incorrect.

In one of his earliest screen roles, Ronald Reagan hints at his sports-announcing success as he and Anita Louise recount one of the famous jockey's death-defying rides. Another amusing scene involves the composition of a "horse song" by Peter, Dexter, Maxie and Droopy. Titling their opus, "Oh, What a Horse Was Charley, Until He Got a Charleyhorse," they all exchange vocal riffs before the unwelcome touts are literally reined-in and driven out the hotel-room door.

Again joyously performing in the face of cinematic bigotry, Louis created the closest thing to a real fictional character he would experience until the early 1950s. His performance of "Jeepers Creepers" helped earn a Best Song Academy Award nomination for Harry Warren and Johnny Mercer.

Conventional wisdom suggests that Louis considered a film appearance just another gig in an endless string of performances. Though it is true that touring was his bread and butter, he consistently gave his all, whether for a live audience, a recording, or a filmed sequence—and his membership in the Negro Actors Guild suggested that he took his acting career seriously.

On October 7, 1938, Fredi Washington wrote to NAG Executive Board Chairman Cab Calloway and other E. B. members, tendering her resignation as Executive Secretary, "due to personal business matters and health," to take effect November 1. However, wanting to remain of service to the organization, she requested that her membership be changed from "associate" to "active."[36] In a letter to Democratic leader and future U.S. Postmaster General Frank C. Walker, Bill Robinson described a NAG benefit event, to be held at New York's 46th Street Theatre on December 11: an "evening's entertainment with stars of the screen, radio, concert stage, etc., that will linger in the memories of those who attend for a long time afterwards."[37]

To commemorate the occasion, NAG published a lavish souvenir program that featured formal photographs of its top

The Negro Actors Guild of America published a lavish souvenir program to commemorate its first benefit event, held at New York's 46th Street Theatre on December 11, 1938.

officers, including Pops. At this time, several white Hollywood luminaries were supporting the union, including Eddie Cantor, Al Jolson, Tyrone Power, Rudy Vallee and Paul Whiteman, who all sat on the Benefit Committee, and Bing Crosby, who joined the Advisory Committee.

Louis' marriage to Lil finally ended on September 30, 1938. Charged with desertion, he escaped paying alimony and, on October 11, wed Alpha before a gig in Houston. Bassist George ("Pops") Foster was best man. This nuptial bliss was not destined to endure, however. As soon as the band returned to Harlem to play the New Cotton Club, Louis became enamored of a lovely chorus girl named Lucille Wilson. Their "relationship" began when he started buying the cookies she sold to help support her mother and siblings. He later wrote:

> One night when Lucille came into my Dressing Room to deliver her Cookies, I just couldn't hold back the deep feeling and the warmth that I had *Accumulated* for her since I first laid eyes on her in the front line on the Cotton Club floor. And about all things— Swinging in that Front Line every night — Looking *beautiful'er* "n" *beautiful'er* every night. Then too— She's doing her dance every night in front of me standing there directing the Band and *Blowing* my Solos on my trumpet whenever it was time for me to *Blow* "n" *Wail*. All of those Beautiful Notes along with Lucille's perfect dancing. Me — diggin those cute *lil* buns of her's.[38]

Calling her "Brown Sugar," Louis told Lucille that he had "eyes for her," and — if any of the other cats were in the running — to at least give him a shot. Soon they were going to the movies together and, after the final show of the evening, driving around town in a rust-colored Packard that Glaser had given him.

For 1939, Glaser cooked up a true extravaganza: "The King of the Trumpet" and the 14-man Luis Russell Orchestra would be accompanied by other powerhouse "colored" acts, including the Dandridge Sisters and Pops' hero, Mr. Bojangles. Now Louis' film career began to affect the content of his concerts, which featured less improvisational jazz and more movie songs, such as "Skeleton in the Closet" and "Jeepers Creepers." (To publicize the upcoming tour, excerpts from "Skeleton," "Swing That Music" and "Confessin'," showing Pops with the Russell band, were included in a "Hearst Metrotone News" short released at the end of 1938.)

The show rang in the New Year at the New York Strand, then went on the road, hitting cities of all sizes, including Baltimore, Buffalo, Indianapolis, Chicago, Kansas City, Madison, St. Paul, Dayton, Cleveland, Atlanta and Miami. Returning to the Cotton Club in October, they played an extended engagement for the next seven months.

The 15-man band recorded "Jeepers Creepers" and the Louis–Horace Gerlach number "What Is This Thing Called Swing?" on January 18, 1939. One month later, Pops and the Casa Loma Orchestra cut a Hoagy Carmichael pair, "Rockin' Chair" and "Lazy Bones." On April 5 he and the Russell aggregation visited Hot Five territory, recording big-band arrangements of "Hear Me Talkin' to Ya," "Save It, Pretty Mama" and "West End Blues," a draggy, far less virtuosic version than the 1928 waxing. Over the course of the year, the band cut 11 more Decca sides, including Kid Ory's "Savoy Blues" and "Baby, Won't You Please Come Home?"

Afforded time to seek other employment, Louis played some radio gigs, including an ASCAP Award Concert at Carnegie Hall on October 6 and a broadcast from the Waldorf-Astoria the following week, performing "Ain't Misbehavin'" with the Benny Goodman Orchestra — the first time the real King of Swing met the officially acknowledged one. Though Pops practically had invented swing, public tastes were gravitating toward the more refined, elegant version played by white big bands led by Goodman, Tommy Dorsey, Harry James and Glenn Miller. However, the success of musicologist William Russell's recent book *Jazzmen*, featuring interviews with pioneering New Orleans musicians, including Bunk Johnson (who, in early 1939, had written to Louis, describing a decade of hard times), revived an interest in traditional, small-group jazz.

Louis also returned to Broadway, as Bottom the Weaver in *Swingin' the Dream*, Gilbert Seldes and Eric Charell's musical adaptation of Shakespeare's *A Midsummer Night's Dream*. Staged at the new Rockefeller Center Theater, the play, set in 1890 Louisiana, featured a primarily black cast, including Pops, Butterfly McQueen (as Puck) and "Moms" Mabley (as Quince). The Jimmy Van Heusen score was performed by Benny Goodman and his sextet, and Walt Disney designed the sets. This talented troupe opened on November 29, 1939, but their combined efforts failed to salvage a script awkwardly combining iambic pentameter with slang phrases unsuitable to both Elizabethan England and 19th-century New Orleans. After the 13th performance, the curtain dropped for the final time. However, Leonard Feather, in his *Down Beat* review, wrote, "From the moment he enters in the red fireman's suit as 'Bottom' and calls, 'Peace, Brother,' until the final scene in which you learn Pyramus kicked the bucket, Louis is the same brilliant actor."[39] In a letter written seven years later, Pops recalled:

> Butterfly McQueen.... She's one of my favorite actresses. We (she and I) worked in a play called *Swinging the Dream*, a Shakespearean play. And every night I'd wait for her to come on the stage and do her act. And it would just knock me completely out. Yea, she's a great little actress.[40]

One day prior to opening in the play, Louis was elected to membership in ASCAP.

For Louis, 1940 was nearly identical to the previous year, combining gigs at the Cotton Club with a cross-country tour and recording dates. On March 14 he led his band in a Decca session, producing five sides, including the Armstrong originals "Hep Cats' Ball," "You've Got Me Voodoo'd" and "Lazy 'Sippi Steamer," all fine examples of bluesy, swingin' trumpet and solid jive. Another original number, "Harlem Stomp," was contributed by trombonist J. C. Higginbotham. Pops then joined the Mills Brothers on April 10 and 11, singing about the lax labor conditions of the "W.P.A.," the mellow jive of "Boog It," and the charms of Don Redman's "Cherry" and Irving Berlin's "Marie."

In its May 1940 newsletter, NAG included an article about "Captain's Courageous," a group of women who were raising money for the Guild. Among the first to join the effort was "Captain" Lil Armstrong. On May Day, Pops and the band recorded three songs, including his own "You Run Your Mouth, I'll Run My Business" and the nonsense number "Cut Off My Legs and Call Me Shorty."

On May 27, Louis assembled a band of New Orleans jazzmen, including Sidney

Bechet, Wellman Braud and Zutty Singleton, to get traditional on four Decca sides: "Perdido Street Blues," "2:19 Blues," "Down in Honky Tonk Town" and "Coal Cart Blues." He was uncomfortable during the sessions; and though Louis sometimes politely deferred to the elder statesman of improvisation, Bechet, jealous of Louis' stardom, later criticized him for championing personality over pure jazz performance.

On March 10, 1941, Pops returned to the small-group format with a new Hot Seven lineup, including Luis Russell and Sidney Catlett (drums). He enjoyed recapturing the 1920s style in his playing and singing on four songs, including "I Cover the Waterfront" and "Long, Long Ago." One month later he recorded another four sides, including the charming blues "Hey, Lawdy Mama" and the ominous "Now, Do You Call That a Buddy?" (a tale of two-timing during which he raps, "Now, lookee here, boy; I don't dig you," and sings, "I'm gonna *shoot* my buddy; he's just a dirty cat").

While on tour that autumn, Louis gathered the full orchestra for a November 16 recording date in Chicago, playing with rhythmic and lyrical brilliance on yet another version of "When It's Sleepy Time Down South," and scolding the "dog" once again during "I'll Be Glad When You're Dead, You Rascal You": "You're the most no-goodest cat I ever met" (because of eating all the red beans and rice, and messing around with his wife, in that order of importance).

Though Louis didn't act in the film, Paramount's *The Birth of the Blues* (1941), released that same month, briefly features him in a concluding montage honoring major jazz innovators, including Duke Ellington, Benny Goodman, Tommy and Jimmy Dorsey, and Paul Whiteman (who couldn't be excluded from a Bing Crosby film). Crosby portrays a New Orleans lad who, in 1898, is drawn to the music of the first African American hot musicians. Defying the protestations and (mild) beatings of his father, he goes on with the help of a trombonist (Pops' future bandmate Jack Teagarden) and a Memphian cornetist (Brian Donlevy) to develop America's first successful white hot band (patterned after the Original Dixieland Jazz Group, an all-white New Orleans band that became popular in New York as early as 1917).

Though the film focuses on the Caucasian contribution, it also includes a surprising amount of material dealing with that devilish "colored music" that so exasperates the "proper" white folks of New Orleans. Thanks to the presence of Crosby, the scenes featuring the black performers are handled evenly, and very little blatant stereotypical behavior is included. (A modicum is contributed by Mantan Moreland, who characteristically rolls his eyes while "playing" a cornet.) Eddie ("Rochester") Anderson, delivering one of his finest performances, is shown teaching Crosby's female friend (Mary Martin) how to sing like a bona fide "colored" person, and — in classic "tom" style — nearly giving his life to help his white pals. (During a nightclub brawl with gangsters he rushes in, only to be brained with a whiskey bottle. A touching and sensitively directed scene later shows Crosby and his cohorts singing over his sickbed — which, of course, in true Hollywood fashion, pulls him through.)

During 1941, Orson Welles, fresh from directing *Citizen Kane*, had met Louis in Hollywood. After discussing the possibility of a film, they had signed a contract with a publisher, Allen, Towne and Heath. Welles then worked on "The Story of Jazz," an epic screenplay depicting the experiences of various musicians over the course of four decades, tied together by the commentary of two "comedian" narrators. Opening in 1899, the early scenes were to focus on young Reggie (based on Louis), who, at one point, meets up with King Jeffers (inspired by King Oliver). While attending a black college in the South, Reggie attracts scorn when trying to work improvisation into the classical repertoire. Subsequent scenes were to depict a courtroom battle between conservative forces believing that jazz is "devil" music and more enlightened folks who recognize its value as a true American art form; the utilization of jazz during World War I; and the challenges faced by several post-war musicians.

At one point Welles again contacted Louis, intending to rewrite the sprawling script as a more accurate depiction of the Armstrong story. He also brought Duke Ellington on board, paying him $1000 per week for three months, auditioned Billie Holiday for a potential role, and cast Hazel Scott in the role of Lil. RKO-Radio signed David Stuart, manager of Hollywood's Jazz Man record shop, as technical advisor, and Welles made plans to shoot portions of the film in Technicolor.

In a letter to Leonard Feather written in Atlanta on September 18, 1941, Louis mentioned the "Story of Jazz" project, as well as his earlier screen roles:

> We're getting ready to play a swell dance here tonight for the colored folks and the white folks are invited as spectators…. Honest they get along down here at these dances just like one beeg family. It would be kicks sometimes if you could dig some of this jive so's you can realize just what I am talking about….
>
> That was real swell news when you told me that you are going out in Hollywood to help me out with my picture…. To show you how glad I was to hear of it — I wrote to Mr. Elliott Paul the producer of this flicker that I'm to make. And man — I sent you sky high. Honest I did. I told him — if there's anyone that knows about my life it's Leonard Feather….
>
> As far as the most important events in Jazz during my 25 years — well, the first one was when Pops booked me for my first commercial program over the NBC for Fleischmann's Yeast…. Then too — those pictures — *Pennies from Heaven, Artists and Models, Everyday Is a Holiday* — And that fine *Going Places, Jeepers Creepersly*–speaking.

Louis also listed some recordings "I personally think were kinda good":

Memories of You
West End Blues
Ol' Man Mose
Swing That Music
Confessin'
Lazy River[41]

Unfortunately, Orson Welles shelved "The Story of Jazz" on October 28, 1941, when shooting began on *The Magnificent Ambersons* (1942).

3

Silver-Screen Swing

What do I want to get famous for? What do I care about famous? The pub-
lic does that. That ain't me. Man, I just blow. I don't care who I'm play-
ing for or where I'm playing. My mind never leaves that tailgate. Every
time I pick up that horn, I can see Joe Oliver, Bunk Johnson, Baby Dodds.
— Louis Armstrong[1]

After the United States declared war on Japan in December 1941, everything on
the homefront — including venues for musical performers — changed. Rather than
nightclubs, theaters and ballrooms, Joe Glaser was booking school gymnasiums and
military bases, where mostly white G.I.s were grateful to hear good music played by
enthusiastic performers. During the conflict, Louis would lend his services to several homefront causes and receive certificates of appreciation from the Hollywood
Canteen (signed by Bette Davis) and the American Theatre Wing of the Stage Door
Canteen of Cleveland (signed by Bob Hope).

In January 1942, Louis was "deserted" by Alpha, whose love of extravagance had
been curtailed by her husband's declining wartime earnings. In fact, Louis reported
to Walter Winchell that she had taken him for "THOUSANDS and THOUSANDS
of dollars" before beginning an affair with an "ofay boy" (Cliff Lehman, the drummer in Charlie Barnet's band).[2] But with Alpha gone, he was free to pursue Lucille
Wilson, whom he called "Ceily."

During a Los Angeles session on April 17, 1942, Louis and the band cut four sides,
including a driving arrangement of "I Never Knew." Three days later they appeared
in four "soundies," promotional short subjects shown between feature films. Once
again filming "I'll Be Glad When You're Dead, You Rascal You" and "Shine," he also
sang "When It's Sleepy Time Down South" and was accompanied by hefty singer
Velma Middleton's trademark "choreography" — which included tumbling around
on the floor while doing the splits — on "Swingin' on Nothing." Trombonist George
Washington joined Middleton on the "Swingin'" vocals, and Sid Catlett played drums.
Incredibly, "Shine" became a lavish production number with several pretty actresses
who either polished a giant shoe in the background or, while Pops played his solo,
had their own footwear shined by youngsters.

Then 16 years old, B. B. King recalled:

> Indianola, Mississippi, had a movie theater. Whites sat in the balcony and blacks sat below until white kids started throwing candy at our heads. Then the positions got switched to protect us black kids. Sitting upstairs, looking down at the big screen, I was wrapped up in the adventures of my old cowboy heroes, not to mention the Phantom and the Three Musketeers. There might also be a short film — they called them soundies— with black entertainers like Cab Calloway or Louis Armstrong or Fats Waller. They were wonderful. Around town you'd also find the ten-cent vendor, a primitive screen attached to a projector that, for a dime, showed three-minute music pieces. I suppose you could call them early videos.[3]

Louis' soundie appearances resurrected his film career, bringing him to the attention of MGM producer Arthur Freed, who was casting the screen adaptation of the all-black musical *Cabin in the Sky*, which had been a critical favorite and a moderate popular success on the New York stage in 1940. On April 30, 1942, Louis signed a contract guaranteeing $7,500 for two weeks' work, plus an additional $2,000 if the shoot ran into a third week.

Joe Glaser pulled this off at an opportune moment. Three months later the American Federation of Musicians went on strike, declaring a ban on instrumental recordings that would last until November 1944. Until the conflict was settled, musicians had to rely on live gigs and radio dates, appearances in films, and supporting the war effort. Count Basie, Benny Goodman, Harry James and other jazz men had been signed by Captain Bob Vincent of the U.S. Army to produce a series of "V-Discs" to be shipped monthly, in boxes of 25, from Special Services headquarters in New York to servicemen in Europe and the Pacific. Like those who performed for the USO, all artists donated their services. Between 1943 and 1949, Louis allowed several radio and concert performances to be recorded, including a version of "Ain't Misbehavin'" with Jack Teagarden, broadcasts of "Black and Blue" and "Do You Know What It Means to Miss New Orleans?" (with Billie Holiday), and all-star jams of "Mop, Mop" and "Back o' Town Blues" (with Teagarden, Roy Eldridge, Coleman Hawkins and Art Tatum) and "Jack-Armstrong Blues" (with Teagarden, Billy Butterfield, Bobby Hackett and Herb Ellis).

One V-Disc, titled "Reminiscin' with Louie" features a brief interview. When the radio announcer mentions his stature and influence as the most important jazz musician, Louis replies, "Say, that's swell, Pops. I appreciate that. That's awful nice. That's my life. I just like to blow this thing. I *love* this thing."

At MGM, Arthur Freed and neophyte director Vincent Minnelli were busy with pre-production on *Cabin in the Sky*. Following the success of the George and Ira Gershwin–Dubose Heyward folk opera *Porgy and Bess* in 1935, screenwriter Lynn Root had written a story titled "Little Joe," which came to the attention of Broadway producer Albert Lewis. Unlike the Pulitzer Prize–winning *The Green Pastures* (1930), which featured an all-black cast but was loaded with negative stereotypes (blacks were barred from theaters during the nationwide tour), the new project, retitled *Cabin in the Sky*, was designed by Root to present a positive, more racially sensitive depiction of African American life.

Vinton Freedley, who had produced many Gershwin–Cole Porter Broadway musicals, was hired as associate producer, and choreographer George Ballanchine co-directed with Lewis. In a major artistic coup, Ballanchine, backed by Lewis and Freedley, integrated his sophisticated balletic style into the dancing, thwarting the efforts of money men like Martin Beck who had insisted that the black hoofers be restricted to tapping. After Root completed the play, his libretto was paired with the music of Vernon Duke, a Gershwin protégé who initially had been intimidated by the "Negro" subject matter. Another Duke — Edward Kennedy Ellington — also was mentioned, but Vernon eventually was won over by the play's universalist message.

Vernon Duke asked his "April in Paris" collaborator E. Y. ("Yip") Harburg to write the lyrics for the songs, but had to settle for his second choice, John Latouche, whose stomping grounds of Virginia Beach provided an arena for their first-hand "research" on African American culture. After wasting most of their time partying, the pair holed up in a cottage in Westport, Connecticut, where they completed the score.

The role of Petunia Jackson, who attempts through prayer to save her husband, Little Joe, from his own worst enemy — himself — was awarded to the great Ethel Waters, whose charisma and determination created an entirely new persona for the character. By the time rehearsals were over, the rather carefree Petunia had become a deeply spiritual and compelling woman.

Dooley Wilson portrayed Little Joe; Rex Ingram played the dual role of "Lucius" and "Lucifer Jr." (son of ol' Beelzebub himself); Todd Duncan was "The Lord's General"; and Katherine Dunham, who doubled as assistant choreographer, became Georgia Brown, Joe's greatest temptation. Staged for the relatively small sum of $50,000, *Cabin in the Sky* opened at the Martin Beck Theatre on October 25, 1940, and ran for 156 performances. The *New York Times*' Brooks Atkinson referred to the premiere as "the peer of any musical in recent years."[4]

Though the content of Root's play had to be toned down by Freed for the film, Minnelli (who was assisted by Andrew Marton) was able to retain Ethel Waters and the powerful Rex Ingram. Dooley Wilson, who recently had played "Sam," Humphrey Bogart's singing sidekick, in *Casablanca* (1942), was considered, but the role of Little Joe ultimately went to the popular Eddie ("Rochester") Anderson. The character of Georgia Brown, who was confined to dancing in the stage version, was given a beautiful singing voice to accommodate the casting of Lena Horne.

Resistance to the film version came from whites and blacks, who had been offended by the 1936 Warner Bros. screen adaptation of *The Green Pastures*, which also features Rex Ingram (as "De Lawd"). Devising a publicity campaign that included giving interviews to African American newspapers, Freed claimed that the film would be "a dignified presentation of a peace-loving and loyal people."[5] He also benefited from the Office of War Information's requirement that the motion picture industry promote domestic, including racial, harmony — a result of President Roosevelt's Executive Order 8802, which forbade racial and religious discrimination in war industries. To please the Production Code Administration, screenwriter Joseph Schrank eliminated some of the hot material involving Georgia Brown.

Wisely, associate producer Albert Lewis sought out an African American adviser,

Cabin in the Sky (1943). Petunia Jackson (Ethel Waters), the General (Kenneth Spencer), "Little Joe" Jackson (Eddie ["Rochester"] Anderson), Georgia Brown (Lena Horne) and Lucifer Jr. (Rex Ingram).

renowned musician and composer Hall Johnson, who commented on the script before filming began. In a July 24, 1942, letter to Lewis, Johnson wrote:

> I had been a bit afraid of finding the comedy exaggerated to the point of burlesque to please white people, or the straight forward earthiness of the story somewhat thinned out to avoid hurting colored people. Happily neither has been done and the *Cabin* remains what it has always been, a delightfully breezy treatment of what is really a very weighty subject—a study in conscience. The subject of your play is a matter of general human experience and the individual characters are everywhere and among every race. ... *The Green Pastures*, a third-hand derivative from a second-hand book, was never more than a white-washed burlesque of the religious thought of the Negro. ... Fortunately, with *Cabin in the Sky*, you are confronted by no such problems. Your story deals basically with emotional urges, not only familiar but common to every human being. The theme is a universal one, which simply gains fresher entertainment values by being interpreted through a Negro medium — for a change.[6]

Impressed with the script, Johnson was hired to provide gospel arrangements for his famed choir to sing on the soundtrack. Only three songs from the original

Cabin in the Sky (1943). MGM's "all-black" musical, featuring a powerhouse all-star cast, including Louis *and* Duke Ellington.

score—"Cabin in the Sky," "Taking a Chance on Love" and "Honey in the Honeycomb"—were retained by Freed and Minnelli. The melodies of "Love Me Tomorrow" and "(In) My Old Virginia Home (On the River Nile)" were included in the incidental score written by studio arranger Roger Edens, but the remaining songs—"Li'l Black Sheep," "Happiness Is a Thing Called Joe" and "Life's Full o' Consequence"—were written by Harold Arlen and Yip Harburg, who had rejected the Broadway offer. Called "the Negro-est white man I have ever known" by Ethel Waters, Arlen proved a wise choice.[7] The twosome also wrote six numbers that went unused. After the songs had been selected and Edens had completed the underscoring, George E. Stoll was assigned to conduct.

Wanting to insure that the film appeal to a wide audience, Freed cast Duke Ellington and his orchestra (to appear in a scene at "Jim Henry's Paradise"), and Louis (to play "The Trumpeter," one of Lucifer Jr.'s "idea men"). Pops arrived at MGM on August 28, 1942, to record "Trumpet Break" and "Ain't It the Truth," one of the Arlen-Harburg songs that eventually was dropped from the film. Rehearsals for the dialogue sequences began the following day, and Minnelli fired up the cameras on August 31, completing principal photography on October 24. Some of the cast members were called back to shoot retakes on October 27 and 28.

Saddled with a B-film budget (the final cost was $662,141.82), Minnelli delivered A-film quality, including an atmospheric visual style, excellent performances from the entire cast, and sterling musical numbers. During Minnelli's absences on October 3 and 5, the Duke Ellington footage (including John W. ["Bubbles"] Sublett singing "Shine") was directed by the legendary Busby Berkeley.

Displeased with the way religion was depicted in the film, Waters was seen as "difficult" by the producers, who did not hire her again. Some of her problems stemmed from on-set "competition" with the beautiful Horne, who indirectly reminded her that she was no longer the svelte, seductive singer she had been 20 years earlier. Waters later wrote, "All through that picture there was so much snarling and scrapping that I don't know how in the world *Cabin in the Sky* ever stayed up there."[8]

Horne also unwittingly became the reason that Louis' one major musical scene ended up on the cutting-room floor. After arguing with art director Cedric Gibbons about the set decorations used in the "Ain't It the Truth" sequence, Minnelli filmed it — including the nude Horne singing in a bathtub — but then was forced by the PCA to eliminate such eroticism (even the suggestion of a naked black woman was unacceptable). Therefore, the major five-minute production number featuring Louis singing the song while surrounded by "the devil's imps" and 26 dancers also was cut. The surviving soundtrack recording, an epic 5:23 musical suite featuring a typically ebullient Pops vocal, stratospheric trumpet solo and hard-swinging instrumental section, suggests how stunning the scene may have been.

After previewing *Cabin in the Sky* in a New York projection room on February 3, 1943, *Variety*'s "Hobe" pointed out:

> Some of the box-office limitations of "Cabin" are inherent in the original work. In the first place, it's fantasy, which is inclined to be tough to sell. Secondly, it's an all–Negro show, making it doubtful material for the South and likely to decrease its audience in other parts of the country.[9]

The formidable cast went some way in compensating for these "negative" elements when the film went into general release on April 9, eventually earning $1,606,624 at the box office.

In an effort to "explain" its production to a mass audience, MGM included a written prologue that is both thoughtful and typical of the "democratic values" emphasized during World War II:

> Throughout the ages, powerful and inspiring thoughts have been preserved and handed down by the medium of the legend, the fable and the fantasy.
> The folklore of America has origins in all lands, all races, all colors.
> This story of faith and devotion springs from that source and seeks to capture those values.

Though the film opens with Petunia escorting Little Joe to church to cleanse him of his sins, namely gambling and cavorting with Georgia Brown, he soon is harassed by former associates who haul him to Jim Henry's joint, where he is nearly killed by Domino Johnson (Sublett). At home in bed, Joe briefly passes away, but a battle between the forces of Heaven (represented by Kenneth Spencer's the General) and Hell (led by Ingram's Lucifer Jr.) for his soul results in a six-month reprieve,

Cabin in the Sky (1943). "Stop that noise!" orders Lucifer Jr. (Rex Ingram, center), as the Trumpeter (Louis) blows away another "idea man" (Mantan Moreland) at the Hotel Hades.

supposedly a sufficient amount of time to prove that his wanton ways are mended. Rallying his "idea men" for a way to corrupt Joe, Lucifer Jr. is inspired by the Trumpeter, who devises a plan to have Joe win a fortune in the Irish Sweepstakes. After winning a heap of bread, Joe is mistakenly accused by Petunia of falling back in with Georgia Brown, so he leaves home and parties furiously with the gold-digging singer. When Petunia saunters into Jim Henry's to give Georgia a dose of her own medicine, a savage tornado levels the joint. After Petunia's soul pleads for the Lord to allow Joe's soul to accompany hers into Heaven, the now-recovered husband wakes up, ready to repent after experiencing a terrible dream. The stage version of *Cabin* ended with Petunia and Little Joe being gunned down, but, in true Hollywood fashion, Schrank added the cyclone (lifted from *The Wizard of Oz* [1939]) and the clichéd dream premise, thus giving the film a happy ending.

Louis' remaining scene is brief, and he plays the trumpet for only a few seconds (Lucifer Jr. orders him to stop "that noise"), but his character is one of the most important in the film. The best "idea man" in the gang that includes Mantan Moreland, Willie Best, Moke (aka Fletcher Rivers) and Poke (aka Leon James), Louis not only suggests the sweepstake idea but is credited with the original-sin plan of Eve biting the apple! He obviously enjoyed the performance, including the wearing of little "horns" on his head.

Waters' superb renditions of "Happiness Is a Thing Called Joe," "Cabin in the

Sky" and "Taking a Chance on Love" are highlights, as is her reprise of Lena Horne's "Honey in the Honeycomb" when Petunia boldly competes for Joe's affection in the climactic scene—a rare treat allowing a stark comparison between the respective seductive vocal approaches of the two singers. Waters was a fine actress and later made cinema history as the first African American to emerge as the true star of a major Hollywood film with a white cast, in Stanley Kramer and Fred Zinnemann's *The Member of the Wedding* (1952).

Eddie Anderson turns in a fine performance, lending his unforgettably bizarre voice to two numbers, including a duet with Horne on "Life's Full o' Consequence." The great Ellington swings his orchestra, featuring tenor saxophone master Ben Webster and trombonist Joe ("Tricky Sam") Nanton, on "Things Ain't What They Used to Be" and "Goin' Up," and behind Sublett on "Shine."

Interestingly, "Hobe" concluded his *Variety* review in somewhat political fashion:

> Regardless of the box-office reception of "Cabin," the sincerity evident in its production may provide an answer to the liberal and Negro groups that criticized Metro for its production of "Tennessee Johnson." And whatever its box-office fate, "Cabin" is a worthwhile picture for Metro to have made, if only as a step toward Hollywood recognition of the colored man in American life.[10]

Referring to Waters as "enthralling" and casting "a magic spell over an audience," the *New York Times* reported that "this first all–Negro screen musical in many a year is a most welcome treat."[11] A critical and popular success, *Cabin* received a Best Song Academy Award nomination for "Happiness Is a Thing Called Joe."

Donald Bogle has evaluated Louis' appearance in *Cabin in the Sky* as merely a specific example of his career-long aping of Stepin Fetchit: "Included also were Willie Best, Mantan Moreland, and Louis Armstrong, all at their incredible coon best."[12] Here Bogle places Pops in the same category with the eye-rolling Moreland and the lazy, imbecilic Best, though Louis' performance has very little in common with the actions of these perennially stereotypical actors. Bogle, however, rightly praises the performance of Anderson:

> Under the sensitive direction of Vincente Minnelli, Anderson hit at an area his predecessors never approached: he touched his audience. ... They were drawn to Rochester's charming, funny and sad diminutive hero. Had he been given an opportunity to explore his wondrous admixture of the comic and the pathetic in other roles, there is no telling how great his contributions to American screen comedy might have been.[13]

Indeed. Likewise, to what extent might Armstrong have excelled in the cinema had he been given more opportunities?

Cabin in the Sky, and its all-black successor *Stormy Weather* (1943), which also features Lena Horne (costarring with Fats Waller, Cab Calloway and the Nicholas Brothers) marked the apex of what Bogle calls the "Negro Entertainer Syndrome": "Indeed, in almost every American movie in which a black had appeared, filmmakers had been trying to maintain the myth that Negroes were naturally rhythmic and natural-born entertainers."[14] Louis' "characterization" in *Cabin in the Sky*, and, for the most part, all his previous screen appearances, falls squarely within the "syndrome." But *Cabin in the Sky* and *Stormy Weather* were unique, and successful enough commercially to reach the black theaters in the South, where enthusiastic filmgoers embraced them.

After completing his work on *Cabin in the Sky*, Louis concentrated on replacing troublesome members of his band, namely drummer Sid Catlett and bassist John Simmons, who apparently had provoked a fight with Louis' valet, Bob Smiley. Simmons was succeeded by Charles Mingus, a prodigiously talented and dead serious musician who dug Pops' playing but was embarrassed by his stage demeanor, which he viewed as "tomming." (Mingus, who became the most singularly inventive bassist-composer in jazz, could not have been reined in by any bandleader for long.)

Following a court appearance in a sleep-deprived, drunken state, Louis was granted a divorce from Alpha on October 2, 1942. After dealing with several priests who refused to marry them, the Catholic Lucille and Baptist Louis were wed by Reverend John E. Vance of the Washington Tabernacle Catholic Church in St. Louis on October 12. After the wedding night — which consisted of a gig at the Tune Town Ballroom — Louis saw Lucille and her mother off to New York before he and the band hit the road for six months of one-nighters.

Lucille caught back up with him on Christmas, and when she decorated their hotel room with a small tree and lights— the first Louis ever had — he wanted to stay up all night staring at them. For two weeks— at Louis' insistence — she set up the tree in a different town each night, so he could see it after the gig. When Lucille tired of the road, Louis sent her back to New York, mailing her money on a regular basis so she could purchase a real home. Without his knowledge, she found a nice three-story house at 34–56 107th Street in the quiet neighborhood of Corona, Queens. The owners— a white family for whom she had worked — sold it to her for $3,900, and Glaser arranged for the payments to be deducted from Pops' paycheck.

When Louis finished the tour in March 1943 he planned to join his wife in his new home, but when the cabbie pulled up to the property in the wee hours, he thought he had been taken to the wrong place. Even while ringing the doorbell he was dumbstruck; but when Lucille emerged, clad in a nightgown and curlers, he finally realized it was their house. He later wrote:

> The house *was* (+ *still* is) so *high* powered and distinctive looking.... *One* look at that big *fine* house, and *right* away I said to the *driver* "*Aw man quit kidding* and *take* me to the address I'm looking for." ... The *more* Lucille *showed* me *around* the *house* the more *thrilled* I got. ... Right then and I felt very grand over it all. A little *higher* on the *horse* (as we expresses it). I've always appreciated the ordinary good things. I noticed Lucille being the same way.[15]

The short *Show Business at War*, an installment of producer Louis de Rochemont's *March of Time* series, teamed Pops with his *Cabin in the Sky* costar, Rochester, as they performed a skit for a G.I. audience during an April 19, 1943, AFRS transcription gig at the Trianon Ballroom in Southgate, California. Filmed during the same period, the Columbia feature *Jam Session* "merely furnishes band music to

Jam Session (1944). As the swinging bartender, Pops is dazzled by a diamond while singing "I Can't Give You Anything but Love" to a bevy of black beauties.

please the hepcats."[16] Directed by Abbott-and-Costello favorite Charles T. Barton, this 1944 release stars Ann Miller as a country girl who wins a trip to Hollywood and then nearly destroys the career but ultimately wins the hand of screenwriter George Carter Haven (Jess Barker) following a series of tinsel town mishaps. The hoary plot fortunately takes a back seat to the impressive parade of musical talent, including Charlie Barnet (whose band plays "Cherokee"), Jan Garber ("I Lost My Sugar"), Teddy Powell ("Murder He Says"), Alvino Rey ("St. Louis Blues") and Pops, who sings "I Can't Give You Anything but Love," which the *New York Times* called a "high spot."[17]

First shown in silhouette, playing his trumpet behind a filmy curtain, Louis slowly swings out into the light, not allowing his status as bartender to affect his serenading of the string of black beauties seated before him. He finally emerges from behind the bar, picks up his trumpet and strolls over to a big band, swapping solos with tenor saxophonist Joe Garland and clarinetist Rupert Cole. Other musicians in the sequence include Lawrence Lucie on guitar and Sid Catlett on drums. Pops concludes the number by singing another verse to a second bevy of beauties.

On January 18, 1944, 15 musical giants gathered at New York's Metropolitan Opera House for the Esquire All-American Jazz Concert. Since 1936, *Esquire* had held a readers' poll to honor the top jazz artists, but now the magazine selected its winners through a critics' jury that included George Avakian, Leonard Feather, Robert

Jam Session (1944). Pops pours his soul into another high note during "I Can't Give You Anything but Love."

Goffin, John Hammond and Bob Thiele. The musicians usually congregated for a recording session, but due to the AFM ban, an all-star concert was planned; and, to make the event even more gala, the name "All-American" was used to promote the sale of war bonds. Louis won the trumpet and male vocalist spots, joining Billie Holiday and Mildred Bailey (female vocalists), Roy Eldridge (second trumpet), Jack Teagarden (trombone), Benny Goodman (clarinet), Barney Bigard (second clarinet), Coleman Hawkins (tenor sax), Red Norvo and Lionel Hampton (tied for vibraphone), Art Tatum (piano), Teddy Wilson ("guest" piano), Al Casey (guitar), Oscar Pettiford (bass) and Sid Catlett (drums). Though Goodman was playing a gig on the West Coast, he joined the jam via a radio hookup. Pops was having an off night, but played on 10 numbers, sang "I Can't Give You Anything but Love," "Basin Street Blues" and "Back o' Town Blues," and introduced Teagarden, who lent his distinctive vocals to "I've Got a Right to Sing the Blues."

By summer 1944, Louis' silver-screen success enabled Joe Glaser to relocate to Los Angeles, where he opened Associated Booking, Inc., at 8278 Sunset Boulevard. Pops' second film of the year, Republic's *Atlantic City*, stars Brad Taylor as an entrepreneur who develops an entertainment empire on the famous Jersey Boardwalk, alienates his friends with his ruthless demeanor, and then sees his dreams go up in flames. Doris Gilbert, Frank Gill, Jr., and George Carlton Brown's disjointed screenplay, awkwardly directed by Ray McCarey, also features Constance Moore, Charley

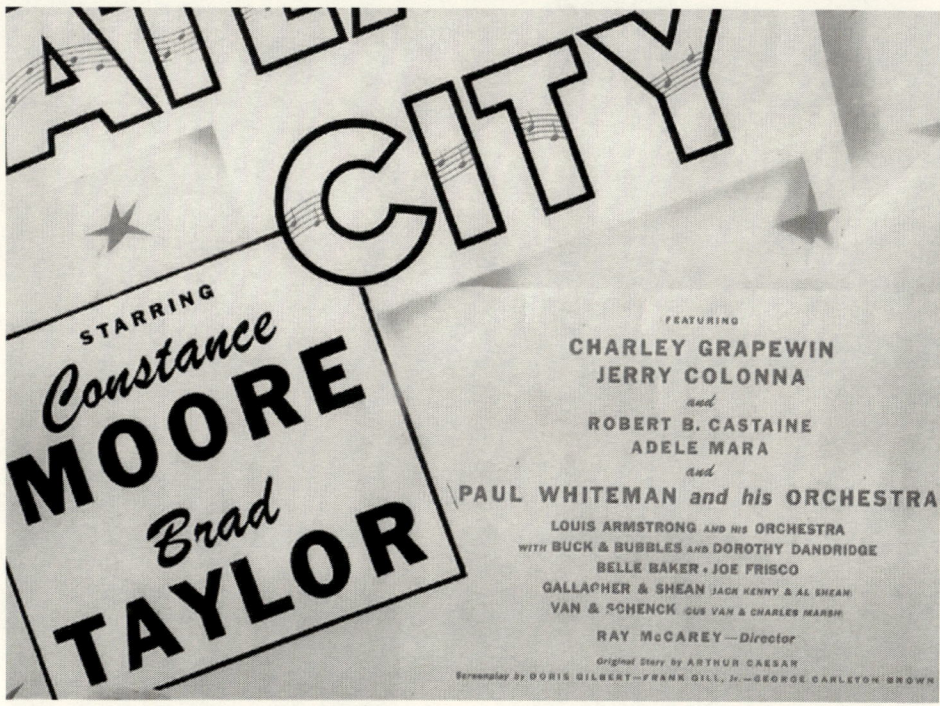

Atlantic City (1944). On the original posters, Louis and the other African American performers are billed in small type below the looming "Paul Whiteman and his Orchestra."

Grapewin and Jerry Colonna, who chews the scenery (in five separate guises) in superfluous "comedy relief" sequences. Referred to as "a stodgy tale, replete with cliché dialog" by *Variety*'s "Abel,"[18] the film, like *Jam Session*, picks up whenever the musicians appear. Though Paul Whiteman "could have phoned his stuff over for all he does,"[19] Louis sparkles on "Ain't Misbehavin'" during a "Harlem on Parade" sequence that also features a gorgeous young Dorothy Dandridge and the furious dancing of Buck and Bubbles. Launching his solo, Pops leans down to play directly into John Alton's camera.

In *Pillow to Post* (1945), Ida Lupino stars as Jean Howard, who becomes the new sales representative for her father's oil-drilling company after all the eligible young men are drafted. Managing one sale to the Black Hills Oil Company, she is stranded in Clayfield, a town housing soldiers stationed at neighboring Camp Clay. To lodge at the local hotel, she must be an Army wife, so she persuades Lt. Don Mallory (William Prince) to register as her husband. Conflict ensues when Colonel Michael Otley (Sidney Greenstreet), Mallory's mother (Regina Wallace) and Jean's father (Paul Harvey) all assume they are married.

Louis appears in a one-and-a-half-minute scene set at the local roadhouse, once again blowing accompaniment for Dorothy Dandridge, here performing "Whatcha Say?" Aiming the seductive lyrics right at Pops, she sings, "Do I get that little kiss? Must you let me down like this?" Shaking off his shyness, he is met with an "Oh, baby."

Atlantic City (1944). Dorothy Dandridge digs Satchmo's solo on "Ain't Misbehavin'."

"Look out here, girl, don't you start that stuff here," he demands with a smile, just before blasting out the final high-register riff.

A very young Dexter Gordon can be glimpsed playing tenor sax in this scene. (More than 40 years later he would receive an Academy Award nomination for his unforgettable performance in Bertrand Tavernier's *Round Midnight* [1986].) Pops and his band pre-recorded "Whatcha Say?" and "Groovin' Baby, Don't You Cry" at Decca studios on August 9, 1944.

A new "Louis Armstrong and His Orchestra," including Billy Butterfield on trumpet and Johnny Blowers on drums, cut two Decca sides in New York on January 14, 1945. Three days later Pops was in New Orleans to play at the Second Esquire All-American Jazz Concert.

Louis often wrote charming letters to Lucille, usually signing his full name and including at least one of his monikers. At one point during 1945 he sent her a close-up portrait from *Cabin in the Sky*, including the inscription: "The Best of Everything in the World—To My Wife Lucille from Her Husband Louis Satchmo Armstrong."[20]

In early 1946 he again was named top trumpeter in the *Esquire* critics' poll. On January 10, two Leonard Feather numbers, "Long, Long Journey" and "Snafu," were recorded for RCA Victor in New York, the former marking the first time that Louis and Duke Ellington played on the same recording. Also in the band were Johnny Hodges (alto sax), Don Byas (tenor sax), Billy Strayhorn (piano) and Sonny Greer (drums). The exquisite combination of Armstrong, Ellington and Hodges provides an all-too-brief trip to Jazz Heaven.

The following week Pops recorded with another jazz virtuoso, Ella Fitzgerald, for the first time, backed by Bob Haggart's Orchestra, and featuring Billy Butterfield, Joe Bushkin (piano) and Cozy Cole (drums). Ella and Louis each sing a verse and chorus on "You Won't Be Satisfied" before he blows a brief solo and they join in a duet on the ending. "The Frim Fram Sauce," popularized by Nat Cole, is a treat, set in a pulsing groove with each of them again singing a verse and chorus.

Glaser kept Louis working constantly. In February 1946, Pops again returned to Louisiana, where he briefly was harassed by local law enforcement in Shreveport. In a letter to Frances Church, Glaser's personal secretary, Louis explained "that awful 'drag' we ran into in Shreveport":

> [T]wo old cracker sheriffs came up to me and said... "Are you Louis Armstrong?" I said: "Yassuh." ... And sho 'nuff, when we finish the dance and finished playing "The Star Spangled Banner" here they come right into me reaching for my trumpet. But I tricked them so pretty. When they asked me—"where's your trumpet?"—I pointed to a trumpet case and said: "There it is." The promoter was kind of hip'd to the jive and asked me: "Are you sure that is your trumpet?" I said: "Yassuh, boss. That's the one I blow every night." But it wasn't. I gave them Joe Jardan's (one of my trumpet men's instead of mine) and that was that.... You see, Joe and I made the switch during our intermission, right under their noses. So they weren't so smart after all.[21]

After pulling a fast one on the fuzz, Pops went on to New Orleans, this time to give his wife and the northern members of the band the Mardi Gras experience. Riding on one of the floats designed by the Zulu Social Aid and Pleasure Club was a real gasser, and he relished their invitation to serve as King at a future Mardi Gras. He wrote:

> You should have seen me bowing an'a waving to the folks and cats as they cheered at the sight of me (their home boy). ... I gotten so full of champagne until I thought I was seeing two floats with a gang of Kings and Satchmo's on it. Haw haw haw. Honest to goodness, we were having so much fun until we almost forgot we had to go to Mobile and play that night—Tee hee. And we did miss the bus.... I was beat for my youth when we gotten on the train.... We arrived in Mobile at 8:45, and hit at nine. Now you can see, we were one maneuvering set of cats![22]

Revisiting his New Orleans roots inspired Louis to create more autobiographical material. Since 1940 he had been corresponding with Belgian émigré Robert Goffin, who had praised him in the 1928 book *Aux Frontieres du Jazz*. Along with financial support, Louis sent Goffin typed reminiscences about the early days in New Orleans—tales of relatives, Black Benny and other colorful characters, pimps and prostitutes—expecting them to be edited into a biography that could be adapted for the silver screen.

On April 27, 1946, Louis officially returned to RCA Victor after 12 years with the Decca label. Fronting a new big band that included Joe Garland (tenor sax) and Arvell Shaw (bass), Louis was joined by his old pal Velma Middleton for a vocal duet on "No Variety Blues," during which he claims, "All the chicks and chippies say I'm a good man!"

After completing *The Magnificent Ambersons*, Orson Welles had considered pruning his "Story of Jazz" script into an anthology film, but again abandoned it to make a wartime propaganda movie. Later he switched his idea from jazz to South American music, proposing a film called "The Story of Samba." For several years Welles toyed with the jazz concept, and while chatting with Louis after a concert in 1945, again asked him to collaborate on a biographical film. Tapping away at his typewriter, Pops sent the director a detailed reminiscence. When Welles began filming *The Stranger* (1946) the following year, screenwriter Elliot Paul, who claimed to have worked with the director on the "Jazz" project, pitched the idea to independent producer Jules Levey, who hired Louis and reworked the project as *New Orleans*.

In the completed film, Paul shares credit with Herbert Biberman (story) and Dick Irving Hyland (screenplay). By the time director Arthur Lubin rolled the cameras at Hal Roach Studios in early September 1946, very little truth about the origins of jazz remained, and the narrative was awkwardly split into two subplots—one showcasing the performances and after-hours activities of the black musicians, and another focusing on a young white woman's attempt to sing music considered "devilish" by her conservative family and friends. Though Louis was still asked to play "himself," the only elements touching on reality are his personal warmth, sense of humor, some of his trademark songs and riffs, and a scene depicting the exodus from Storyville.

The majority of the production was filmed in Culver City, but a second unit was sent to New Orleans to shoot several sequences, including an authentic funeral and street parade featuring George Lewis and Kid Howard's Brass Band. Unfortunately, all of these scenes were judged too "liberal" by studio suits worried about the current "Red Scare." Bassist Red Callender recalled:

> It was gradual the way McCarthyism seeped in. ... In the original script Louis' band was slated to appear on the same bill as Woody Herman's at the big stage concert. We ... filmed it, but thanks to McCarthyism it was never shown. Later, in 1947, Biberman was one of the "Hollywood Ten" ... and was sent to jail.[23]

The opening credits feature a panel billing "Louis Armstrong and His Band and Billie Holiday," as a stilted Caucasian choral rendition of Edgar De Lange and Louis Alter's "Do You Know What It Means to Miss New Orleans?" fills the soundtrack. The first sound heard in the narrative is that of Pops' cornet wafting the (severely shortened) introduction to "West End Blues" from a tonk as the scene fades in on a sign marked "Basin Street" and a superimposed "1917." As a worker at the tonk opens the door to the rear entrance, Louis' legendary sustained high note accompanies him; then Pops plays "West End" again, this time the complete intro, for Nick Duquesne, "The King of Basin Street" (Arturo de Cordova).

The next scene depicts Louis and his band blowing "Maryland, My Maryland" on a Mississippi riverboat, as young Miralee Smith (Dorothy Patrick) is informed by her conservative companion that, "In Maryland, there'd be a price on their heads." At the Smith mansion, Endie (Billie Holiday), the maid, is reprimanded by Mrs.

New Orleans (1947). Though the film is a disappointment, the original poster art justifiably bills "Louis Armstrong and His Band and Billie Holiday" above "Woody Herman and His Orchestra."

Smith (Irene Rich) for playing a "devil" tune ("Do You Know What It Means to Miss New Orleans?") on the piano instead of tending to her duties. Soon Endie admits that she's in love with Louis.

Having agreed to sponsor a "legitimate" concert for Miralee, Henri Ferber (composer Richard Hageman, who subsequently wrote the masterful scores for John Ford's *Fort Apache* [1948] and *She Wore a Yellow Ribbon* [1949]) ducks into the back entrance of Nick's, where he finds Louis alone, playing his cornet.

As Ferber sits at the piano, he marvels at the melodies flowing from the horn. "That note's not in the diatonic scale," he observes.

"Diatonic?" asks Pops.

Referring to his blue notes, Ferber explains that the pitches are "between natural and flat." Of course, Louis had just been playing what came naturally to him.

Impressed by Endie's music, Miralee accompanies her to Storyville and drops in to hear the band at Nick's. Now the maid is transformed into the singer as Endie performs "Do You Know What It Means to Miss New Orleans?" with her compatriots. A highlight of the film, this sequence is the first of three comprising the only footage of Louis and Billie performing together — historical records of two jazz phenomena that make it possible for audiences to sit through the remainder of *New*

New Orleans (1947). *Top:* Endie (Billie Holiday) sings "Do You Know What It Means to Miss New Orleans," accompanied by the solos of Louis and Barney Bigard. *Bottom:* Pops admires the blowing of his home boy, Edward ("Kid") Ory.

Orleans. Also relevant to the history of jazz are the appearances of Kid Ory, Zutty Singleton, Barney Bigard and Red Callender.

Though the musicians are playing Louis' brand of New Orleans jazz, the music is referred to as "ragtime" at this point in the film (depicting a 42-year-old Pops blowing in 1917 is a bit anachronistic). When Miralee asks Nick where "this music" came from, he replies, "work songs, the Gold Coast of Africa, little Christian churches, riverboats" (slavery is not mentioned).

Following a visit from Mrs. Smith, who tries to bribe him to keep Miralee out of his tonk, Nick gives the unsuspecting girl a tour of "the real Basin Street." Although she is repelled by the sight of drunks and prostitutes, she grows closer to Nick and refuses to stay away. In league with Colonel McArdle (John Alexander), Mrs. Smith is aided further by local authorities who decide to close down Storyville. Just before the exodus begins, Louis speaks to the people forced out of their homes and businesses, mentioning the "loss of jobs and good music in the nighttime." As police march in, the folks begin to move on, accompanied by Louis and Billie's duet on "Goodbye to Storyville." Louis later described the real event in his memoir *Satchmo: My Life in New Orleans* (1954):

> Some sailors on leave got mixed up in a fight and two of them were killed. The Navy started a war on Storyville, and even as a boy I could see that the end was near. The police began to raid all the houses and cabarets....
> It sure was a sad scene to watch the law run all those people out of Storyville. They reminded me of a gang of refugees. Some of them had spent the best part of their lives there. Others had never known any other kind of life....
> A new generation was about to take over in Storyville. My little crowd had begun to look forward to other kicks, like our jazz band....[24]

The encore of Miralee's concert provides a fitting coda to the Storyville exodus, as she stiltedly butchers "Do You Know What It Means to Miss New Orleans?" (Though the patrons get up and leave because of her performance of African American music, a modern audience might get up and leave because she sings it so badly.)

As part of the Great Migration to Chicago, Louis helps Nick finish the Orleans Club, formerly a "burnt-out chop suey dive." Piano great Meade ("Lux") Lewis has a brief cameo in this scene. When the club opens, local youth enthusiastically follow the sound of Pops' cornet wafting through the air. "Go to it, Satchmo," urges Nick. "Convert the Philistines."

Louis wouldn't be "Satchmo" for another 15 years, but perhaps the most ludicrous moment of the film occurs when an inebriated patron stumbles into the club and babbles, "Jass it up, boys! Jass it up."

"What did you say?" Nick inquires. (A more asinine depiction of the origin of the term jazz [originally spelled "jass"] cannot be imagined.)

Having lost track of Endie after the Storyville migration, Louis finally is reunited with her at the club, where they perform "The Blues Are Brewing." A lengthy montage sequence shows him and the gang on the road across the United States; then segues to Woody Herman and his orchestra playing a white version; then dissolves back to Louis, now singing "Endie" in Paris, where Merilee appears, holding a copy of Pops' book *Swing That Music*. Hard times have gotten better: Louis and Endie are married, and Nick now is a successful music promoter in New York. The film then concludes in the Big Apple with another whitewashed version of "Do You Know What It Means to Miss New Orleans?" as Merilee is joined by Woody Herman and company. (A young Shelley Winters can be glimpsed in a non-speaking bit part as an audience member. Other uncredited bit players include Ethel Waters and Sammy Davis, Jr.)

When shooting wrapped on *New Orleans* in late 1946, Louis had high hopes for the film. In a letter to his friend, Madeleine Berard, a Swiss journalist and dancer, he wrote:

> [L]et me tell you, I think it's going to be a pretty good lecture on this music called jazz. It starts way [down] there in Storyville in the good old days of 1917 in New Orleans, where this real jazz started. You'll witness a seven-piece band playing some of the finest old tunes you ever heard. ... "Farewell to Storyville" ... was taken from the recording of "Good Time Flat Blues." Probably you've heard this recording by Maggie Jones. I played the accompaniment with my trumpet on this recording way back there in 1924. Billy Holiday sings this tune, she sings it so beautifully. ... Another tune Billy Holiday sings is called "Do You Know What It Means to Miss New Orleans?"—a very beautiful tune. ... So until you see the film, which I do hope you will, I'll leave the rest up to you. Of course Billy and I are doing quite a bit of acting (ahem); she's also my sweetheart in the picture... Ump Ump Ump. Now isn't that something? The great Billy Holiday, my sweetheart? ... The picture will have its premiere in New Orleans during the Mardi Gras. And we're going down there for the event. Now isn't that nice? I always sez to myself. Good things come to those who wait. Just think — me in New Orleans during carnival time. My home town. All the old folks and the young folks too will be so glad to see me and have me there — Yass Lawd.[25]

On December 21, Louis expressed similar sentiments in a letter to *Melody Maker* magazine:

> This year will probably be the biggest part that I've ever had in any flicker (I mean) picture. I've just finished making a movie for the Goldwyn Studio called "NEW ORLEANS." Billie Holiday the colored recording artist is in the picture. And she plays the part of my sweetheart. She sings some beautiful tunes in this film. As for myself — I am all through the picture — New Orleans — is a picture that's written all about the good old days in Storyville. Where the blues were born....[26]

Billie Holiday did not relish her *New Orleans* experience, which began with soundtrack sessions at Studio and Artists Recorders on September 11, 1946. She also was managed by Joe Glaser, who had booked her for the role, but when she called him to complain about the demeaning depiction, he told her that she'd never work in Hollywood again. The fact that she did hang around the studio long enough to complete her scenes (while unfortunately feeding her severe alcohol and heroin addictions) did very little for her career: *New Orleans* was her one and only feature film. In her 1956 autobiography *Lady Sings the Blues*, she recalled:

I should have known better. When I saw the script, I did. You just tell me one Negro girl who's made movies who didn't play a maid or a whore. I don't know any. I found out I was going to do a little singing, but I was still playing the part of a maid....

Don't get me wrong. I've got nothing against maids—or whores—whether they're black or white. My mother was a maid, a good one, one of the greatest. My stepmother is Tallulah Bankhead's maid right now, and that's a part I'd even consider when they do her life story. I've been what I've been. But I don't think I'm the type for maid parts; I don't feel it. I didn't feel this damn part. How could I, after going through hell from being one when I was twelve....

So the scuffle at the studio began. They sent me to a dramatic coach on the lot to coach me in my lines. ... And about the only lines I had called for me to say, "Yes, Miss Marylee. No, Miss Marylee," in twenty-three different kinds of ways. So this coach was trying to brief me on how to get the right kind of Tom feeling into this thing.[27]

Much of Holiday's disgust stemmed from the way she was treated by Dorothy Patrick:

I never did set very well with women. This chick must have been from somewhere South or on the border. Some people don't actually love Negroes and don't want to make love to them, but they don't actually hate them neither. This girl wasn't one of those. She wanted nothing to do with me....

After the "star" looked at a few days' rushes she decided I was stealing scenes from her. This was a laugh. I was no actress, never had been one, never pretended to be one....

I kept calling Joe Glaser every day, and I worked all night every night. Finally one day on the set I took about all I could from Blondie. I was tired of her giving me a hard time. They had me cornered. I couldn't walk off like I wanted to. So I bust out crying.

This time Louis Armstrong blew the whistle.

"Better look out," he said to the director. "I know Lady and when she starts crying, the next thing she's going to do is start fighting."

Anyway, the picture was finished some kind of way and I was glad to split the hell out of there and be gone. I saw it later—much later—and found out Blondie must have had her way. They had taken miles of footage of music and scenes in New Orleans, but none of it was left in the picture. And very damn little of me. ... I never made another movie. And I'm in no hurry.[28]

However, on February 8, 1947, Holiday appeared on stage with Louis at Carnegie Hall to promote *New Orleans*, and attended the April 26 premiere at the Saenger Theatre in Crescent City, California, where she and Pops sang a duet on "Do You Know What It Means to Miss New Orleans?" and was accompanied by Bobby Tucker on "Don't Explain."

New Orleans is one of the few films to draw its finest card within the first minute. As a cultural triumph, Louis' "West End Blues" introduction far outdistances the artistic quality of this entire film, not to mention just about any other American musical or cinematic achievement. But the majority of 1947 filmgoers knew nothing of Louis' significance, viewing the picture merely as another musical entertainment. Contemporary critics, however, did realize his importance to the film. *Variety*'s "Brog" noted:

> Star names—Arturo de Cordova and Dorothy Patrick—won't mean a lot on the marquee, and some special sales effort is going to be required to draw audiences, outside the hep set, to whom the names of Armstrong, Herman and Billie Holiday would ordinarily be no magnet. Actually, as it turns out, "Satchmo" Armstrong is the star of the film, proving as solid in a generous dramatic role as he is on the trumpet.

In a comment indicative of the era in which it was written, "Brog" added:

> Arthur Lubin's direction is generally well-paced to take advantage of the best aspects of the story and musical interludes. He gets a credit, too, for those lingering close-ups of the expressive faces of the Negro musicians.[29]

Bosley Crowther, in his *New York Times* review, accurately called the film "a far-from-inspired screen endeavor to trace the birth and evolution of jazz from Basin Street in New Orleans to the capitals of the world." In particular, he criticized the "wretchedly routine romance intended to represent the conflict of 'long-haired' music and jazz," and advised, "Put it down as a fizzle in every respect but one. That is the frequent tooting of Louis Armstrong on his horn." However, the old critical curmudgeon couldn't help but take a little backhanded shot at jazz:

> When the old Satchmo blasts upon his trumpet, it is music to strong and durable ears—providing those ears are attached to a reasonable admirer of jazz. And a good bit of circumambient drizzle may be forgiven for those electric bursts.[30]

While appearing in *New Orleans*, Louis led several Los Angeles recording sessions. On September 6 his Hot Seven, with Vic Dickerson (trombone), Barney Bigard (clarinet), Charlie Beal or Leonard Feather (piano), Allan Reuss (guitar), Red Callender (bass) and Zutty Singleton (drums), cut "I Want a Little Girl," "Sugar," "Blues for Yesterday" and "Blues in the South." With the big band he waxed versions of the *New Orleans* numbers "Endie" and "The Blues are Brewin'" on October 17, followed by small-group arrangements of "Do You Know What It Means to Miss New Orleans?" "Where the Blues Were Born in New Orleans" and "Mahogany Hall Stomp" fronting the Dixieland Seven, his cohorts from the film shoot, with Minor Hall taking over Zutty's drum chair.

When Robert Goffin's book *Horn of Plenty* finally saw publication that year, the result was nearly as ludicrous as the *New Orleans* film. Though he had used the material Louis wrote, he replaced actual incidents with embellished passages, and, worst of all—being unfamiliar with the United States and its language—he rewrote the dialogue in a contrived dialect.

After his autobiographical aspirations became Hollywood whitewash, Louis was pleased to accept an offer pairing him with clarinetist Edmond Hall's Cafe Society Uptown Orchestra for the February 8, 1947, gig at Carnegie Hall. Pops played the entire Saturday evening concert, splitting the material between Hall's band and—at Glaser's insistence—his own 16-piece outfit. In general, the date was a rousing success; but, specifically, it proved that Louis was at his finest playing with a New Orleans–style combo.

The first set opened ominously with Pops and the Hall band playing the New Orleans funeral classics "Flee as a Bird" and "Oh, Didn't He Ramble?" then kicking into high gear with "Dipper Mouth Blues," "Mahogany Hall Stomp," "Muskrat Ramble" and "St. Louis Blues." Bassist Johnny Williams sang the duet with Louis on "Rockin' Chair," then Pops unleashed drummer Jimmy Crawford on "Tiger Rag," beat out "Black and Blue," and played a soaring solo on the standard "I'm Confessin'." Back in 1920s mode, he began "Struttin' with Some Barbecue" and sailed "(Up the) Lazy River" before closing the stirring set with "I'll Be Glad When You're Dead, You Rascal You," "Save It, Pretty Mama" and "Ain't Misbehavin'."

The big band set opened with a brief instrumental version of "When It's Sleepy Time Down South," then swung into Benny Goodman's "Stompin' at the Savoy" before Pops vocalized "I Can't Give You Anything but Love." Sid Catlett thrashed away on "Mop, Mop," then Louis delivered a masterful, low-down vocal on "Back o' Town Blues" and was joined by Velma Middleton on "You Won't Be Satisfied." The show closed with two versions of "Do You Know What It Means to Miss New Orleans?" the first with Pops on vocals, followed by Billie Holiday's appearance with the rhythm section and a few of the horn players.

"Miss Billie Holiday, my costar in the picture *New Orleans*!" announced Louis before the band blasted into the driving instrumental "Roll 'em."

On March 12 he was back with the big band, cutting five sides for Victor. Sammy Cahn and Jule Styne's "I Believe," recently sung by Frank Sinatra and Jimmy Durante in MGM's *It Happened in Brooklyn* (1947), features a powerful, high-register solo. Though Glaser assumed this approach was the most profitable, he was convinced otherwise by publicist Ernest Anderson, a jazz purist who wanted to move Louis back into the small-group format. Having befriended Pops, Anderson learned that Glaser's company was commanding only $350 per weeknight and $600 per Saturday gig — usually overworking the band to clear enough cash.

Walking into Glaser's office, Anderson offered him a $1,000 cashier's check for Louis—without the band —for a single gig, at New York's Town Hall, at midnight on May 17. Glaser scoffed when Anderson described backing Pops with only six musicians, hand-picked jazz masters. Promised that Louis' fee would soon jump from $350 to $2,500 per night, Glaser finally capitulated, and Anderson hired Bobby Hackett (cornet), Jack Teagarden (trombone), Peanuts Hucko (clarinet), Dick Carey (piano), Bob Haggart (bass), Sid Catlett and George Wettling (drums) for $60–$75 each. Sidney Bechet also was hired, but bowed out prior to the performance, which went on without any rehearsals. Louis not only blew his improvisational best, but also achieved a musical first in his career, playing a public concert with an integrated band (Teagarden, along with fellow whites Eddie Lang and Joe Sullivan, had first recorded with Louis at Okeh in 1929).

The program included a rollicking version of "Ain't Misbehavin'," the Pops–Big Tea duet on "Rockin' Chair," "Back o' Town Blues," "Pennies from Heaven," "Save It, Pretty Mama" and "St. James Infirmary." Having witnessed the success of the combo from a choice seat in the hall, Glaser nonetheless wanted Louis to return to the big-band format to draw larger crowds. Anderson, however — backed by Leonard Feather — continued to lobby Glaser to hire an "all-star" group based on the Town Hall model.

On June 10, Pops, Teagarden, Hackett and Hucko were joined by Ernie Caceres (clarinet and baritone sax), Johnny Guarnieri (piano), Al Casey (guitar), Al Hall (bass) and Cozy Cole (drums) to record four Victor sides. Pops and Tea's "Jack-Armstrong Blues" and "Rockin' Chair," two numbers they had been blowing live, were given the studio treatment. Louis' ballad "Someday (You'll Be Sorry)," introduced by Guarnieri on celeste, offers a soothing vocal and a brief Teagarden solo, and "Fifty-Fifty Blues" reunites both of them on vocals.

Nine days later, Louis and the Town Hall band, with Jack Lesberg on bass, played a concert at New York's Winter Garden Theater to promote the premiere of *New Orleans*. Broadcast by NBC radio, this tribute to the Big Easy was hosted by Fred Robbins and featured high-energy renditions of "Way Down Yonder in New Orleans," "Muskrat Ramble" and "Tiger Rag." Big Tea sang and Pops scatted the familiar "Basin Street Blues"; the trombonist favored "Do You Know What It Means to Miss New Orleans?" with two beautiful solos; and Louis sang "Someday." A rare performance of the instrumental duet "Dear Old Southland," with Dick Carey playing the piano accompaniment originated by "Buck" Washington Lee on the 1930 studio recording, was a moving high point.

Convinced of the financial possibilities of forming a small "all-star" group, Joe Glaser hired Pierre Tallerie, a meddlesome snitch the band dubbed "Frenchy," and signed Teagarden, insisting that he accept a seven-year contract at $500 per week. He also agreed to add Dick Carey and Sid Catlett from the Town hall band, Barney Bigard on clarinet and Arvell Shaw on bass. Of the "mixed band" concept, Mezz Mezzrow wrote, "Louis and I used to talk about it all the time — it was our idea of the millennium."[31]

4

To Hell with That

I say my prayers every night, my blessings for everything I eat, and I believe in treating my fellow man right. A man's a man until he proves different.

— Louis Armstrong[1]

Recently separated from his wife, writer Sylvia Fine, Danny Kaye was neck deep in depression when he worked for director Howard Hawks on the set of *A Song Is Born*, which began shooting at Goldwyn Studios in August 1947. Blessed with none of Fine's usual comic material, Kaye had signed a contract with Warner Bros., and now was making his cinematic swan song for Samuel Goldwyn, the mogul who had made him a star.

Reworking the story "From A to Z" by Billy Wilder and Thomas Monroe that Hawks had filmed as *Ball of Fire* with Gary Cooper and Barbara Stanwyck in 1941, Goldwyn cast Kaye as "Professor Hobart Frisbee," a member of an academic group who are writing "The Totten Musical Encyclopedia." (Though Harry Tugend wrote the script, he received no on-screen credit.) To properly visualize Frisbee's quest to learn about "modern jazz," the producer cast Benny Goodman as one of the professors, and Louis, Tommy Dorsey, Lionel Hampton, Charlie Barnet, Mel Powell, Louis Bellson, Buck and Bubbles, the Page Cavanaugh Trio, the Golden Gate Quartet, and Russo and the Samba Kings as the hepcats who sit in with the old longhairs. On August 6, Louis joined Dorsey, Goodman and Hampton to pre-record their numbers, including "A Song Was Born," "Goldwyn Stomp" and "Flying Home."

Accustomed to producing his own films, Hawks was not fond of Goldwyn, who often arrived on the set with "suggestions." Forced to use Virginia Mayo in the original Stanwyck role, the formidable director was not about to give in to additional pressure. When Goldwyn told him not to film the white performers standing too close to the black musicians, Hawks insulted him until he left the set. The director claimed:

> I said, "Get yourself another director, will you? I'm not going to pay any attention to that. To hell with you. As far as I'm concerned, the Negroes belong in music because they're part of this kind of music." Well, the whole thing was unfortunate. Only one good thing happened. Satchmo and I became such good friends. I was over

in Africa making a picture [*Hatari*] once, and I got a strange fever. I went over to the nursing home — they didn't have hospitals, they had nursing homes—for a couple of days, and Satchmo was touring over there, and he heard I was there. He came up to the hospital to see me, and that made me a hero with all of the Negroes in Africa. A got a lot more respect from the Negroes after that.[2]

Hawks circumvented Goldwyn's "orders" whenever possible, keeping the film refreshingly devoid of overt racial stereotypes. Progressive in his social views, Hawks usually included strong female characters in his films (Katharine Hepburn in *Bringing Up Baby* [1938], Jean Arthur in *Only Angels Have Wings* [1939], Rosalind Russell in *His Girl Friday* [1940] and Joanne Dru in *Red River* [1948], among others), and now attempted to integrate his performers. When asked why the musicians weren't featured in more scenes, he replied, "Well, we'd get something all ready, and then I'd get orders to do a different thing."[3] Persuaded to make the film by Goldwyn's offer of $25,000 per week, Hawks admitted:

> I think Goldwyn realized that he'd made a silly contract with me, that he'd made a fool of himself, and he was so mad at having made it, that he wanted to try and gum things up. He certainly did. And it wasn't easy. Danny Kaye had always done his wife's material. He'd separated from his wife, and he was a basket case, stopping work to see a psychiatrist twice a day. Now you can imagine working with that. He was about as funny as a crutch. It was an altogether horrible experience. I've never seen the picture.[4]

Though critics have faulted the film for its lack of Fine's trademark songs and gags, their absence actually allowed Kaye to develop a somewhat subtle and atypical character. Rather than mugging and singing nonsense songs— and dropping out of character to become Danny Kaye — he maintains his Hobart Frisbee persona throughout, leaving the musical thunder in the hands of the Olympian group of maestros. Mayo plays nightclub singer Honey Swanson, who is engaged to mob boss Tony Crow (Steve Cochran) but eventually falls for "Frizzy." While Benny Goodman is a comic treat as Professor Magenbruch, Louis, Dorsey, Hampton, Powell, Barnet, Bellson, and Buck and Bubbles are smoothly integrated into the script, appearing at strategic moments to bring real harmony to the film.

After Frisbee decides to research the history of jazz, he haunts nightclubs and dives, where he begins to dig the aforementioned masters. This montage is one of three major segments featuring the musicians, and the only one set outside the walls of the Totten Foundation. "A Song Was Born" opens with Mayo lip-synching Jeri Sullivan's vocal, Louis singing a verse, then a succession of brief solos by Dorsey, Pops, Barnet, Goodman, Hampton, Powell and Bellson. The second Totten sequence, occurring after the gangsters take over the mansion for the shotgun wedding of Honey and Crow, involves Frisbee's demonstration of musical vibration, meant to cause a heavy artifact to topple from the wall onto the head of one of the goons.

"What are hepcats doing in a place like this?" the criminal asks before the band launches into "Flying Home."

"Our hope is that, in the words of Mr. Armstrong," explains Frisbee, "this particular music might send you out of this world." Before blowing, Louis has a brief opportunity to display his nonverbal acting skills, glancing up at the artifact and then nodding affirmatively to Kaye.

United Artists' trailer celebrated "an all–American musical aggregation that sets the pace for an exciting, romantic escapade," singling out "the wail of Benny Goodman's clarinet, the moan of Tommy Dorsey's trombone, the call of Louis Armstrong's trumpet, the lilt of Lionel Hampton's vibraphone, the lament of Charlie Barnet's saxophone, the rhythm of Mel Powell's piano, and the harmony and tempo of Buck and Bubbles." Hawks critic Gerald Mast called the musical sequences the film's one saving grace: "Hawks delights in documenting the way that musicians make music — in the same way he documents the ways that people fly planes, catch tuna, drive cattle, chase game. No film with all those musicians can be *all* bad."[5] (Happily for Danny Kaye, he reconciled with Sylvia Fine, who stuck it out until his death in 1987.)

During the *A Song Is Born* shoot, on August 13, 1947, Louis and the All Stars debuted at Billy Berg's club in Los Angeles, where Hoagy Carmichael, Woody Herman, Benny Goodman and Johnny Mercer paid their respects. *Down Beat*'s George Hoefer reported that, "Satchmo's superb stage presence binds together a showcase of jazz stars into a jazz production that warmed the hearts of nostalgic music lovers (Louis is playing and singing with more heart and inspiration than he has for years)."[6]

Hitting the road for another nationwide tour, the All Stars—bowing to another of Glaser's "moneymaking" gimmicks—added Velma Middleton to the act. In the middle of a number, she would do her "dance" (gyrating, rolling around on the stage and doing the splits) and exchange witticisms with Pops.

In New York on October 16 the band recorded four songs, beginning the session with "A Song Is Born," featuring Jack Teagarden and Pops on vocals. "Please Stop Playin' Those Blues, Boy," opens with the trombone of "Mr. T," who is scolded by Louis for making him "depressed."

"I feel bad enough, without you makin' me feel worse, Gate," Teagarden laments as Pops blows some low-down licks.

On Sunday, November 30, Pops and the band again performed for Ernest Anderson, this time at Boston's Symphony Hall. "Mahogany Hall Stomp" opened the show in energetic fashion, with Louis giving Dick Carey and Arvell Shaw a chance to flex their improvisational muscles before blowing into a high note that he sustained for a solid 10 measures. "Hold it! Hold it!" urged his bandmates.

The oft-played "Black and Blue" followed, proving that Louis considered it an important part of his live repertoire. Four instrumentals—"Royal Garden Blues," "Lover," an epic "Body and Soul" (featuring sublime soloing by Barney Bigard) and "Muskrat Ramble"—were succeeded by the vocals of Teagarden ("Stars Fell on Alabama") and Middleton ("Since I Fell for You").

Bigard led the band into a driving "Tea for Two," continuing to solo as Pops joined in with the original melody, and taking it home accompanied only by Catlett's drums. A lengthy jam on the traditional blues number "Steak Face," also spotlighting Catlett, was followed by Pops' second vocal of the night, "On the Sunny Side of the Street," and a trip back to New Orleans on "High Society." Bigard again led off, using his years as a member of Ellington's band to great effect on Duke's "C-Jam

Blues"; Big Tea sang "Baby, Won't You Please Come Home?"; and the entire band wailed on the closer, Coleman Hawkins' "Boff Boff."

Just as Louis was successfully "reverting" to the classic New Orleans sound, the "new jazz," bebop, was gaining a foothold. Incubated in Harlem by musicians who veered away from traditional polyphony and the Armstrong style toward harmonic experimentation—further improvising on the chord changes in a tune, rather than on the melody, and favoring the "flatted fifth" (flatting the fifth note in a scale)— this interesting, sometimes wild, and often *un*-danceable music was being powerfully advocated by bop trumpeter John Birks ("Dizzy") Gillespie and alto saxophonist Charlie ("Bird") Parker (who first hit upon the chord change–improvisation idea after listening to Art Tatum's piano playing). Gillespie inaugurated the term "bebop" after a listener, who heard him instructively scatting a melody to his band, thought he had told them to play a song with that name. Eventually, bop would revolutionize jazz, creating a new generation of outstanding soloists and composers, including one of the finest in American music, Thelonious Monk, whose complex harmonies and displaced rhythms comprise a 180-degree turn from Armstrong's music, yet swing formidably.

Louis was beginning to listen to more recordings—his own, and even those waxed by up-and-coming beboppers. He said:

> I'd never play the bebop because I don't like it. Don't get me wrong; I think some of them cats who play it play real good, like Dizzy, especially. But bebop is the easy way out. Instead of holding notes the way they should be held, they just play a lot of little notes. They sorta fake out of it. You won't find many of them cats who can blow a straight lead. They never learned right. It's all just flash. It doesn't come from the heart the way real music should.[7]

He also commented:

> Very personally, I don't care for most bop, except maybe for Parker, some Miles Davis, some Thelonious Monk. But some people who I'd swear to be of sound mind are very high on it, and I suspect that if I understand it, which I largely don't, I'd be in a better position to make up my mind about bop.[8]

Miles Davis said of Louis *and* Dizzy Gillespie:

> I hated the way they used to laugh and grin for audiences. I know *why* they did it— to make money and because they were entertainers as well as trumpet players. They had families to feed. Plus they both liked acting the clown. … I was younger than them and didn't have to go through the shit they had to go through to get accepted in the music industry. They had opened up a whole lot of doors for people like me to go through.[9]

While Louis was touring with his so-called "moldy fig" jazz, Bill Robinson again was drumming up financial support for the annual benefit staged by the Negro Actors Guild, to be held Sunday, December 5, at New York's Imperial Theatre. Intending to raise money for NAG's "badly depleted" Welfare Fund, the show, again promising appearances by "Stars of Radio, Stage and Screen," was to be emceed by Ed Sullivan, who also produced.

Mainstream America was experiencing the effects of McCarthyism, and African American performers usually were offered the same tired stereotyped characters in Hollywood, but a few white heavyweights, including Sullivan and Crosby, continued to throw in their lot with NAG. By this time, NAG had greatly expanded its list of officers, including Dooley Wilson, who joined the vice-president ranks, Mabel Mercer, Mary McLeod Bethune and Claude Barnet.

Celebrating its 10th anniversary, NAG issued an official policy regarding members who picketed theaters practicing segregation. Speaking out against protests aimed at "theatres in which plays are playing with Negro casts"—which only led to unemployment for African American performers—the Guild requested "a unified fight against all the theatres and other institutions which maintain the practice of racial and color discrimination." Stating its support for "every type of protest against discrimination and segregation which is lawful," NAG stressed the need to "fight against segregation in the public schools … the hotels and restaurants and other public places … the laws which compel segregation and which have remained unchanged on the statute books of these cities and states for half a century."[10]

NAG recently had given an award to vocal director Hall Johnson, a major player in the success of *Cabin in the Sky*. In his letter of appreciation to Guild secretary Mabel A. Roane, Johnson's remarks about traditional African American culture can be applied specifically to Armstrong's career as an "entertainer":

> [M]any of our "smart" young people—the future hope of the race—regard me as old-fashioned and reactionary because I insist on stressing the importance of our folklore and folk music and the culture that is really ours and belongs to nobody else. These people are ashamed of their rightful heritage only because they don't know the value of it. It is my constant hope and belief that, at some future day, they will learn that no man can claim to be really *free* so long as he wishes to forget or deny something that is really his own. When that day of realization comes, these same people will be glad that a few of us have worked to preserve these priceless treasures of great art which prove, as nothing else can, that Negroes have always been wonderful people whether they themselves knew it or not.[11]

In February 1948, Louis was guest of honor at the first International Jazz Festival in Nice, France. On behalf of President Vincent Auriol, French singer Yves Montand presented Pops with the prestigious Golden Vase.

On April 30, John Lester, President of the National Jazz Foundation, Inc., of New Orleans, wrote a press release declaring that Louis was "one of the most extraordinary geniuses that all music has ever known," and conferred upon him the titles of "Honorary Life Member," "Doctor of Music," "Honorary Member of the Board" and "Honorary Vice President."[12]

On Sunday, November 21, Louis and the All Stars, making their television debut, plugged *A Song Is Born* on the CBS *Toast of the Town* program, hosted by Ed Sullivan. *Variety* reported that the show had taken "a definite upswing … with a talent-laden bill and some pleasant surprises," but thought that Pops could have done better with his own material:

Louis Armstrong and his orchestra, all name musicians in their own right, did a brace of songs in their usual fine fashion but they would have pleased more with something like Satchmo's disk smash "Can't Give You Anything but Love," instead of plugging "Song Is Born," Danny Kaye starrer in which Armstrong appears, with the tired little song.[13]

Two days later Pops made a similar small-screen appearance on the *Eddie Condon Floor Show*. He became so popular with Eddie that he repeated the act four times the following summer. On December 11 he and the band were at Chicago's Blue Note, playing a benefit for the Damon Runyan Cancer Fund. Broadcast nationally, the performance, hosted by Dave Garroway, roared in with "Muskrat Ramble."

"Did you see the picture *A Song Is Born*, in which Louis is just as pretty as he plays?" Garroway asked his radio audience, noting that all proceeds from the sound-track album were being donated to the Runyan Fund. Teagarden then opened the film's title song with a brief solo and vocal, then improvised a new opening verse for "Basin Street Blues." Earl Hines swung into his nightly feature, "Boogie Woogie on the St. Louis Blues," before Louis led the standby "High Society" and, after calling Garroway "Pops," "Royal Garden Blues." The band closed the program with a brief "I've Got a Right to Sing the Blues."

On February 21, 1949, Louis became the first jazz musician to grace the cover of *Time* magazine. The full-color artwork showed his world-famous visage decked out as King of the Zulus, a role he long had dreamed of playing during Mardi Gras, and the lengthy article touched on his early years and musical accomplishments, King Oliver, bebop, Lucille, Joe Glaser and racism. Six days later he was greeted in New Orleans by Mayor DeLesseps Morrison, who presented him with the key to the city. As he relaxed in his hotel room, a member of the Zulus made him up in blackface and a grass skirt for the parade. Though some African Americans viewed his Zulu Kingship as a throwback to minstrelsy, Pops was honored to cast a joyous, humorous light on the Mardi Gras celebration; as he often did, Louis relished playing the trickster.

The All Stars joined him on the float, and he was thrilled by the arrival of jazz historian Hughes Panassie, who had traveled from France to be with him. That evening Pops entertained 500 patrons—including his ex-wife Daisy Parker—at Booker T. Washington Auditorium. The next morning the All Stars, accompanied by Panassie, hit the road for a series of one-nighters in Jackson, Tulsa and Dallas before reaching Las Vegas for a two-week engagement at the Flamingo, Benjamin ("Bugsy") Siegel's "dream in the desert" which, two years earlier, had cost the mobster his life at age 41.

In San Francisco on March 16, Pops made his first guest appearance on Bing Crosby's "Chesterfield" radio show. From March 23 to April 3, he and the All Stars played the Hollywood Empire Room on Vine Street between Hollywood and Sunset boulevards. One of the best shows of the engagement was broadcast live on the AFRS *Jubilee* program, and cost each of the patrons one dollar plus tax. The crowd enthusiastically applauded after hearing a few notes of "When It's Sleepy Time Down South." Following an introduction by the radio announcer, the band swung into "Panama" before Pops admitted to blowing the feathers off the Flamingo in Vegas: "I made it look like one of them plucked ducks."

"We're takin' 'em to New Orleans this time," he announced before singing "Back o' Town Blues." Earl Hines was featured on "Pale Moon"; Velma Middleton and Pops improvised some suggestive rap during their "Don't Fence Me In" duet; Big Tea played furious solos on "Lover"; and Bigard again offered his "Body and Soul." Louis and Tea sang and blew a lively "A Song Was Born," settled into "Whispering," and did the "Mahogany Hall Stomp" before Pops had the audience roaring with laughter during "Me and Brother Bill." During a stop-time scat break, Louis' bizarre verbalizations even caused *him* to break down laughing. Bigard again led off a breakneck "C-Jam Blues"; Tea warbled through "A Hundred Years from Today"; Hines, Shaw and Catlett tore it up on "Boogie Woogie on St. Louis Blues"; and Middleton returned for Irving Berlin's "Blue Skies." Pops mimicked Tea's Texas twang while they sang "Rockin' Chair," so the trombonist took over the vocal and changed the tempo during "The Sheik of Araby." Bumped from the singer spot on the previous number, Louis closed with "Confessin'."

On March 27, Eslanda (Mrs. Paul Robeson) delivered a lecture entitled "The Negro Contribution to Culture" at NAG's 12th Annual Meeting at the Grand Street Boys Association in New York. Focusing on "the treatment of Negroes in films," she mentioned several current Hollywood productions, including *Lost Boundaries*, *Quality*, *No Way Out*, *Intruder in the Dust* and *Home of the Brave*:

> This kind of program in Hollywood, and *South Pacific* for Broadway, certainly make things look up for the Negro actor, and certainly make things look up for the 15 million Negroes who have been so misrepresented on stage and screen for so many years.
>
> It does seem to be taking a long time for us Negroes to find our rightful place in our country. We know, of course, that we are not all Uncle Toms and Aunt Jemimas, any more than all Irishmen are policemen, all Chinese laundrymen, all Italians fruit vendors, and so on. Along with other Americans, we can look back into our history, and find much to be proud of, and can be reassured when we see what substantial contributions we have made to the culture of our country, and of the world.[14]

After closing at the Hollywood Empire, the All Stars played a week of one-nighters on their way to Chicago, where Glaser had booked a week-long run at the Blue Note. Back in New York, they again guested on the *Eddie Condon Floor Show*, appearing on the June 11, August 27, September 3 and September 10 broadcasts.

Pops cut two Decca sides, "Maybe It's Because" and "I'll Keep the Lovelight Burning (in My Heart)," with the Sy Oliver Orchestra on September 1. Five days later he waxed two more with the Gordon Jenkins Orchestra, which featured Billy Butterfield and Yank Lawson (trumpets), Jack Lesberg (bass) and Johnny Blowers (drums). Unfortunately, both songs—his first recordings of "That Lucky Old Sun" and "Blueberry Hill—are bogged down by an overwrought, stilted chorus. Far more hip are two Sy Oliver recordings from a September 30 session, pairing Pops with Billie Holiday: "You Can't Lose a Broken Heart" and "My Sweet Hunk o' Trash," the latter especially capturing their delightful chemistry.

"Now, listen, Pops!" commands Lady Day, in top form.

"Look out, baby. Watch it, honey," warns Louis.

Pops also appeared on a television program broadcast from the Apollo Theater in September. During the autumn, the 1949 All Stars European tour opened in Stockholm, Sweden, and closed in Palermo, Sicily. During the Italian stint, Pops allowed their October 26 concert in Rome to be filmed for release as the feature *La Botta e Risposta*. While in the Italian capitol, Louis and Lucille had an audience with Pope Pius XII. Arvell Shaw recalled:

> I guess the people and the Pope had been listening to the broadcasts. He found out we were going to play Rome so he asked to meet [them] 'cause he said that when he was a young priest he was a fan, he had Louis Armstrong records. He liked jazz.... So he would like to talk with Louis. So it was arranged through the American Embassy in the Sistine Chapel. And all the diplomats and all the press was there. The Pope was telling Louis how he loved his records and how he had his records when he was a young priest and everything. And he was asking Louis and Lucille about their life in the U.S. And he said, "Mr. Armstrong, you and Mrs. Armstrong, do you have any children?" And Louis said, "No, but we're having a hell of a lot of fun trying." There was complete, shocked silence for a minute. It could have been a disaster. Then everybody looked at Pope Pius; he burst out in a guffaw, then everybody.... I bet the American ambassador must have lost three years of his life.[15]

Shaw also claimed that the "feud" between Louis and beboppers like Dizzy Gillespie was inflated, perhaps even manufactured, by music journalists:

> I think what Louis did by himself was to make jazz into a soloist's art form. Before Louis, when they improvised, they would just state the melody and then what they would do, they would get "hot"; they would heavily syncopate the melody. Louis started improvising on the chord structure of a tune. The old guys used to think he was crazy.
>
> Dizzy and Louis lived maybe two blocks away from each other in Corona. They were very dear friends. ... That competition, that thing that Louis was against bebop, that was created by the jazz writers to have something to write about — "the moldy fig thing."[16]

"We're gettin' ready to jump those good old good ones!" announced Pops as the All Stars tore into "Royal Garden Blues" at a November 9 concert in Trieste, Italy. The first line of "Black and Blue" drew applause, as did each bit of scat and a brilliant solo. Louis' superb playing continued on "Twelfth Street Rag" and "Baby, Won't You Please Come Home?" (on which Teagarden also excelled). The enthusiastic audience gave Velma Middleton a hearty welcome when she sang "Don't Worry About Me," and they were thrilled further by Hines' frenetic version of "I Got Rhythm" and Bigard's lyrical "Body and Soul," on which the clarinetist held the concluding high note for a staggering 32 seconds. The band concluded the show with "High Society" and Irving Berlin's "Russian Lullaby," on which Shaw rocked the house with a thunderous bass solo.

Back in the States, the All Stars, with Cozy Cole on drums, recorded 10 numbers at Decca's New York studio on April 26–27, 1950 — comprising one of the best sessions of Louis' career. The instrumentals "Panama," "New Orleans Function" (a medley of "Flee as a Bird" and "Didn't He Ramble?") and "Twelfth Street Rag" opened the dates in hot fashion, with Cole and Shaw driving the band with forceful rhythmic precision.

As Hines plays ominous-sounding chords on the piano, Pops introduces the medley in fine fashion:

> And now, folks, we gonna take you down to New Orleans, Louisiana. Tell you the story about "Didn't He Ramble?" Of course, you know there was a funeral march in front of "Didn't He Ramble?" where they take the body to the cemetery, and they lower ol' Brother Gate in the ground. And, a — dig it!

Bridging the two tunes, Pops adds:

> And as the family is cryin', as they lower ol' Brother Gate in the ground, and ol' Reverend say, "Ashes to ashes. Dust to dust. It's too bad ol' Gate couldn't have stayed on Earth with us." And the snare drum player, he takes the handkerchief out of the snare, and rolls up so the members can form in line to swing back to the hall, playin' "Didn't He Ramble?"

Pops is in beautiful voice on the Rodgers and Hammerstein ballad "That's for Me," and equally eloquent blowing through the epic "Bugle Call Rag/Ole Miss," featuring powerhouse drum solos by Cole. Bigard opens "I Surrender, Dear" with a typically sumptuous clarinet solo, then kicks into high gear as the band swings up a storm, finally shifting into a 6/8 blues tempo and playing one of his virtuoso high notes on the ending. The band gets supremely funky on "Russian Lullaby," one of the numbers they had been working out during gigs, allowing space for a Shaw and Cole jam, and a harmonically stunning section featuring Pops, Bigard and Hines. A driving rendition of "Baby, Won't You Please Come Home?" presents Teagarden at his vocal and instrumental best, and a formidably swinging yet lightsome "Fine and Dandy" allows Hines to stretch out. The session closer, Clarence Williams' "booze blues" "My Bucket's Got a Hole in It," had been recorded by Hank Williams the previous August. Both Pops and Big Tea get exquisitely low-down while taking it home.

On Saturday, May 13, Louis visited the *Ken Murray Show* on CBS. Pops was an admirer of Murray, one of the most versatile talents in show business. Though his television program ran only three seasons during the medium's early years, Murray was also a capable character actor in Hollywood films, a comedian, a photographer and a director.

Ten days after appearing on Murray's 30-minute variety show, Louis, while at the Horse Shoe Bar in Rock Island, Illinois (an area he first visited during his riverboat excursions more than 30 years earlier), typed a letter to his fellow actor. Laced with his idiosyncratic jargon, autobiographical reminiscences, witticisms and warmth, the missive indicates Pops' true appreciation of another entertainer's abilities. Addressed to Ken "Stuff" Murray, the letter reads:

Horse Shoe Bar
Rock Island, Ill.
May 24th, 1950

Dear Stuff Murray:

Just a little Scribblings, to let you know how you "knocked Ol' Satchmo" completely out. … I've worked with a lot of great stars like yourself, but you have a certain something, when a person works with you they feel so at ease, and stuff like that. … You make a guy forget he's working and just "jiving" with one of the neighborhood big shots.…

Honest, "Stuff"—you remind me of a very popular guy down in New Orleans in our neighborhood called "Slippers" … "Yea Man" Slippers was his name. … He was the kind of a fellow who could mingle with everybody—musicians—church folks, he could dance, swim, had all the gals, was crazy about us kids, was very good on the dukes, had a very wonderful sense of humor, aw hell, he was a living aspirin. … Tee Hee…

I won't take up too much of your time… Because I know you're busier than a cat on a tin roof. … Ha ha ha. … You're the busiest man I've ever met in New York. … Honest, you're busier than Joe Glaser (my boss) he even books attractions while on his vacations. … I dug you in your Blackouts, on the Coast. … You "gassed" me. … My regards to the cast. … Nightie night and *God Bless Ya*.

Am Ulceratedly Yours,
Louis Armstrong

Though Pops played all his live gigs with the All Stars, he balanced his recording work fronting sessions with larger orchestras. On June 26 he was back in New York, cutting two "French" sides, "La Vie en Rose" and "C'est Si Bon," with Sy Oliver. Earl Hines was the sole member of the All Stars to join the session, spurring on Pops to his vocal and instrumental best. Both songs conclude with him soaring into goosebump-raising solos.

Louis played for his own 50th birthday bash (though he still was only 48) at New York's Bop City on July 4. Articles celebrating his achievements appeared in many national publications, including *Down Beat*, which dedicated an issue to him. On August 23 he recorded two songs, "Life Is So Peculiar" and yet another "I'll Be Glad When You're Dead, You Rascal You," with Louis Jordan and His Tympany Five. Two days later Pops enjoyed his second meeting with Ella Fitzgerald, recording Sy Oliver's arrangements of "Dream a Little Dream of Me" and "Can Anyone Explain" with an octet. The sublime "Dream" opens with Pops' trumpet and Ella's scat, then runs the vocal gamut, with each singer scatting around the other, trading off lyrics, and harmonizing perfectly.

"Say, Pops! Oh, Pops, put that horn down and listen!" Ella commands during the second number. "I want to ask you a question."

"What's buggin' you, baby?" asks Louis.

"Well, have you ever been in love?" she replies.

"Ha, ha, ha, ha, ha, ha. How you sound!" says Pops. "I've been in love four times. But, tell me," he continues, gently swinging into the lyric.

On August 31, Louis and Sy Oliver cut two more numbers, "Sit Down, You're Rocking the Boat" and "That's What the Man Said." During the autumn, he guested on four television programs: *Ted Steele's Cavalcade of Bands* (October 10); an unknown show (late October); the *Kay Kyser Show* (November 19); and NBC's *The Big Show* (December 17), broadcast from Hollywood. The original contract for the latter, signed on December 11, guaranteed $1,000 for his appearance on this 90-minute variety program.

Louis had returned to Hollywood, with Teagarden, Hines, Bigard and Cole to pre-record soundtrack performances for MGM's *The Strip* on December 26, 28 and 29, 1950. For their collective work, the All Stars received $20,000. In between, Pops helped throw a televised birthday party for an old pal on the December 27 *Bing Crosby Chesterfield Show*. Broadcast from San Francisco, the show also featured Joe Venuti and Dinah Shore.

Directed by Leslie Kardos and produced by Joe Pasternak, *The Strip* stars Mickey Rooney as Stanley Maxton, a World War II veteran who lands in tinsel

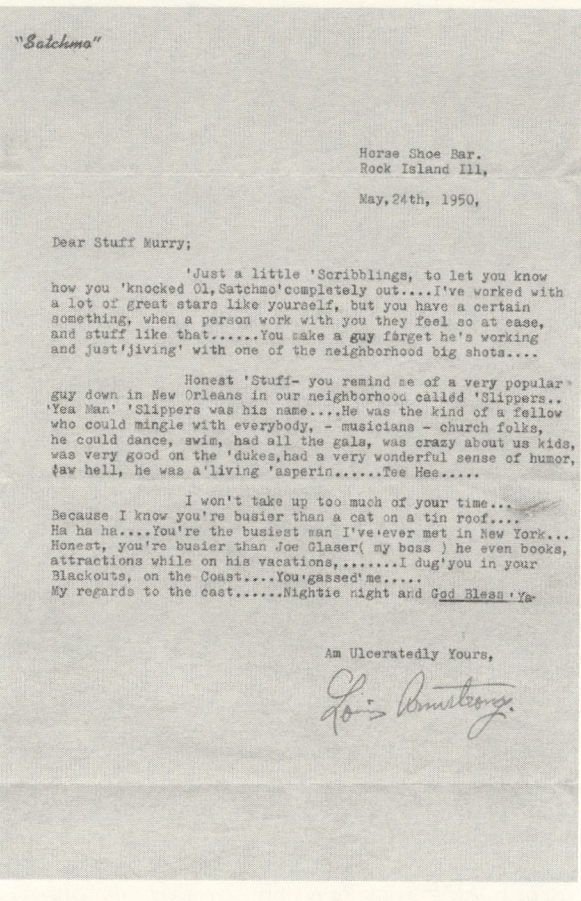

Top: Letter from Louis to actor Ken Murray, typed at the Horse Shoe Bar, Rock Island, Illinois, May 24, 1950. Laced with jive, autobiographical reminiscences, witticisms and warmth, it shows Pops' appreciation of another entertainer's talent. *Bottom:* Louis always carried stationery printed only with his name, so he could type in his daily address — here, the Horse Shoe Bar in Rock Island, Illinois — a fascinating aspect of the ceaseless autobiographer.

The Strip (1951). MGM's title lobby card features Louis, Earl ("Fatha") Hines, Jack Teagarden and Barney Bigard.

town, hoping to make a living as a jazz drummer, but soon resorts to working for local bookie Delwyn ("Sonny") Johnson (James Craig). While drumming at a Dixieland club owned by "Fluff" (William Demarest), Maxton falls for Jane Tafford (Sally Forrest), a would-be actress whom he introduces to Johnson. When the mobster makes a play for Jane, the outraged Maxton is beaten to a pulp and she is fatally wounded after killing her attacker. The film concludes with Maxton returning to swing on the skins.

The *noir* crime melodrama is ineffectively directed and acted, the performance sequences are a highlight, with George E. Stoll's musical direction and Nick Castle's choreography creating an authentic jazz club atmosphere. Louis, who has no dialogue, and the band recorded 12 numbers for the film, nine of which are used on the soundtrack. "Ole Miss," featuring Cozy Cole's blazing drum solo (well-mimed by Mickey Rooney), provides one of several joyous moments Pops brings to the film's downbeat mood, as does Teagarden, who sings and plays his trombone coda on "Basin Street Blues."

The ballad "A Kiss to Build a Dream On" had been written 15 years earlier by Bert Kalmar, Harry Ruby and Oscar Hammerstein II for possible inclusion in the Marx Bros. classic *A Night at the Opera* (1935), but had been languishing at MGM ever since. Though Pops performs it in the final scene, the song is first sung by Wil-

The Strip (1951). Stanley Maxton (Mickey Rooney, at the drums) "jams" with Jack Teagarden, Barney Bigard and Louis.

liam Demarest, who is joined by Rooney in mangling the melody, then by a hatch-eck girl (Kay Brown), and can be heard in the background at various moments.

A religious medley includes "Shadrack" and "When the Saints Go Marching In," bridged by a brief drum solo by Cole/Rooney. The former, telling the tale of "three children of Israel"—Shadrack, Meschach and Abednigo—who encounter the wrath of the Babylonian king Nebuchadnezzar, includes Pops' admission, "Well, you couldn't burn a hair on the head of Shadrack," during which Barney Bigard injects some humor by displaying his bald pate.

The instrumentals "That's a Plenty," "Hines' Retreat," "Fatha's Time" (a sensual blues) and "J. T. Jive" (including another drum solo) are also heard during the film. Rooney's casting accounts for Cole's visual absence, but the presence of a white actor in Arvell's Shaw's bassist spot is a mystery. "Ain't Misbehavin'," an arrangement of Count Basie's "One O'Clock Jump," and "I'm Coming Virginia" were dropped from the score. Vic Damone and Monica Lewis also are on hand to sing "Don't Blame Me" and "La Bota," respectively.

In his first television performance of the New Year, Louis was back with Bing Crosby on the January 17, 1951, *Chesterfield Show*. Two weeks later, he and the All Stars played the Pasadena Civic Auditorium, a "Just Jazz" concert organized by Gene Norman and recorded for a Decca album release. Following the band's "When It's

Sleepy Time Down South"/"(Back Home Again in) Indiana" introduction, Pops announced, "We gonna knock out one of them little, cute little old numbers I kind of wrote myself ... 'Someday'!" blowing the melody with Tea's harmonic accompaniment and gorgeous Bigard obbligati.

For some hometown cats he met prior to the concert, Pops "draped" "Back o' Town Blues" on them, blowing a sublime solo. After singing a lyric which warns a man against mistreating his woman, "because it's gonna bounce right back on you," he added, "That ain't no stage joke, either, Homes!" Then, for all the "gumbo eaters," he launched into "Way Down Yonder in New Orleans."

"Lord have mercy! Them cats is good!" Louis raved at the end of the tune, turning the spotlight on Teagarden for a trombone-led "Stardust." Velma "jump[ed] that new dance—'the Hucklebuck'"; Earl Hines breezed through a brilliant version of Fats Waller's "Honeysuckle Rose"; Arvell Shaw tore it up on a cookin' "How High the Moon"; Bigard got virtuosic on "Just You, Just Me"; Cole played an astounding array of rudiments during the jam "Bugle Blues"; and Pops, Tea and Bigard blew a heavy wind on Hines' own "My Monday Date."

Pops' inspired vocal on "You Can Depend on Me" was followed by the band's furious jam on "That's a Plenty" and Big Tea's "Body and Soul." Velma Middleton finally appeared to lay on the "Big Daddy Blues," then announced, "Baby, It's Cold Outside" before she and Pops sang and rapped some improvised shtick. On the closer, "Muskrat Ramble," Louis welcomed the Firehouse Five, Walt Disney employees who moonlighted as jazz musicians. Eleven of the numbers were released on 45-rpm EP records by Decca.

On February 6, Pops again joined arranger-conductor Gordon Jenkins, a major Armstrong admirer, for a Los Angeles recording session that yielded three Decca sides: Irving Berlin's "You're Just in Love," a swinging vocal duet with Velma; "If," a tender ballad with trumpet solo; and the classic "Big Butter and Egg Man," with Pops soloing and scatting around Velma's fine vocal.

Bing was digging ol' Pops so much that he invited him for several more *Chesterfield* appearances—on April 11 and 25 (during which they sang "Gone Fishin," a duet they also recorded in Los Angeles two days later), and May 23. On April 23, Louis and the All Stars recorded two ballads, "Unless" and "You're the Apple of My Eye" (cowritten by Pops, who shares another vocal with Velma), at a Decca session.

In the midst of these projects, Crosby induced Frank Capra to give Louis a cameo in their current feature-film collaboration *Here Comes the Groom* (1951), costarring Jane Wyman, Alexis Smith and Franchot Tone. Some filmgoers who stepped out for refreshments could have missed this unbilled "role." Released by Paramount, this tale of a war correspondent who adopts two French orphans (Jacques Gencel and Beverly Washburn), assuming he will be wed to his longtime sweetheart (Wyman) back in the States, is pure "Capracorn" from the first frame to the last. But it's entertaining hokum nonetheless, particularly when Crosby's Pete Garvey teaches proper and bashful socialite Winifred Stanley (Smith) how to lure "cousin Wilbur" (Tone) away from marrying *his* fiancée. Johnny Mercer and Hoagy Carmichael's "In the Cool, Cool, Cool of the Evening," a leitmotif performed in various incarnations, won the Best Song Academy Award that year.

Louis suddenly appears (alongside Bing, Dorothy Lamour, Phil Harris, Frank Fontaine and Cass Daley), singing and blowing a few notes on "Misto Cristofo Columbo" during a Transatlantic flight. Bosley Crowther, in his *New York Times* review, wrote, "With all due respect to these worthies, they are obvious 'ringers' in the film. It could get along just as well without them."[17] Driven by a breezy, likeable Crosby performance, the film was popular with audiences and critics.

Back in New York on July 24, 1951, Pops cut two more Decca sides with Sy Oliver—"(When We Are Dancin') I Get Ideas," offering a charming two-beat ending with his laughter as he tickles himself with his own vocal, and his first official release of "A Kiss to Build a Dream On." The following month he and an octet recorded a gently grooving version of Hank Williams' masterful "Cold, Cold Heart" and the ballad "Because of You," on which he overdubbed trumpet obbligati.

Louis joined Milton Berle on the September 25 broadcast of his popular absurdist television show. As a contrast to "Uncle Milty's" "lapses into grotesque femme," Basil Rathbone's Horatio Hornblower satire (during which the great English actor "permitted himself to become somewhat ludicrous"[18]), and some unconventional vocalizing by Metropolitan Opera soprano Patrice Munsel, Pops sang "Jeepers Creepers," "On the Sunny Side of the Street" and the popular "Gone Fishin'."

For his next film role—as trumpet-blowing boxing trainer "Shadow" Johnson in MGM's *Glory Alley* (1952)—Louis earned $25,000 for working a solid two weeks, November 14–27, 1951, under the direction of the formidable Raoul Walsh. Once again Pops' performances are the highlight of a mediocre film, fortunately set in New Orleans but unfortunately marred by a ludicrous Art Cohn screenplay. Even the name of the protagonist—Socks Barbarrosa (Ralph Meeker)—stretches the bounds of absurdity. After Barbarrosa ditches a prize fight, he is branded a coward by "the Judge" (Kurt Kasznar), the blind father of his girlfriend Angela (Leslie Caron, fresh from Gene Kelly's *An American in Paris* [1951]), and then runs off to fight in Korea. Returning a hero, with the Congressional Medal of Honor pinned to his chest, he admits to Angela that his earlier display of cowardice stemmed from an embarrassing facial disfigurement, and then he promptly defeats his opponent in the ring.

As in *The Strip*, Louis buoys the film with several outstanding musical numbers, but also enjoys a few dramatic moments as Shadow Johnson (rather than being relegated to portraying "himself" in the background). The only African American character in the film, "Shad" is treated respectfully, though he typically addresses the whites with formal titles.

"That's What the Man Said" is performed by Pops and Jack Teagarden, backed by a chorus and orchestra. "Glory Alley," written for the score by Jay Livingston and Mack David, opens with piano and Pops' vocal, then gains strings and brass before Louis blows a solo that, unfortunately, is drowned out by dialogue. New Orleans material heard during various scenes includes "South Rampart Street Parade," "Flee as a Bird" and "Oh, Didn't He Ramble?" One song, Jimmy McHugh and Harold Adamson's "It's a Most Unusual Day," was dropped from the film.

In his *New York Times* review, Bosley Crowther referred to the acting as "callow, arrogant and ponderous," reserving praise for Pops: "Louis Armstrong sticks

his broad, beaming face into the frame and sings or blasts a bit on his trumpet. That makes the only sense in the whole film."[19]

Ralph Meeker enjoyed their collaboration, and inscribed a portrait to Pops, "Moviley Yours. Hope we fly on another *cinematic venture*."[20] Philip ("Monk") Friedman also presented him with an 8x10, signing, "My warmest admiration for a great artist and friend."[21]

While working on *Glory Alley*, Pops joined Ella Fitzgerald and guitarist Dave Barbour's orchestra for a November 23 session in Los Angeles. The day after he walked off the MGM set, Louis and Ella guested on Bing Crosby's radio show.

"What are you doin' in Hollywood this trip, Louis?" asked Cros. "You making a picture or something?"

"I'm working on a picture out at MGM called *Glory Alley*," replied Pops. "It's a story about New Orleans."

"I read about that picture, *Glory Alley*," said Bing. "I understand that you have a very, very dramatic part in the picture."

"Yeah," laughed Louis, "this old cat has gone legit there!"

Following Pops' performance of "I Get Ideas," Bing observed, "I don't think you've become a legitimate actor; you've become a legitimate singer!"

"No, Daddy, no," countered Louis. "That's your racket!"

Producer Milt Gabler, a jazz record mogul who joined Decca in 1945, was attempting to make Louis a more bankable pop singer. On November 28 he reunited his artist with Gordon Jenkins to cut four sides: "When It's Sleepy Time Down South," on which (after an introduction by the arranger-conductor's trademark string sound) Louis blends some fantastic low vocal tones with scat and then blows a powerhouse solo; "It's All in the Game" (with a melody written by Coolidge vice-president Charles Dawes); "Jeannine (I Dream of Lilac Time)"; and "Indian Love Call." After recording these numbers, Pops again paired up with Ella, on Crosby's *Chesterfield* TV show.

During 1951, the FBI, which had been conducting surveillance on Louis for the past three years, turned up the heat when they discovered his name on the NAG letterhead. J. Edgar Hoover began suspecting that he had leftist tendencies when his name was discovered in the address book of a "suspected Communist."

New Year's Day 1952 was rung in with an historic musical pairing, that of Ol' Gate and the future Ol' Blue Eyes on CBS-TV's *The Frank Sinatra Show*, which also featured Yvonne DeCarlo and the Three Stooges (Moe Howard, Shemp Howard and Larry Fine). Unable to hire help for his New Year's Eve Party, Frank was "pleasantly" surprised when the Stooges, dressed in white tie and tails, knocked at his apartment door. Soon after his guests filed in, Pops arrived to sing "I'm Confessin'" with the pianist and blow some lightly swinging solos.

After guest George DeWitt tried to impersonate Perry Como, Mel Torme, Vaughan Monroe, Billy Eckstine and Billy Daniels, he and Frank collaborated on

Opposite, top: Glory Alley (1952). "Louis (Satchmo) Armstrong and His Trumpet" are featured on this original lobby card from the MGM boxing drama set in New Orleans. *Bottom: Glory Alley* (1952). Louis and Jack Teagarden perform during the celebration for Socks Barbarrosa (Ralph Meeker).

some "mutual impressions" of James Cagney, President Harry Truman and others. Sinatra also sang a duet version of "Getting to Know You" with DeCarlo before everything blacked out.

Waking up on the couch with an ice bag on his aching head, and attempting to talk into a shoe, Frank unleashed a severely "hungover" vocal on an alcohol-altered "Oh, Look at Me Now," including a lyric that warns you're in trouble when Ava begins to look like Marjorie Main.

Pops re-entered, looking for his abandoned trumpet, admitting to Frank that, at a late-night club session, "I was halfway through a solo before I realized that I didn't have it in my hand." Frank sat down at the piano, and the two sang a duet on "Someone to Call My Own." Sinatra capably scatted alongside Satch, who blew some fine blue notes and sang out, "Oh, yeahhhhh!" while nuzzling cheek to cheek with the Voice, creating a memorable musical moment. Joyously wishing the audience, "Happy New Year," Pops told Frank, "Don't forget to come see us at the [Club] Hangover when you come up to Frisco."

While in Denver on March 19, 1952, Louis and the All Stars—now featuring Bigard, Cole, Russ Phillips (trombone), Donald Ruffell (clarinet and tenor sax), Marty Napoleon (piano) and session bassist Dale Jones—recorded two Decca sides: the Sammy Cahn–Jule Styne torch song "I'll Walk Alone"; and the romantic, "Spanish"-tinged "Kiss of Fire," with Pops commanding, "Ah, *burn* me!" at the end.

Back in New York during the summer, Pops made three television guest appearances. On June 8 he was featured on *The U.S. Royal Showcase*. Two days later the work of Louis' supporter Ed Sullivan was discussed at a NAG meeting. Agents for Sullivan's *Toast of the Town* had requested that the Guild send a congratulatory fourth-anniversary cake to the television studio. The motion was carried unanimously.

Louis made his debut on the *Colgate Comedy Hour* on June 28, enduring the *Buck Privates*–derived shtick of Abbott and Costello. After inanely arguing with a bogus cameraman, Bud and Lou attempted to recreate the magic they cast at Universal a decade earlier, but guest tough guy George Raft nearly killed Costello when he got too rough in the "basic training" scene, jerking the comic's portly body all over the soundstage before his victim admitted, "I saw you do this in *Scarface*!"

When the homesick, drafted, would-be soldiers sought solace by contemplating where Basin Street is, Louis wandered onto the stage, decked out in an Army uniform, to musically inform them about New Orleans. The cameraman was able to cut to a tight close-up of Pops as he played, providing an excellent view of his right hand at work on the valves. Following a brief tap dance by one of the soldiers, Costello ran onstage and grabbed a toy trumpet, which Abbott hastily knocked to the floor.

More re-creations of classic comedy routines ensued, including the familiar "pack that grip" gag, during which Bud's self-debate over "should we stay or should we go" causes Lou repeatedly to load and unload a suitcase with increasingly feverish abandon. A number by singer Rosetta Shaw; some ballroom terpsichore by Raft and Costello (whose partner was a dummy); a musical visit to the Old Soldiers Home, featuring a tap dance by "Civil War veterans" in various stages of decrepitude; and a dice game (another rehash of *Buck Privates* material) were capped off by the return of Louis, who first played reveille and then tore into a swinging solo at an Army training camp.

At an August 25 session in New York, Pops and Sy Oliver collaborated on two more songs, "I Laughed at Love" and "It Takes Two to Tango," a Satchmo hoot: "Do that dance of love. Oh, *zet!*" he sings, just before blowing an inspired solo and shouting, "Them cats was rompin' that time!"

During his next television appearance, Pops survived a visit to "The Great One" on the September 20 *Jackie Gleason Show*. Following his usual "Honeymooners" skit with Art Carney, Audrey Meadows and Joyce Randolph, Gleason, a fan of big-band jazz (but also possessed by infinite ego and a love for thickly sliced ham), made mincemeat out of one of Pops' performances. *Variety*'s "Trau" reported:

> Poorest showcasing framed Louis Armstrong with his Dixieland quartet. Satchmo fronted in trumpet and vocal on "Kiss to Build a Dream On" but the second workout, on "That's-a-Plenty," was thrown off via the P. S. trumpet participation of Gleason that made no sense and impaired the otherwise impressive Armstrong jazz exercises.[22]

Two days after his Jackie experience, Pops recorded four more songs with Gordon Jenkins: two holiday numbers, "White Christmas" and "Winter Wonderland"; and a pair of ballads (featuring Arvell Shaw and Cozy Cole), "Chloe (Song of the Swamp)"—including backing singers who shift from singing "Chloe, Chloe" to "Louie, Louie"—and "Listen to the Mocking Bird." As the chorus repeats the title of the latter, Pops scats in between the lyrics, a prime example of his ability effortlessly to merge jazz improvisation with any pop song arrangement.

Compiled three years earlier, the short film *The Negro in Entertainment*—touted as "a motion picture dedicated to Negro Americans," but actually a lengthy advertisement for Chesterfield cigarettes—was released in 1952. Filmed standing in front of a stage curtain, Louis is accompanied by another trumpeter on the soundtrack, and appears on screen for a total of 12 seconds.

During the 1952 All Stars tour of Europe, Pops and the band headlined another Italian concert film, *Saluti e Baci* (aka *La Route du Bonheur*), shot at Rome's Cinecittà Studios during the final week of October and released the following September. Also appearing in the film are the orchestras of Claude Luter and Aime Barelli.

Back in New York, Pops made a Yuletide appearance on NBC's December 20 broadcast of *All Star Revue*, hosted by Tallulah Bankhead and costarring Jack Carson, Patsy Kelly and Phil Foster. Louis received the script on December 9, along with the notice of a rehearsal scheduled for Wednesday, December 17, from 5 to 9 P.M. in the Garden Room of the Paramount Caterers at 138 West 43rd Street. Executive produced by Sam Fuller and directed by Dee Englebach, this special Christmas show included numbers by musical director Meredith Wilson, Pops performing with the Ron Fletcher Orchestra, and an "Antony and Cleopatra" skit featuring Bankhead as "Cleo" and Louis as "the Soothsayer."

"I crave word of my beloved, Marc Antony," announced Bankhead. "What sayest thou, Soothsayer?"

"Sooth!" replied Pops.

"Soothsayer, surely thou hast divined the fate of my lord," she observed.

"Yea, verily," Louis added.

"Then speak, o sage, where is my Antony?" she asked.

"Forsooth," Pops responded, "he approaches from Alexandria with Agrippa and a few other cats!"

Later in the skit, Bankhead, inquiring further about her lover, admitted, "I fear for his safety. What sayest thou, o Soothsayer?"

"Fear not, o Queen," Louis answered. "Thou knowest Antony. He digs the most!"

"Well said, Soothsayer," she praised.

When introducing him to the audience, Bankhead said:

> And we have the great Louis Armstrong. I just adore his style. He's the only singer in the world with a voice lower than mine. You know, last week a Music Hall of Fame was established in the Chicago Museum of Natural Science and Industry, and the first one to be elected was Louis Armstrong. He nosed out two other well-known musicians—Bach and Beethoven. Louis accepted victory like a true champion, he sent beautiful consolation telegrams to Bach and Beethoven. The thing that makes Armstrong such a magnificent artist is that he's such a conscientious performer, so intense about his work ... and right now he's going over every little phrase, every little nuance.

The camera then cut to Louis, fast asleep in a chair. Later he sang one of Wilson's songs, "Who Needs What Moonlight?"

Bankhead had been one of Louis' most ardent fans since the early 1930s, when she used his records to alleviate boredom on film sets. She referred to her favorite tune, "Potato Head Blues," as "one of the greatest things in life," and played it during the second act of Noel Coward's Broadway play *Private Lives* (1948). In 1950 she had written an "appreciation" that later was published in *Flair* magazine and reprinted in the All Stars tour programs:

> It seems to me that the greatest factor contributing to the chaos prevailing in the world is the lack of a real basis of communication among people. And it is the function of the occasional transcendent genius to surmount the natural and manmade barriers that separate people and to invest their lives with meaning by illuminating the mysteries of human existence — which is in itself, to the aware person, a profoundly unnerving, even terrifying proposition. Such a genius is Louis Armstrong. ... Louis Armstrong is that *rara avis*, a great man. And by greatness I mean that fine shade of difference existing where genius is present. Fortunately for humanity at large and jazz lovers in particular, Louis Armstrong is both genius and great in the ordinary sense. By this I don't mean to minimize his genius as a creative artist in his field, but to say that if Satchmo had never heard of a high F or if he thought a trumpet was a minor bridge bid or couldn't sing a note, I would still dig him because he is an authentically great man embodying all of the best human qualities and instincts by which people should conduct their lives.[23]

Bankhead also commented on Pops' prowess as a screen performer:

> I suppose it might be interesting and possibly even expected of me to evaluate Louis Armstrong as an actor. If I were to draw an analogy, I should mention Charlie Chap-

lin. The magic of Chaplin's art is that he illustrates the tragedy inherent in life—man trapped by circumstance and buffeted by fate—by using his own comic personage in the most ridiculous and hilarious situations. It is the coexistence of the sad and the funny that makes one want to cry while rocking with belly laughs. Anyone who has heard Louis Armstrong at his best will experience a similar emotion. In musical terms, undiscerning people think of Mozart's music as exclusively gay and frothy; happy, full of laughter. It is—sometimes—but underlying it is a profound sadness. Such is Louis' art.[24]

At this time, rumors circulated about the production of a musical biopic based on Louis' career. In a May 1944 letter to Robert Goffin, Pops had written:

> I am stopping at Mrs. Louise Beavers' Home out there [Los Angeles]. ... She certainly is a swell person.... And incidentally—if ever you should film the story of my life you should see that Mrs. Beavers get a good part in the picture.... She could really play the part of my mother since she looks so much like Mary Ann (my mother) and acts just like her.... And as great an actress as Mrs. Beavers is—why she and I could get together and really make a big thing in a film together.[25]

Unfortunately, no such film was made; but, considering the whitewashing of history that occurred in *New Orleans*, perhaps it was a blessing.

Before going on tour during the winter of 1953, Louis hired a new permanent trombonist for the All Stars. Full of youthful exuberance, James ("Trummy") Young had spent six years playing and singing with Jimmie Lunceford, one of the true architects of big-band swing, whose arrangers had included Sy Oliver (eventually stolen away by the formidable Tommy Dorsey). Marty Napoleon retained the piano bench, alongside Bigard, Shaw and Cole. While in Detroit on February 23, Pops, the band and members of Sy Oliver's orchestra recorded "Congratulations to Someone," a light yet dynamic swing ballad that features two powerful trumpet solos, and Louis' second stab at a Hank Williams two-beater, layin' down bluesy licks on "Your Cheatin' Heart," which the Alabama wild man had waxed exactly five months earlier. Pops' respectful version came upon the heels of the tragically alcoholic Hank's untimely death at age 29 on New Years' Day.

During the spring, Universal and director Anthony Mann began production on a biopic about another doomed musician, *The Glenn Miller Story*, giving the Hollywood treatment to Valentine Davies and Oscar Brodney's faithful script recounting the bandleader's professional beginnings in Los Angeles during the mid–1920s to his death while flying from England to Paris on December 15, 1944. Mann cast one of his favorite leading men, James Stewart, as Miller (who was born in Clarinda, Iowa, in 1904).

Prior to filming this musical, Mann had created a new, more rugged, screen persona for Stewart in several successful Westerns, including *Winchester 73* (1950), *Bend of the River* (1952) and *The Naked Spur* (1953). (After casting his star as the all–American hero in *Miller*, Mann returned him to more morally ambiguous territory in *The Far Country* [1954] and *The Man from Laramie* [1955].)

Before returning to Hollywood, Louis and the All Stars (complemented by five session musicians) recorded "April in Portugal" and "Ramona" during an April 21 Decca session.

For *The Glenn Miller Story*, Pops received $5,000 to play himself in one scene of the Universal epic, during which Miller and his bride, Helen (June Allyson), are taken to Connie's Inn to see ol' Gate blow with his band. Billed second on the list of "guests" in the opening credits, he joined a group of performers that included Frances Langford, Ben Pollack, Gene Krupa, the Modernaires, the Archie Savage Dancers, and the All Stars. Louis and his cohorts, with Krupa sitting in on drums, pre-recorded their brief soundtrack contribution in early June. On the 24th, he and the band played another of Gene Norman's "Just Jazz" concerts at the Pasadena Civic Auditorium.

The Glenn Miller Story opens in a Los Angeles pawnshop, where Miller is reclaiming his trombone from Mr. Krantz (Sig Ruman). Possessing just enough money for the horn, Miller nonetheless inquires about a string of pearls for his "girlfriend" in Boulder, Colorado, whom he hasn't seen in two years. He and his pal Chummy Mac-Gregor (Henry Morgan) then play a gig with Mark Minton and His Mellow Music at the Sunset Hotel.

Tired of playing lame society soirees, the pair audition with Ben Pollack's band at the Venice Pier, and Miller lands the job after Chummy slips one of his buddy's arrangements onto the music stand. Prior to a gig at the Denver Palace, Miller calls Helen for a date, which he finally keeps in the wee hours, after the disgusted girl has gone to sleep. The couple visits the University of Colorado campus and Miller's parents (Irving Bacon and Kathleen Lockhart) before he goes on the road. Prior to leaving, he tells Helen that his goal is to be the arranger for his own band — to find "the right sound," one he has yet to hear.

Two years later Miller is playing a Pollack gig in New York. Fed up with the conventional arrangements, Miller tells the bandleader to go on without him. After pawning his trombone once more, Miller runs into Don Haynes (Charles Drake), who tells him about a pit band that "Red" Nichols is forming with Benny Goodman and Gene Krupa. Miller then calls Helen — who is engaged to a local yokel — and orders her to take a train to New York and marry him. (He gives her his phone number: "Pennsylvania 6-5000.")

Following a whirlwind ceremony, the Millers are surprised by a mob of friends hiding in their hotel room. Pollack, Krupa and others insist they go to Connie's Inn for some real entertainment — that is, Louis Armstrong and his band. As the Miller party enters the club, Pops performs "Basin St. Blues" with Bigard, Young, Napoleon, Shaw and Cole.

"Who's he?" Helen asks.

"Louis Armstrong!" Miller replies, just before Pops asks Krupa, Pollack and saxophonist Babe Russin to sit in. Soon Glenn climbs onto the stage to play a solo on Trummy's trombone. During the jam, Krupa and Cole play a rousing duet on the drum kit.

Returning to his seat, Miller tells a tipsy Helen, "When I start playing jazz with the likes of Louis Armstrong and Gene Krupa, I'm lucky if I come in third."

Disappointed that her husband has failed to pursue his dream of creating "that sound," she inspires him to study with Dr. Schillinger (Leo Mostovoy) and write his own arrangements. Soon he composes "Moonlight Serenade," but is appalled by the stiff, hoochie-coochie version he hears in a local cabaret. Informed by Haynes that

The Glenn Miller Story (1953). James Stewart "jams" with Trummy Young and Louis in the Connie's Inn nightclub scene.

he could start his own band for $1,800, Miller is surprised when Helen gives him the stash she has saved by "stealing" the loose money from his pants pockets.

On the road to a Boston gig, the band is stranded in a blizzard. While waiting to get their truck repaired, Helen falls ill and loses the baby she was carrying. In an act of desperation, Miller and MacGregor sell their vehicles to pay off the musicians, but soon promoter Si Schribman (George Tobias) gives Glenn enough cash to form a new band—to create "something radical"—as long as the kids can dance to it. When his trumpeter cuts his lip during a rehearsal, Miller rewrites the "Moonlight Serenade" lead part for clarinet and "harmonize[s] everything real tight in the same octave."

"That's it. That's the sound," Helen comments.

A montage of newspaper headlines and record covers follows, and soon the Millers are celebrating their 10th wedding anniversary, during which the band plays the brand-new "Pennsylvania 6-5000." Next, the orchestra is seen waxing "Tuxedo Junction" for a Hollywood film soundtrack. During the session, Glenn receives a notice from the U.S. War Department commissioning him as "Captain Alden G. Miller."

Assigned to conduct an Army Air Corps marching band, Miller balks at playing the standard John Philip Sousa material. During a parade for General Hap Arnold (Barton MacLane), he crosses in front of a marching column and kicks the band into his own arrangement of "St. Louis Blues." Following a good bawling out by his C.O.,

Colonel Spaulding (Dayton Lummis), he is praised by the General for providing a "great morale builder, giving the men music they like." He then asks Arnold if he may form his own band to give the troops overseas "a piece of home."

At his quarters in Bedford, England, Miller and "The American Band of the AEF" perform "In the Mood" as an air-raid siren blares away. Although an enemy plane drops a buzz bomb close to the bandstand, the musicians impress the audience by calmly playing through the attack. Another performance features Frances Langford and the Modernaires singing "Chattanooga Choo Choo" with the band.

After Miller is promoted to Major, he boards a flight to France, intending to stage a special Christmas Day show in liberated Paris. When his plane fails to arrive, the orchestra, whose members took a separate flight, carry on without him. During the performance, they play Miller's new swing arrangement of "Little Brown Jug," Helen's favorite tune, which she hears over the radio at their home in the States.

James Stewart gives an admirable performance in this well-made film, convincingly miming Miller's trombone and piano playing. (The actual trombone work was recorded by Joe Yukl.) But, at one point during production, complications arose from his extensive contact with the trombone mouthpiece. When Stewart asked the trumpet master how to keep his lips from getting sore, Pops replied, "Yeah, Daddy, when you go home tonight, have your old lady sit on your face."[26]

Davies and Brodney's screenplay takes few liberties with Miller's life story (the actual Chummy MacGregor served as technical adviser), but other historical facts are distorted, such as the presence of the 1953 All Stars with Louis at Connie's Inn. Though this anachronism may easily be excused, the inclusion of an integrated Air Corps during the parade sequence (set in 1943) is pure fantasy. (Including the African Americans as extras in this scene is noble, but such a whitewashing of history ignores the reality of military segregation during World War II.)

Louis has only one line of dialogue in his brief scene, but his musical effect on Miller is at least indirectly addressed, and it is difficult to fault the production in any department, except perhaps for the absence of Miller vocalist Tex Benecke, who led the orchestra after the bandleader's untimely death. Most importantly, the film tells a coherent story accompanied by music, rather than stringing together a series of tunes with narrative interludes, as do other musical biopics.

The Glenn Miller Story was released by Universal-International on December 10, 1953. During its initial run, the film grossed $7.7 million at the box office. *Variety*'s "Brog" wrote, "One of the big musical moments ... has nothing to do with the Miller music. It is a red-hot jam session that has Louis Armstrong ... socking "Basin Street Blues."[27] Bosley Crowther praised the film in his *New York Times* review:

> Sweet is the word the modern swingsters would apply to the type of music played in the Thirties and Forties by the late Glenn Miller and his band. And that is the word, beyond question, for the picture.... In the way of atmospheric sidelight, there is a wonderful jam session ... performed in a smoky New York hot spot, with Louis Armstrong and Gene Krupa.... Bathed in a flow of changing colors—purple, dark blue, sultry red—it flashes and rocks with the wild beat of the fanciful horns and drums.[28]

The Glenn Miller Story (1953). Gene Krupa on the drums behind Barney Bigard (left) and Louis.

Louis had been scheduled to tour with Benny Goodman during 1953. Following the sale of more than $1 million in advanced tickets, Goodman told Pops that he would be running the show.

"You're nothing," Louis replied, and then, night after night, proceeded to blow the clarinet man off the stage. Goodman's subsequent depression and anger actually made him physically ill.

Trumpeter Bobby Hackett recalled, "Pops came close to killing him without touching him, just playing."[29]

Host Eddie Albert welcomed Louis, backed by the Skitch Henderson Orchestra, on the July 7 New York telecast of *Nothing but the Best*. While performing at the Massachusetts State Fair in Springfield on September 27, 1953, Pops wrote to his friend Marili Mardon, mentioning his attempts to focus on his autobiographical writings—clear evidence that documenting his career was more important than affairs of the moment:

> Why—in my dressing rooms—I just about do a dozen things at once, uncon-
> sciously—f'rinstance, giving an interview, to some wiseguy who barged in just at
> the time I'm typing some of my life's story, and right into a real deep chapter, that
> I didn't want to lose, and probably wouldn't ever get a hold of that particular phrase
> again. Ya Dig? But, I love my dear public.[30]

On October 22, Louis and "the Commanders," featuring the talents of trumpeter Billy Butterfield and arranger-conductor Toots Camarata, recorded two funky, hard-driving Christmas swingers, "'Zat You, Santa Claus?" and "Cool Yule," ending with Louis reciting the title and laughing into the fade-out. The band also cut two non–Yuletide big-band ballads, "I Can't Afford to Miss This Dream" and a vibrant, pulsing arrangement of Pops' classic "Someday (You'll Be Sorry)." The next day he guested on the TV show *Life Begins at Eighty*.

Then Louis and the All Stars—now with Billy Kyle (piano), Milt Hinton (bass) and Kenny Jones (drums)—returned to some serious globetrotting. On New Years' Eve, NBC Radio broadcast their gig from Yokohama, Japan. Back in the States on January 16, 1954, they were captured on their closing night at San Francisco's Hangover Club by CBS Radio. The obligatory "Sleepy Time" introduction led to some swinging treats—the "Shadrack"/"When the Saints Go Marching In" medley and a rare live performance of "West End Blues"—a comic collaboration between Pops and Velma on "Dummy Song," and a brief vocal by Barney Bigard on "My Bucket's Got a Hole in It."

Four days later Pops was interviewed by CKNW Radio in Vancouver. On March 19 in New York, he and the band cut four numbers, "Basin Street Blues," "Otchi-Tchor-Ni-Ya," "Struttin' with Some Barbecue" and "Margie." Louis again collaborated with Gordon Jenkins on April 5, recording his bebop parody version of "The Whiffenpoof Song" (during which he lays down some hilarious bop scat) and three other numbers: "Spooks"; a ballad arrangement of Joyce Kilmer's "Trees"; and his own swinger about Jazz Heaven, "Bye and Bye."

Louis welcomed a new permanent drummer, Barrett Deems—who returned the All Stars to integrated status—in May 1954, just in time to play on one of the finest records of his career. Producer George Avakian had made a deal with Decca, who released Pops to make one album for Columbia, the company that now owned the original Okeh sides he had waxed during the 1920s. Guaranteeing him royalties on the earlier recordings and the promise of a term contract in the future, Avakian landed him for a set of songs by W. C. Handy, whose legendary work had yet to be recorded by a major label.

Louis told Avakian to pick the songs, which he and the band would rehearse on the road. During a layover in Chicago on July 12–14, they cut 11 numbers that were selected for the album, *Louis Armstrong Plays W. C. Handy*. Several rehearsals were also recorded, but left unreleased.

While listening to the tapes in Columbia's Times Square editing room in New York, W. C. Handy wept. "I never thought I'd hear my blues like this," he said. "Truly wonderful! Truly wonderful! Nobody could have done it but my boy Louis!"

Seated next to the sightless composer, Pops characteristically took no credit for the brilliant performances: "Ain't no work, making records like this! Them old time good ones, they play themselves, Mr. Handy. You get to blowing those beautiful changes right, and you have to play good. We was just having a ball, that's all."[31]

At the end of the first evening's work, Avakian let the tape machines roll, capturing Louis practicing, selecting keys, directing the other musicians, and jamming lyrics with Velma while rehearsing three numbers. A famous story recounting Pops' childhood encounter with an alligator also was recorded.

The album begins with an epic eight-minute-fifty-second version of Handy's most famous song, "St. Louis Blues." Pops opens up with incomparable power and a big, fat tone, instantly proving that this will be a profound listening experience. After two instrumental choruses, Velma Middleton enters with one of her finest vocals, occasionally improvising lyrics. Pops then blows again before singing, setting up a superb Bigard solo. The number ends with a Louis-Velma improvised vocal duet, a low-down Trummy Young solo, a stratospheric trumpet chorus and a brief Deems drum break before Pops blasts back in on the coda.

Louis sings all of "Yellow Dog," another Handy masterpiece, before blowing a solo over the crescendoing band. Based on an old African American folk melody, "Loveless Love" features another Pops-Velma vocal pairing; while the spiritual-like "Aunt Hagar's Blues," which Handy wrote after hearing a Chicago washwoman speak of her relationship troubles, is a tale wonderfully sung by Pops, who lays down some joyously mournful blue notes in his closing solo. Velma again joins Pops on "Long Gone (from the Bowlin' Green)," a swingin' bit of levity, with the band contributing a gang vocal to the choruses and a pair of rousing Trummy trombone breaks.

Handy's two portraits of his hometown follow — "Memphis Blues," his very first blues number, and "Beale Street Blues," which paints an atmospheric portrait of the city's equivalent of Bourbon Street — both featuring splendid Pops solos. Shaw and Deems enjoy brief breaks on "Ole Miss," a 1916 tune honoring the speediest train that ran between Memphis and New Orleans; and Young, overcome by the momentum of his boss' high-register blowing, drives the Cajun-inspired "Chantez Les Bas (Sing 'Em Low)" eight bars past the arranged ending, with Pops effortlessly continuing to soar skyward.

Handy wrote "Hesitating Blues" in 1915, after hearing an itinerant musician playing a folk melody in Memphis. Louis and Velma sing only the verses before Pops plays another superb solo. The band closes the album with "Atlanta Blues (Make Me One Pallet on Your Floor)" on which Louis overdubbed trumpet obbligati behind his vocal, then — for the first time — also multi-tracked a second voice part, scatting around and finally doubling his lead vocal.

After returning to New York, Louis, Bigard, Shaw and Deems, supplemented by 10 musicians, recorded "Skokiaan (South African Song)" on August 13. Though the number begins as a serious Sy Oliver arrangement, Pops laughs his way through the vocal, pianist Dave Martin adds some wild flourishes, and the entire band kicks into a raving swinger. That evening the All Stars played a Basin Street East gig broadcast by NBC Radio, an event repeated weekly through early September.

On August 21, Louis dropped in on *The Dorsey Brothers Show* at CBS, swinging alongside Tommy and Jimmy. Later he remembered a delightful *faux pas* that occurred on the air:

> We was going to play "Rampart Street Parade," and we're discussing what tempo to play it, and I say, "Why don't you play it not too slow, not too fast, just half fast." The audience finally picked it up. Some people got that on their tape. From then on — couldn't nothing follow it.[32]

On September 1, Pops and the All Stars recorded "Muskrat Ramble" and an instrumental medley of "Tenderly" and "You'll Never Walk Alone." Four days later he had the privilege of portraying King Oliver in the "Emergence of Jazz" episode of the popular television series *You Are There*, which attempted to re-create some special New Orleans moments.

On the September 19 broadcast of NBC's *Colgate Comedy Hour*, Louis was one of several guests who joined host Eddie Fisher at the Hollywood Bowl, which was being used as a television stage for the first time. Backed by the Gordon Jenkins Orchestra, Fisher opened the program in typically stilted fashion. Following performances by the Vagabonds and a Native American ballerina, Peggy Lee emerged to establish a groove with "Love, You Didn't Do Right by Me" and "From This Moment On." Classical violinist Mischa Elman then contributed some Slavic solemnity to the proceedings.

In his most infamous television appearance, Pops, in a mockery of Dizzy Gillespie's trademark beret, ran onto the stage wearing an absurd knitted cap with a large yarn ball on top. Singing his altered version of "The Whiffenpoof Song," he took satirical shots at flatted fifths and Birdland before concluding with some bop scatting. Fisher then joined him for a duet on "The Birth of the Blues." Managing to inject a modicum of feeling into his vocal, Eddie laid some skin on Pops.

After Rocky Marciano (whom Fisher nearly had forgotten to introduce at the beginning of the show) and his manager discussed the champ's recent heavyweight victory, the cast collaborated on a production number about the history of the Hollywood Bowl, including Peggy Lee on "Lover," Pops soloing along with a "New Orleans" chorus, and Fisher ludicrously closing with an ultra-wooden rendition of the lachrymose "Oh, My Papa!"

During a September 15–October 5, 1954, engagement at the Sands Copa Room, Louis was filmed with singer Robert Merrill and other performers for inclusion in a 60-minute Quality Films production about Las Vegas. Though completed, the film was not distributed.

Louis' final screen-oriented assignment of 1954 teamed him with Frank Sinatra to record a number for *Finian's Rainbow*, a proposed animated feature version of Burton Lane and E. Y. Harburg's 1947 Broadway hit. The film was to feature a soundtrack that included Ella Fitzgerald, Sonny Terry and Brownie McGhee, Oscar Peterson, and Red Norvo. Though Sinatra recorded nine tracks—including a scat duet with Pops on "Ad Lib Blues" and a pairing with Fitzgerald on "Necessity"—they remained unheard when the film was scrapped by Walt Disney, who objected to its left-wing political content. The November 20 session marked the only time Louis and Frank worked together in a recording studio.

Louis' second autobiography, *Satchmo: My Life in New Orleans*, was published in the United States during 1954. This candid, colorful and occasionally ribald reminiscence was initially too hot for American consumption, and had been translated into colloquial French and published by Editions Rene Julliard two years earlier.

Pops and the All Stars played their 1954 New Years' Eve gig at the Down Beat in San Francisco. During the CBS Radio broadcast, their set included "Sleepy Time"/"Indiana," "Big Butter and Egg Man," "High Society" and "Auld Lang Syne." On January 21, 1955, they played three lengthy sets at the Crescendo Club in Los Angeles, offering an eclectic mix of traditional New Orleans tunes, swingers, comic numbers, pop standards and movie songs, all recorded for a Decca album release. First-set highlights included "Tin Roof Blues," a Billy Kyle–led "Perdido," and a version of "Me and Brother Bill" ending with a ferocious scat-fest. Trummy Young demonstrated his vocal and scat prowess on a raging "'Taint What You Do (It's the Way That Cha Do It)," and Pops and Velma steamed up "Don't Fence Me In."

The second set opened with an in-the-pocket "Shadrack"/"When the Saints Go Marching In" medley that built in intensity from start to finish. Pops again bashed bop with "The Whiffenpoof Song," and Trummy's enthusiasm injected new life into Big Tea's former part on the "Rockin' Chair" duet.

"Lookee here, folks," Pops advised. "We're gonna take you way back this time. It's even before my time." Looking at Billy Kyle, he added, "You played it with Buddy Bolden. A little 'Twelfth Street Rag'!" and then blew beautifully on the old Hot Seven number. They also excelled on "Muskrat Ramble," which Pops dedicated to "all the musicians in the house," quoting "Bye, Bye, Blackbird" during a soaring solo. The band also offered their innovative arrangements: the "St. Louis Blues" piano work-out for Kyle; and Shaw turning "The Man I Love" into a bass extravaganza, eventually joining Deems in propelling the tune to a blistering tempo.

Pops characteristically got supremely low-down on "Back o' Town Blues," then lightened up on "Old Man Mose" and, mentioning *Going Places* and Dick Powell, "Jeepers Creepers." The band opened the final set with "Struttin' with Some Barbecue"; Louis blew like mad "(Up the) Lazy River"; and they repeated three numbers requested by the recording engineer. The evening ended with a speed-of-sound "Mop Mop," featuring Deems, and a final reprise of "Sleepy Time," concluded by Pops singing a goodnight to the audience in place of the usual "Ohhh, yeahhhhhhhh!"

"They shoulda' stayed in bed, or at least back in Hollywood," *Variety*'s "Chan"[33] reported about the special Mardi Gras edition of *Colgate Comedy Hour*, broadcast from New Orleans on Sunday, February 20. Intending to share some of the famous festival with viewers across America, producer Ted Bates merely managed to include brief shots of the Court of the Two Sisters, the Absinthe House and an un-costumed crowd of revelers in between performances by Gordon MacRae, Peggy Lee, Louis, street dancers Skeet and Pete, a teenage Dixieland band, pantomimist Gene Sheldon, and the Carmen Dragon orchestra. NBC featured Pops in another broadcast from the Big Easy, on the February 26 *Horace Heidt Show*.

Ed Sullivan featured Louis and Robert Merrill on the Sunday, April 17, broadcast of *Toast of the Town*. On April 25 the All Stars cut some numbers at a New York session. Pops and Billy Kyle wrote "Pretty Little Missy," a smooth swinger featuring a charming horn arrangement, some nimble piano licks, and exhilarating solos by Bigard and Young. The same day, the band began a series of dates to record a new album for Columbia, and, as a follow-up to the sublime W. C. Handy set, chose the songs of Fats Waller. The initial session produced versions of "Black and Blue" and "I've Got a Feeling I'm Falling" that were left off the finished record.

The nine tracks comprising the release *Satch Plays Fats: A Tribute to the Immortal Fats Waller by Louis Armstrong and His All Stars*, were cut April 26–27 and May 3. Kyle and Middleton open the set with Waller and Andy Razaf's "Honeysuckle Rose," as Pops enters with trumpet accompaniment, then kicks the song into a swinging groove as he and Velma trade off on the vocal. Everyone is solidly in-the-pocket on this number; and, though her vocal is brief, the much-maligned Middleton jazzes it beautifully, refuting those anti–Velma-ites who have labeled her a detriment to the All Stars.

Pops had sung "Honeysuckle" in *Hot Chocolates* 26 years earlier. The next number, the ballad "Blue Turning Grey Over You" (also written by Waller and Razaf in 1929), was the personal favorite of Lucille Armstrong. Pops runs the gamut on this one, opening with a muted solo, singing, scatting, then digging in for a dynamic, full-range solo the final time through. He sings "I'm Crazy About My Baby," then scats around Young's trombone solo before blowing his own killer break. "Squeeze Me," cowritten with Clarence Williams in 1925, was Waller's first published song. This arrangement features a Pops and Velma duet, and fine solos by Bigard, Young and Louis.

Pops contributed another of his rare trumpet obbligati overdubs to "Keepin' Out of Mischief Now," a bouncy swinger in the "Ain't Misbehavin'" mode. (At that time, overdubs were achieved by "patching" between two tape machines.) Velma returns for a duet on the double entendre classic "All That Meat and No Potatoes," featuring nearly impenetrable lyrics by E. Kirkeby. Louis laid down another overdub — a scat overlapping his lead vocal — on "I've Got a Feeling I'm Falling," a swing ballad featuring soaring solos from the entire group.

The album concludes with the two Waller songs most associated with Pops, "Black and Blue" and "Ain't Misbehavin'," the latter a hard-swinging version cut in a single take on May 3. Louis had honed it so much over the years that he didn't bother to listen to the playback. He had to know full well that both his singing and playing were peerless. The funky final chorus alone is worth the price of the album.

During the month of May, Pops and the All Stars enjoyed another weekly NBC Radio gig at New York's Basin Street East. Ed Sullivan was back as "a heavy booker of Negro talent"[34] on May 15, when he welcomed Louis, the Will Mastin Trio, starring Sammy Davis, Jr., Senor Wences and Richard Hearne. *Variety*'s "Jess" noted that "Sullivan ... did some firstrate pitching for Negro performers via a spiel on their fight against Commie inroads into TV."[35] Gary Crosby (Bing's 21-year-old son) also guested, singing a duet "just like a chip off the old block" with Pops: "Working together casually and effectively they provided the stanza with a sock windup. In addition to giving out with his gravel-voiced lyricising, Armstrong also took a couple of snappy trumpet solos."[36]

NBC captured Pops performing with Woody Herman's orchestra in Washington, D.C., for *Producer's Showcase — Wide Wide World*, on June 27, 1955. On "That's My Desire," Louis shared vocals with Woody and Velma, and soloed on "When the Saints Go Marching In." The following week, on July 2, Paul Whiteman introduced Louis and the All Stars as one of *America's Greatest Bands*, in a broadcast from New York. That evening they began a two-night gig at Basin Street East before hitting the road on another tour.

In Los Angeles on September 8 and 9, Pops recorded two Yuletide songs with Benny Carter's Orchestra and two numbers with Gary Crosby and the All Stars. Back in New York three weeks later, he cut versions of "Back o' Town Blues" and "Mack the Knife" with the band; then they all flew to Sweden to begin a major European tour. The lineup remained the same, except for Barney Bigard, who was succeeded by clarinetist Edmond Hall.

A concert in Amsterdam on October 29, and an after-show performance in Milan on December 19, were recorded by Philips for inclusion on the Columbia album *Ambassador Satch*. While Pops and the gang were swinging in Switzerland, *New York Times* correspondent Felix Belair, who was covering an East-West summit in Geneva, wrote:

> America's secret weapon is a blue note in a minor key. Right now its most effective ambassador is Louis (Satchmo) Armstrong. … What many thoughtful Europeans cannot understand is why the United States Government, with all the money it spends for so-called propaganda to promote democracy, does not use more of it to subsidize the continental travels of jazz bands…. American jazz has now become a universal language. It knows no national boundaries, but everyone knows where it comes from…[37]

While at the Vieux Colombier Club in Paris, Louis was interviewed by Edward R. Murrow, who was preparing "Two American Originals," a special one-hour episode of the CBS-TV show *See It Now*. In November, *Variety*'s "Herm" reported:

> The inclusion of the primitive artist Grandma Moses and that equally primitive jazz man Louis Armstrong … was such a solid accomplishment … that nothing could undermine it. Not even Edward R. Murrow's awkwardness on his end of the interviews. But if Murrow got somewhat lost in trying to find common ground with his subjects, both Grandma Moses and Satchmo were able to project their personalities with a naturalness and a warmth that was all the more striking because of Murrow's stiffness.[38]

The second half-hour was dedicated to the European tour, including some performance and audience footage filmed at the Vieux Colombier. "Herm" added:

> Here … the inflexible Murrow manner was juxtaposed to Satchmo's free wheeling jive talk. Murrow's queries about the difference between this and gut bucket were hardly as important as Armstrong's expression of his own feelings about jazz and his audiences. Satchmo, as always, was swinging even though Murrow laid down a very cool, cerebral beat.[39]

CBS re-ran the program on Tuesday, December 13.

Though the Milan recordings include overdubbed audience reactions, the material on the *Ambassador Satch* album is uniformly excellent. Three of the 10 numbers—"Royal Garden Blues," "Muskrat Ramble" and "Twelfth Street Rag"—were cut in a Hollywood studio after the band returned to the States, and also were overdubbed with applause. "Royal Garden" is an invigorating opener, followed by "Tin Roof Blues" from Amsterdam. Though Pops calls the German melody he picked up on tour "Huzzah Cuzzar," the tune's actual title is "The Faithful Hussar." His vocal, comprised entirely of scat, prefaces several blazing solos. "Muskrat" again includes Louis' "Blackbird" jam, which is picked up by Young. Though Velma usually sang "All of Me," Louis does so here, improvising, "You have your *Pops*. Now don't abuse them chops!" Arvell Shaw tosses in some Dizzy Gillespie bop scat during the final chorus of "Twelfth Street Rag," adding an unexpected comical contrast to this New Orleans cornerstone. Two more Amsterdam tracks—"Undecided" and "Dardanella"—allow the band to stretch out; then Louis takes another valiant stab at "West

End Blues," featuring a gut-bucket solo by Young and lightsome Kyle piano that provides a perfect dynamic contrast to Pops' Promethean solo. The album closes with a furious "Tiger Rag." Three songs—"Clarinet Marmalade," "Someday" and "When the Red, Red Robin Comes Bob, Bob, Bobbin' Along"—were not included on the record.

Though it contains golden-age Hollywood's usual amount of whitewash, Universal-International's *The Benny Goodman Story* (1955), from a musical standpoint, remains tinsel town's best biopic of a jazz legend. Louis is mentioned in two scenes (once by Kid Ory himself; and, again, by Sammy Davis, Sr., who plays Fletcher Henderson), but it is unfortunate that writer-director Valentine Davies didn't actually work him into a scene. Perhaps Pops would have refused such an offer, considering that, years later, when Goodman wanted to atone for the 1953 tour fiasco, Louis reportedly told Lucille, "Are you crazy? I don't want to have dinner with that motherfucker."[40]

The racism faced by Teddy Wilson and Lionel Hampton is never addressed, but their supporting roles are a highlight, as are the performances of Gene Krupa and Ben Pollack. The screenplay follows Goodman's development as a musician, particularly his drive to get hot music recognized by the public, from the age of 10 to the groundbreaking 1938 Carnegie Hall concert. Admirably, the film remains focused on the music, and smoothly integrates the romance between Goodman (a fine performance by Steve Allen) and John Hammond's sister, Alice (Donna Reed). Goodman re-recorded many of his classics for the score, and the Carnegie Hall numbers feature standout solos by Krupa and Harry James.

Louis returned from his European tour on the final day of 1955, and rang in the New Year by appearing on a special January 1 broadcast of *Toast of the Town*. "I got a chance to let all the cats know I was back," he recalled.[41]

In his celebration of 1956—which would shape up as one of his very good years—Frank Sinatra returned to MGM to costar in *High Society*, a musical remake of *The Philadelphia Story* (1940). Producer Sol C. Siegel already had the (alphabetically billed) Bing Crosby and Grace Kelly on board, and wanted to add Sinatra, who was thrilled at the prospect of starring with his boyhood idol.

Commissioned for $250,000 to write the score for the film (Sinatra and Crosby each were paid $200,000), Cole Porter invited the three costars to his home to listen to the songs. Though Porter wrote nine new songs for the film, musical director Saul Chaplin added an extra number, the composer's "Well, Did You Evah?" which originally had been written for the 1938 Broadway show *Dubarry Was a Lady*, for a Sinatra and Crosby duet scene.

High Society features a simple story about ice-cold young divorcee Tracy Lord (Kelly), who plans to marry stiff suitor George Kittredge (John Lund), has a drunken evening's "fling" with reporter Mike Connor (Sinatra) and finally re-marries C. K. Dexter-Haven (Crosby), who has returned to Newport for the jazz festival featuring Louis, who acts as the musical narrator.

On Monday, January 2, Louis and Lucille flew to Hollywood, where he began rehearsing the songs the following morning. After pre-recording his musical performances on January 7–18, he and the All Stars reported to the MGM set. Though

High Society (1956). Pops is prominently featured alongside Frank Sinatra, Bing Crosby and Grace Kelly on this original title lobby card.

Pops had attempted to land a part for Velma Middleton, the studio refused. He recalled:

> Of course, we tried everything to get Velma in, but, after all, it was one of these pictures that was already set. Mr. Glaser tried to pull all kinds of strings—and I got with Johnny Green and Bing Crosby and all the bigwigs. We tried to figure out a scene, but, you know, sometimes a picture's already set—so Mr. Glaser put her on half salary. She had to hang around two weeks in California.[42]

The film opens with an aerial shot of Newport, then cuts to Louis' band bus as it snakes its way to "Dex's" mansion. As his personality jumps off the screen, Pops is shown in close-up, his rendition of "High Society Calypso" providing a charming introduction to the wonderful Porter score. Concluding the number, he adds, "Can you dig old Satchmo swingin' in the beautiful High So-ci-yu-tee!" He later recalled, "I got carried away … and I was so busy swingin' with my cigarette holder, while singing the 'High Society Calypso,' and the director kept saying, 'Keep it in,' you know."[43]

While recounting the making of the film for Hughes Panassie, Pops explained:

> We're in this bus, going up there to play for this festival—and as we go up that road, among those fine homes … that's when I start telling the boys [sings "High Society

Calypso"]. That's in the beginning of the picture — and you're talkin' about a bunch of cats — you know, your boys, how they can ham up a thing. You know, they're all tryin' to steal that scene. Trummy Young mugged so much — I tell ya — even when the director was *explaining the scene*, he was muggin'. Oh, we had the greatest laugh. Everybody was tryin' to steal the scene, you know?

The purpose of Armstrong's presence in this once-fashionable playground of the wealthy — a certain amount of the background of our story — is revealed in this musical dissertation, timed with the arrival of the bus at their destination. We get out of the bus, we ham it up, quite naturally. We see this beautiful room, and I say, "Man, look at this. Will you dig that big ol' rehearsal hall?"

Trummy said, "Man, that's a big pile of bricks."

I said, "But I ain't goin' in there. I don't have my library card!"

And this butler comes out with this dried prune face — and, quite naturally, we're all so happy-go-lucky — and he's got a hat on, you know. And this cat's standin' all erect: "Are you the musicians?"

"Yeah, Daddy, that's what the man said."

"Well, who will I tell 'em is out here?" Talkin' about Dexter. That's Bing.

I said, "Tell Dexter, man. Tell Dexter, 'Satchelmouth'."

And he turns around, just as erect, and says, "Will you follow me, Mr. Satchelmouth?" That killed me, man.

And we go in this house, boy, and turn it on, see? So, now, the first thing we're playing is "Calypso— High Society." That's the one we sing in front of the picture … quite naturally, after we finish this song, I say, "End of song, beginning of story," and then they go on, see, with their lines…. And then, all through the story, they've got this music, see?[44]

Cinematically segregated throughout the film, Louis and his cohorts interact only with Crosby in a few scenes — when first arriving at the estate and, most memorably, during a party in which the two musical giants perform "Now You Has Jazz," a swinging number that enlivens the proceedings whenever Louis launches into one of his solos. (Crosby calls him Pops during the scene.) Louis said, "Even when Bing got on the stand with us, doing this big number, I had to tell him to lighten up. You can tell from the music, he's wailin'."[45]

Another highlight is the song "Little One," which Crosby begins a cappella. After Louis adds his obbligati, a full orchestra joins in, shifting the scene from realism to classic Hollywood "musical reality." As Bing roams around the patio in the foreground, Pops can be seen playing inside the hall behind him. Later, after Sinatra sings "You're Sensational" to Grace Kelly, Louis blows some "change of pace music," leading into Crosby's performance of "Samantha" — providing a bridge between two great jazz-pop singers. Pops' last musical flourish occurs when he and the band blast in during Dex and Tracy's wedding ceremony. "End of story!" Pops announces just before the final fade-out.

Several publicity photos were taken to show Louis palling around with Crosby, including one of them "jamming" on the set (with Bing on drums), and another with a grimacing Pops standing over Bing as the latter attempted to "play" the trumpet. Of his entire experience of working with the cast, Louis said:

Well, we had a lot of fun, and everybody was so wonderful. Grace Kelly, she's just a doll. And Frank Sinatra — regular devil, you know. Quite naturally, ol' Bing was

High Society (1956). Edmond Hall (background, left) and Barrett Deems swing behind Bing Crosby and Pops on "Now You Has Jazz."

right in there with us, you know, tellin' jokes on the set, and everybody — Johnny Green, the [musical] director — I think the whole MGM lot was in our corner.

I had the pleasure of telling Grace Kelly, Bing Crosby and Frank Sinatra how well they did their acting, and how *real* they made it look. You wouldn't think they was acting. You'd think they was really, you know, living their parts.

And I told them I haven't seen any actor make a scene seem so real since the last time I saw Raymond Massey on Broadway when he was playing the part of *Abe Lincoln in Illinois*. He did that scene so real, until, one night, after his last performance, he went uptown in Harlem and freed the Cotton Club girls! Yuk, yuk, yuk, yuk![46]

Variety's "Abel" considered the film "a solid entertainment every minute of its footage":

The original Philip Barry play, *The Philadelphia Story*, holds up in its transmutation from the Main Line to a Newport jazz bash ... casting of Satchmo Armstrong for the jazz festivities was an inspired booking.... Crosby makes "Now You Has Jazz" (aided by Armstrong) as his standout solo.... The romantic scenes are capitally done in every sequence...[47]

During the return trip to New York, Louis' beloved typewriter was smashed, so he compensated by recording reminiscences on his home reel-to-reel recorder. On February 6, 1956, he made his lengthy "audio letter" for Hughes and Madeleine Panassie, recalling the *High Society* production, and playing the soundtrack recordings on his turntable, including "High Society Calypso," "Samantha," "Little One" and "Now You Has Jazz." He also blasted away on his trumpet as he played a record by Italian crooner Ray Martino.

On March 23, 1956, Louis guested on NBC's *Perry Como Show* in New York, before he and the All Stars embarked on another overseas tour, this time including dates in Australia and Africa. Having taken enough time from his hectic tour schedule to record the Handy and Waller theme albums for Columbia, he agreed to participate in another major project, this time a lavish benefit for the Multiple Sclerosis Society at Chicago's Medina Temple on June 1. Planned as a two-part concert, the event would combine the script "50 Years of Jazz," to be read by actress Helen Hayes and augmented by the playing of Pops and the All Stars, with a full-length concert. Joe Glaser phoned George Avakian to pitch the idea for a Columbia album, but the producer initially thought the pairing a bit strange:

> [D]espite [Hayes'] marquee value and standing as the first lady of the American stage, the narration might not be something which record buyers would be anxious to hear again and again, if only because Miss Hayes and jazz were a tenuous stretch. So I was not exactly enthused about the idea...[48]

Avakian had little time to prepare the project. Columbia's engineering personnel were already on assignment, so the task of recording the event fell to the local CBS radio station in Chicago. Pops and the band were still touring overseas, enjoying their historic visit to the Gold Coast of Africa, and being filmed for Edward R. Murrow's feature-length expansion of his *See It Now* documentary.

The concert went on as planned, but the transitions between Hayes' stiff narration and the All Stars' numbers were a bit shaky, and some unexpected choreography and a New Orleans–style funeral parade contributed to several problems with microphone placement. Disappointed that the overworked Louis hadn't had time to rehearse much "new" material, Avakian shelved the album. (A Columbia LP of the music eventually was released in 1980.)

The All Stars lineup remained the same, except for bassist Dale Jones filling Arvell Shaw's spot, and the program didn't stray too far from their usual set. The opening parade marched to the tune of "Flee as a Bird"/"Oh, Didn't He Ramble?" As the musicians reached the stage, they began a medley of "Memphis Blues," "Frankie and Johnny" and "Tiger Rag." During the narrated section, the cats really cooked on "Basin Street Blues," "West End Blues" and "Struttin' with Some Barbecue."

Highlights of the uninterrupted concert included a blistering "Indiana"; "My Bucket's Got a Hole in It"; Edmond Hall stretching out on "Clarinet Marmalade"; and "Ko Ko Mo (I Love You So)," featuring a comic duet between Velma and Louis, who briefly blew a little "Chicago" during one of his solos. Pops and Trummy Young expanded on their "Rockin' Chair" shtick, with the trombonist claiming, "I'm gonna stay right chere in Chicago. I sure dig it the most, man."

Pops was back with Ed Sullivan on Sunday, June 24. This eighth anniversary celebration was a momentous occasion featuring an unbilled Pops, who surprised the great TV emcee by singing "Happy Birthday," and guests Desi Arnaz and Lucille Ball, Harry Belafonte, Teresa Brewer, Walt Disney, Ruth Gordon, Sam Levy, Ethel Merman, Jack Paar, Gregory Peck, Ronald Reagan, Phil Silvers, Robert Walker, Shelley Winters and Natalie Wood.

On July 6, Louis and the All Stars played a set at the Newport Jazz Festival in Rhode Island. With Ed Murrow and the CBS cameras still on their trail, they performed with Leonard Bernstein and the New York Philharmonic at a July 14 Lewisohn Stadium concert, where W. C. Handy was in the audience to hear "St. Louis Blues." The following evening Louis hit the Sullivan stage once again, to help promote *High Society*. Shown in a filmed interview with the host, Crosby plugged the picture before Pops performed "Muskrat Ramble," "The Faithful Hussar," "Stompin' at the Savoy" and "Basin Street Blues." All this classic jazz was followed by even older traditional music when the Iowa Highlanders, a Scottish bagpipe and drum brigade from the University of Iowa, regaled the audience.

Another highlight of 1956 was the beginning of Louis' collaboration with record producer Norman Granz, a jazz purist who founded the Verve label and included anti-discrimination clauses in his contracts. Pops' lengthy association with the company would produce some of his finest records, including several innovative concept albums. Now that Joe Glaser had freed his client from the exclusive Decca contract, Louis was recording for several labels as a freelance artist.

On August 15, 1956, Pops and Ella Fitzgerald — the two greatest jazz singers ever, each with a unique, unrelated style (but sharing a formidable talent for scatting) — performed together at a Hollywood Bowl concert. Backed by the All Stars, they collaborated on "You Won't Be Satisfied (Until You Break My Heart)" and "Undecided." The following day they recorded an entire album, *Ella and Louis*, for Verve. Gone were the All Stars, the "greatest hits" and the shtick — and back were the supreme vocals and restrained virtuoso solos. Though Pops was interpreting Tin Pan Alley classics selected by Norman Granz, he also was back blowing pure jazz.

Granz was the best jazz producer in the business. Refusing to compromise the spontaneity of the music, he never used overdubbing, nor held rehearsals prior to recording. After gathering the musicians — in this case, the Oscar Peterson Trio and drummer Buddy Rich — he worked with Ella and Louis to select appropriate keys for their respective vocal ranges (some of the songs switch between two keys) and then let the tape roll while they all swung "head" arrangements. If the first run-through was fine, that became the take. If not, that became the rehearsal. Pure jazz indeed.

Eleven songs, all of them standards from the "interwar period," were accepted as master takes that day. The album opens with Oscar Peterson's unmistakable piano on the light swinger "Can't We Be Friends?" Every aspect of the song — the effortless playing, the peerless vocals, the melodic, tasteful trumpet solo, the sterling recording — is musical perfection; and the album keeps getting better. Peterson, the epitome of taste and restraint, was the perfect accompanist for Fitzgerald. Here, he and Herb Ellis (guitar), Ray Brown (bass) and Rich provide a welcome change to the Dixieland thunder usually backing Louis.

Ella and Oscar open Irving Berlin's ballad "Isn't This a Lovely Day?" "Yeesss," intones Louis, as he, Brown, Ellis and Rich join in. The tonality of Louis' voice is like a warm, slightly crackling fire as he delivers the most intimate singing of his career; then Ella returns with her instrument of perfect pitch, precisely yet naturally delivering every syllable.

The exquisite "Moonlight in Vermont" features three extraordinary instruments: Pops' warm, melodic trumpet and the two voices — her sensual saxophone and his pleasantly tremulous baritone. The Gershwins' "They Can't Take That Away from

Me" begins with Louis soloing between Ella's vocals, then scatting his way into the second verse. "Swing it, boys," he tells the band as he returns to the trumpet, finally joining Ella to sing the closing verse.

"Under a Blanket of Blue" opens with a Pops vocal, then trumpet obbligati as Ella takes over, closing with another vocal duet. Having honed the tune in concert, Pops offers his trumpet "Tenderly," before Ella's voice sets the band lightly swinging. "You took my chops, away from Pops," Louis improvises prior to playing a trumpet coda. Ella grabs the last word — if you can call it that — by scatting Pops' famous "*Bobba Ba Zoe Ba Doe Ba Zet*, Ohhhh, Yeesssss!" in a gravelly tone.

The second Gershwin number, "A Foggy Day," offers Louis bracketing Ella's verse with a smoothly growling vocal and a swinging, economical solo. The trumpet introduces the melody of "Stars Fell on Alabama," during which the disparate singers harmonize beautifully before Ella scats around Pops' vocal. The band pulses gracefully on Berlin's "Cheek to Cheek," steadily building the groove as the singers turn up the heat. The album ends with two lovely ballads, Hoagy Carmichael and Ned Washington's "The Nearness of You," and the Vernon Duke–E. Y. Harburg masterpiece "April in Paris," during which Pops plays a wonderfully sensitive solo before Ella closes with a superlative chorus.

Louis returned to the *Producer's Showcase* for a dramatic performance in "The Lord Don't Play No Favorites" on September 17, 1956. Robert Stack, Dick Haymes, Buster Keaton and Kay Starr also starred in this tale of a traveling circus stranded in a small Kansas town during a drought. Planning to enter a trick horse in the county races, the circus ringmaster, posing as a "professional rainmaker," tried to dupe the local yokels out of their hard-earned cash.

In "You're the Top," a *Ford Star Jubilee* tribute to Cole Porter broadcast from Hollywood on October 6, Louis joined an all-star cast including Bing Crosby, George Sanders, Shirley Jones, Gordon MacRae, Dolores Gray, Mary Healy, Peter Lind Hayes, Sally Forrest and George Chakiris. During the opening number, which featured the entire cast honoring Porter, Pops sang arm in arm with Dorothy Dandridge, who later performed "You Do Something to Me" and "My Heart Belongs to Daddy."

Sanders, the Oscar-winning actor and celebrated "cad," played piano, sang "C'est Magnifique" and "Let's Do It," and engaged in dual narration of Shakespeare's *Taming of the Shrew* (which Porter used as a basis for *Kiss Me, Kate*) with Louis, who translated the proper English into jive. Introduced by Sanders as "My Associate, Lou*is* Armstrong," Pops, referring to Petruchio, explained, "So this cat croons under the balcony of Shrewsville," just before MacRae serenaded Jones with a number from the Porter show.

Pops also played a number with the All Stars, giving solo spots to Hall, Young and Deems, and blew a brief introduction for Crosby, who joined the program via a live feed from the Pebble Beach Country Club, where he was competing in the famed golf tournament. "Thanks to Sol C. Siegal," said Crosby, he was able to televise the "Now You Has Jazz" scene from *High Society*, in lieu of actually singing it with Pops.

Cole Porter appeared on stage during the closing number, quoting some lyrics to "Well, Did You Evah?" as the cast performed the song. One month later, Pops again joined Ed Sullivan, in a Chicago version of his show, on November 11.

During the waning days of the year, Louis dropped back in on Decca to begin recording the multi-disc *Satchmo: A Musical Autobiography* for producer Milt Gabler—a project dear to the wallet of Joe Glaser, who preferred a true "star" effort to the artistic collaborations his client was beginning to wax at Verve. The sessions were held at Decca's Studio A, at 50 West 47th Street in New York, on December 11–14, 1956, and January 23–24 and 28, 1957. The All Stars, with Squire Gersh (bass) and several additional musicians, cut dozens of classic jazz and Tin Pan Alley numbers, and Pops recorded introductions to the songs (partly improvised, partly penned by Leonard Feather) covering his first 10 years of record-making. After the narration was completed, Billy Kyle added piano accompaniment, tying together the words and music.

The album opens with Kyle playing "When It's Sleepy Time Down South" and Pops reminiscing about New Orleans and King Oliver, represented by "Dipper Mouth Blues," with Yank Lawson blowing Papa Joe's cornet part. Other French Quarter fare are "Canal Street Blues," "High Society" and "Flee as a Bird"/"Oh, Didn't He Ramble?" (the 1950 Decca side). Chicago rightfully occupies a large portion of the presentation, beginning with an instrumental arrangement of "All the Wrongs You've Done to Me," which Louis originally waxed with Clarence Williams' Blue Five in 1924. "Everybody Loves My Baby" rates a mention of the Red Onion Jazz Babies, and "Mandy, Make Up Your Mind" brings up Sidney Bechet, "who's now wailin' in Paris."

Pops pays tribute to the great blues singers he accompanied in New York, including Ma Rainey ("See See Rider"), Bessie Smith ("Reckless Blues") and Clara Smith ("Court House Blues"). Returning to the Windy City, they recall Bertha ("Chippie") Hill with "Trouble in Mind." Velma Middleton gives restrained performances on all four.

The Hot Five and Seven numbers fill a third of the album. The early material includes "Gut Bucket Blues," "Cornet Chop Suey" and "Heebie Jeebies"—Louis' explanation of scat follows the "dropping the sheet music" myth. He mentions his marriage to Lil Hardin while introducing "Georgia Grind," on which Velma fills in for the ex–Mrs. Armstrong. Though Pops wrote "Muskrat Ramble" (the 1947 Symphony Hall recording is used), he again attributes authorship to Kid Ory. Trummy Young re-creates the "West Indian" patter on "King of the Zulus," for which Pops recalls his election to that rare New Orleans accolade. Yank Lawson again plays an Oliver part on "Snag It," a 1926 tune new to the Armstrong repertoire.

Other 1920s classics include "Wild Man Blues," "Gully Low Blues" (Pops mentions the original title, "S.O.L. Blues"), "Hotter Than That," featuring Louis scatting over the guitar work of George Barnes, and "Mahogany Hall Stomp." Referring to "Potato Head Blues" as Tallulah Bankhead's favorite record, Pops adds, "kinda like this one myself," and he notes the original "Knockin' a Jug" as his first "mixed band" session. The big-band numbers, filling another third of the running time, include "Some of These Days," "When You're Smiling," "If I Could Be with You," "I'll Be Glad When You're Dead, You Rascal You" and "Hobo, You Can't Ride This Train." Introducing "Body and Soul," Louis mentions songwriter Johnny Green and his role as musical director for *High Society*, one of two films he recalls during the narration (the other is *The Glenn Miller Story*). On "Dear Old Southland," Pops blows a duet with Billy Kyle, who plays the piano accompaniment originally beat out by "Buck" Washington Lee; and Young plays one of his gentlest melodic solos during "On the Sunny Side of the Street," just before Pops blasts into orbit.

"Well, folks," Louis wraps up, "it sure has been a thrill livin' my life over again," and thanks his arrangers and fellow musicians: "Without [their] help ... I would be like the cat in the hall—nowhere at all!" Joe Glaser and Milt Gabler also rate high praise, the latter for "put[ting] all of this jive together." With characteristic humility, Louis adds, "I also want to thank all of my fans, all over the world, for acceptin' my little offerings. ... Remember, I love you all, always. And I'm 'Red Beans and Ricely Yours,' Ol' Satchmo! Ha, ha, ha, ha, ha."

5

Take Me Along, Daddy

As far as religion, I'm a Baptist and a good friend of the Pope, and I always wear a Jewish star for luck. Those people who make the restrictions, they don't know nothing about music; it's no crime for cats of any color to get together and blow.

— Louis Armstrong[1]

When Ella Fitzgerald was hospitalized with appendicitis, Pops filled in for her on the Sunday, January 27, 1957, broadcast of *The Ed Sullivan Show*. Providing a musical contrast to Dorothy Kirsten and Mario Del Monaco's performance from Puccini's *Madame Butterfly*, Louis and his cats swung several favorites, including "On the Sunny Side of the Street," which the band dedicated to Lady Ella.

Two days later, Pops and Billy Kyle returned to Decca to record the concept album *Louis and the Angels*, a collection of 12 popular love songs about heavenly beings. On January 29 and 30 they worked with Sy Oliver, who wrote arrangements for a lush string section, a woodwind ensemble and an angelic choir. Though the subject seemed serious, and the production was hurried, Louis enjoyed the experience.

Lavish orchestrations might seem out of place in the Armstrong idiom, but the results are a charming blend of pop and swing, juxtaposing Louis' rhythmic solos and scat with 1940s sweet-band sounds. During "You're a Heavenly Thing," Oliver actually had the violinists play Louis' most familiar riff. Of course, there is a version of "Fools Rush In (Where Angels Fear to Tread)," with Louis soaring and scatting away. "The Prisoner's Song," included for its lyric, "If I had the wings of an angel," is an odd track ("Angel?" Pops asks, "I was wonderin' how this song got on here"), but kicks into a rhythm-and-blues groove. Louis bids farewell with "Good Night, Angel," opening and closing the chorus-driven song with some powerhouse scat.

Again Louis tempers a mainstream pop project with his distinct cultural stylings. In the hands of a performer like Nat Cole (who made clear-cut divisions between his pop and jazz recordings), it would have fallen more easily into the Frank Sinatra–Bing Crosby camp, but Pops' consistent ability to integrate his improvisations, both vocal and instrumental, into Oliver's written charts results in artistic innovation. The

Louis and the All Stars' official 1957 tour program.

album's original cover art features Louis, trumpet in hand, seated in front of a painted pair of angel's wings, singing skyward as he glances at a halo suspended above his head!

During a concert in Knoxville, Tennessee, at 10:40 P.M. on February 19, a stick of dynamite tossed from a passing car blasted a four-foot crater about 200 yards from the municipal building where Pops was playing "Back o' Town Blues." Calmly approaching the microphone, he told the segregated audience — 2,000 whites on one side and 1,000 blacks on the other — "That's all right, folks. It's just the phone."[2] Less than a month later, on March 14, he was back on television, guesting on the popular quiz show *What's My Line?*

On the Fourth of July, Louis and the All Stars returned to the Newport Jazz Festival. When they first arrived, Pops learned that he was expected to perform not only with his band, but with many other musicians, most of whom he hadn't seen in years. Exhausted from his never-ending schedule, he was in no mood to be exploited; but when the festival producers asked him to exclude Velma from the lineup, the shuzzit really hit the fan. Emerging from the dressing tent, the King of Jazz appeared for all in the vicinity to see, swearing loudly and wearing nothing but a rag tied around his sweaty head. People took off in all directions.

On stage — and dressed appropriately — Pops was back in top form, laughing and blowing with massive authority. After opening with the familiar "Sleepy Time" and "Indiana," he performed a pair of *High Society* numbers, reprising Crosby's introductory shtick to "Now You Has Jazz" and grooving through "High Society Calypso." Following a ferocious "Mahogany Hall Stomp," Kyle, Deems and Squire Gersh played a laid-back "Blue Moon," joined by the horn players on the final chorus. Edmond Hall tore up "Sweet Georgia Brown"; Louis dedicated "(Up the) Lazy River" to Joe Glaser; and Deems bashed away on "Stompin' at the Savoy."

Three days after playing Newport, Pops paid yet another visit to Ed Sullivan's show, performing "Beautiful Dreamer" solo and "Sweet Adeline" with Teresa Brewer, Pat Rooney and Enzo Duarte. This eclectic episode also welcomed Gary Cooper, Betty Madigan, Jack Paar, Pigmeat Markham and the 1957 Miss Universe contestants.

On July 23, 1957, Pops again answered the call of Norman Granz, to follow up the successful *Ella and Louis* album (which had reached number 12 on the *Billboard* chart) with the appropriately titled *Ella and Louis Again*. Additional sessions were held on July 31 and August 13. Granz planned a double album of standards this time, to include a dozen duets and several solo numbers by each artist. The Oscar Peterson Trio were back, augmented by Louis Bellson on drums. A formidable showboat percussionist, Bellson is at his subtle best throughout the set, anchoring Peterson's crack combo with basic, tasteful grooves.

"Autumn in New York," sublimely waxed by Sinatra that year, is also a treat from the antipodal pipes of Lady Ella and Papa Dip. Cole Porter's humorous double-entendre masterpiece "Let's Do It" is a Louis vocal tour de force. Captured in a single take, "Stompin' at the Savoy," opening with an Ella vocal, builds into a major swinger as she scats into a blazing Pops solo and they simultaneously improvise their way to the end. "Norman Granz say, 'One more!'" interjects Pops. "One more, Daddy!"

"I Won't Dance" provides a charming melodic dialogue between Ella and Louis, who has a blast singing, "merci beaucoup." His trumpet work is sporadic on the album, but he opens "Gee, Baby, Ain't I Good to You" with a dynamic, bluesy solo, climbing into the high register before he and Ella trade off verses, and then rides in around her vocal on the ending. The album's best toe-tapper, the Gershwin classic "Let's Call the Whole Thing Off," is also another enchanting musical conversation.

Ella's lovely solo take on a full-length "These Foolish Things" (which Ray Brown concludes with some beautifully bowed bass) is followed by another fiercely swinging duet on Irving Berlin's "I've Got My Love to Keep Me Warm." Berlin's "I'm Putting All My Eggs in One Basket," Jerome Kern and Dorothy Fields' "A Fine Romance," and the Gershwins' "Our Love is Here to Stay" are also potent duets. "Learnin' the Blues" closes the album with low-down elegance, offering a fiery Pops fanfare and two stunning lessons in blues singing.

The day after completing the Ella session, Pops was back in the studio with Norman Granz, recording an unprecedented 20 numbers to be released on two full-length Verve albums, *I've Got the World on a String* and *Louis Under the Stars*, both featuring arrangements and an orchestra conducted by Russell Garcia. Rushed out when several new Satchmo records were already on the shelves, these collections of lavish standards unfortunately faded from view rather quickly.

Pops' performances—the potent trumpet, the soaring scat, the gargling vibrato—blend very well with Garcia's robust big-band sound arranged for stereo. On *String*, "Don't Get Around Much Anymore" and "Do Nothin' Till You Hear from Me" take him on rare visits to Duke Ellington territory; "Nobody Knows the Trouble I've Seen" offers the reverent Louis, singing and blowing like he really wants Gabriel to dig him; and the title song has him driving a high-power swinger with the rhythmic force of his voice.

On *Stars*, Pops swings with Irving Berlin's "'Top Hat, White Tie and Tails"; "Stormy Weather" brews some atmospheric, orchestrated blues that explode with two trumpet cascades; and the idle, unresponsive mate in "You're Blasé" is nonetheless a "hot mama" and ultimately "*bop a do do do*—blasé."

In overdrive mode, Norman Granz allowed only four days to pass before he had

Compact-disc booklet for *The Complete Ella Fitzgerald and Louis Armstrong on Verve*, signed by pianist Oscar Peterson.

Pops in the studio *again*—for nothing less than another album with Ella Fitzgerald, this time an LP-version of *Porgy and Bess*. No jazz version of the 1935 folk opera, set in Charleston, South Carolina, had ever been performed, and Granz was searching for something "different" that still would allow Ella and Louis to work the duet magic they had created so effortlessly on the previous albums.

The growing civil rights movement provided the impetus for producing a musical featuring African Americans. Three months earlier, Samuel Goldwyn had bought the film rights from Ira Gershwin, and was planning a big-budget feature when Granz reunited Pops with Ella and Russell Garcia's orchestra. The vocal duets for *Porgy and Bess* were recorded on August 18, 1957, though the session was hectic due to Louis' jam-packed schedule. He returned the next day to cut his solo vocals, and Ella completed her performances on August 28. The recordings were finally in the can on October 14, when Pops sang two of the Gershwin songs prior to a session for another Verve album, *Louis Armstrong Meets Oscar Peterson*.

While producing the record, Granz played the tracks for Ira Gershwin, who was impressed and moved by Louis' singing. The album opens with an 11-minute overture adapted by Garcia from several of the songs. Having enough material for three LP sides, Granz wanted to extend the work to double-album length. He also "thought it would be nice as a prologue, as one might find at a concert or theater."[3] The overture provides an ideal dramatic, moody introduction for the veteran duet, again intertwining their talents as musicians; and, now, as *actors*.

Louis is first heard blowing the melody of "Summertime." Ella takes the first verse and Pops the second, singing with a rhythm flowing more fluidly and swingingly than la Fitzgerald's. He then scats around her sumptuous reprise of the initial verse. She sings "I Wants to Stay Here" and "My Man's Gone Now" before Louis introduces "I Got Plenty o' Nuttin'" with another trumpet solo. "Yeesss! I got plenty o' nothin'," he begins, turning the second verse over to Ella, who then performs the ominous "Buzzard Song."

Louis is particularly poignant on "Bess, You Is My Woman Now," sharing a melodic dialogue with Ella before again embracing her beautifully enunciated voice with warm, gravelly scat. He then blows some moody blues on the superb "It Ain't Necessarily So," and rips into the swinging "A Woman Is a Sometime Thing" and "There's a Boat Dat's Leavin' Soon for New York," before closing the album with the heartfelt "Oh, Bess, Oh Where's My Bess?" and "Oh, Lawd, I'm on My Way."

On September 5, 1957, United Artists previewed the expanded, theatrical version of the *See It Now* segment that CBS had broadcast nearly two years earlier. Retitled *Satchmo the Great*, this 63-minute feature compiled by Fred W. Friendly and hosted by Edward R. Murrow includes the original scenes filmed during the 1955 European tour (highlighting Stockholm, Paris and London); added footage of Louis at work, between gigs, and answering various questions about jazz; and a lengthy representation of the All Stars' 1956 trip to Africa's Gold Coast. Nat Hentoff, in his liner notes to the original soundtrack album, wrote, "*Satchmo the Great* is ... the first feature film to be devoted entirely to the international hegemony of a jazz musician."[4]

The film opens with Pops playing a trumpet solo, then segues to Africa as Murrow, in voice-over, speaks of "Louis' ancestors ... probably being dragged away in chains" and the fact that one of 10 Americans can trace his lineage back to the Dark Continent. After a glimpse of Louis during the Gold Coast trip, the scene shifts to Storyville, a mention of "Daniel Louis Armstrong," and then footage of the All Stars jamming as they fly to Switzerland. Murrow narrates, "Hannibal crossed the Alps in 218 B.C. with 37 elephants and 12,000 horses. Louis Armstrong crossed the Alps in the mid–twentieth century with one trumpet and five musicians."

As Pops disembarks, he asks, "Whatcha say, Gate?" and then jams "When the Saints Go Marching In" with a local Swiss band. After a brief "Blueberry Hill," scenes of dates in Sweden, Italy and France are included. After Louis sings "C'est Si Bon" at a Paris club, he is shown in a revealing dressing-room shot, tending to his ravaged lip. In a scene filmed in the club at 6 A.M. one morning, he blows a bit before settling into an interview with Murrow.

Though some of the questions now seem banal, Louis' comments provide a

Satchmo the Great (1957). Louis blows a blue note on this original lobby card.

glimpse of his calm and friendly off-stage demeanor. He describes gut bucket, cool jazz and bop, refers to Verdi and Wagner as "big cats," and asks Murrow, "You dig?"

"Yeah, I dig that," the journalist replies.

"Okay, Daddy," assures Pops. Asked to define a "cat," he explains, "a cat can be anybody from the guy in the gutter to a lawyer, doctor, the biggest man and the lowest man, but if he's in there with a good heart and enjoyin' the same music together, he's a cat." When queried about different styles of music, he replies:

> The only way to sum up music — there ain't but two things in music — good and bad. Now, if it sounds good, you don't worry what it is. You just go on and enjoy it. See what I mean? And anything you can pat your foot to, it's good music.

A description of New Orleans funerals is followed by a 1956 "Mack the Knife" performance at London's Empress Hall, where he played for King George V: "Well, I looked up there and said, 'This one's for you, Rex,' and I laid 'You Rascal, You' on him." Pops, Hall, Young, Kyle, Shaw and Deems are then shown playing "My Bucket's Got a Hole in It."

The Gold Coast footage features his May 1956 arrival in the Ghanaian capital of Accra, where a vehicle named "Satchmo No. 1" awaits to transport him and the All Stars to their hotel. As local musicians play a traditional song rearranged as "All for You, Louis," Pops and the boys join in. Louis tells the gathering, "Ladies and gen-

Satchmo the Great (1957). After landing in Switzerland, Louis jams "When the Saints Go Marching In" with a local band.

tlemen. It really knocks me out to be down here swingin' with you cats," then induces the entire crowd to yell "Oh, yesssssss!" before leading them in a parade.

As Murrow announces that the "seventeenth and twentieth centuries touched hands," Louis is entertained by tribal chieftains before he and the band swing out in the middle of a field, where Lucille joins an aged Ghanaian man in a dance. Soon Velma Middleton is seen cutting some mud with another dancer. Following a visit to a school in Accra, Louis rejoins the All Stars at an evening concert for 100,000 spectators, including Ghanaian Prime Minister Nkrumah. During this unprecedented Gold Coast event—Murrow claims that it "may well have set the world's record in the entire history of music"—Pops sings a moving rendition of "Black and Blue" as he sweats profusely. (In a later interview, Louis explained, "I always sweat all my life. That's the greatest thing for me. You get all them impurities out of your system. Any time you can't sweat you ought to go to a doctor and see what's wrong."[5])

Introducing "Black and Blue" (noted by *Variety*'s "Herm" as "a number cued to the theme of racial discrimination and one which must have had special meaning for this audience"[6]), Pops announces, "We'd like to lay this next one on the Prime Minister."

Referring to the other members of the band, Herm, who called Louis "America's greatest jazzman and most effective ambassador of goodwill," added, "Deems and [Jack] Lesberg are white and nobody in the Gold Coast Negro republic objected to Satchmo's desegregation policy towards whites."[7] Effective footage of audience members smiling, grooving and dancing wildly is intercut with the band's performance.

Referring to Africa, Murrow narrates, "He is convinced that jazz came from here," before Louis describes playing at Chicago's Lincoln Gardens. Stating that the Gold Coast trip was the "second" greatest event in his life, he elaborates on *the greatest*:

> We'd be walking up Rampart Street and run into Joe Oliver. We might have a lesson or a piece of music that was bugging us. And I said, "Papa Joe?" ... and he'd stop, no matter where he was going, and show it to us—while the rest of the musicians would say, "Boy, I ain't got no time," breaking their neck to get to the Eagle Saloon, you see? That's why we all loved Joe Oliver.

When Murrow quizzes Louis about performing in the Soviet Union, he responds:

> After all, my public is the same all over the world. I've played in all the countries, and all languages. They know that I don't speak but one language—and that's bad English. But still, in all, they know the music's gonna be great—so the government is thinking about sending me to Russia.
>
> In Fifty-three, I played Berlin, and I can't count the Russians that came through the Iron Curtain to hear "Our Louis." That's the way they expressed it when we all met at the Hot Club ... "Our Louis." And anyone who says the Russians don't like good jazz, you send them to me, you know?

The film concludes with a performance from the July 14, 1956, Lewisohn Stadium concert with Leonard Bernstein and the New York Philharmonic. Presented in its entirety, this version of "St. Louis Blues" is one of the truly sublime filmed moments in the history of music. W. C. Handy is seen in the audience as the orchestra begins the overture. Then Pops plays a solo introduction before the band kicks in, the scene cutting to the smiling Handy. Louis soars through some magnificent solos, and Edmond Hall swings a beautiful break as Handy again is shown, now searching for a handkerchief, which he finally discovers under his hat, so he may wipe the tears from his sightless eyes. The entire scene is chill-inducing.

Concluding the performance, Bernstein announces:

> Ladies and gentlemen. Louis Armstrong has told me that his most honored ambition is being fulfilled tonight in playing with the New York Philharmonic. I should say that it is rather we on the longer-haired side of the fence who are honored, in that, when we play the "St. Louis Blues," we are only doing a blown-up imitation of what he does. And what he does is real and true and honest and simple—and even noble. Every time this man puts his trumpet to his lips, even to practice three notes, he does it with his whole soul. This is a dedicated man—and *we* are honored.

Louis adds, "I'd like to say, 'Thanks very much' to Mr. Bernstein, and it is the first time playing with a symphony orchestra, and, as we cats say, 'It gassed me, man. It gassed me!'" After he and Bernstein hug, Pops thanks Handy for being their guest, because "[I've] been playing his music for a long time."

Satchmo the Great (1957). Louis rehearses with Leonard Bernstein and the New York Philharmonic at Lewisohn Stadium, July 14, 1956.

The overall image quality of the theatrical release was praised for being superior to that of the earlier video broadcast. As usual, Bosley Crowther added his somewhat acerbic comments to the *New York Times*:

> Whether this film tells you much more about Mr. Armstrong or jazz than you know, it is colorful, comical and genial and has plenty of numbers in it to make you pat your foot. The black-and-white camera work is candid at times, when it catches Mr. Armstrong in close-up, bubbling saliva and perspiring copiously.[8]

The proposed State Department–sponsored Soviet tour was canceled by Louis after he caught wind of what had transpired in Arkansas on September 19, 1957. He was playing a gig in Grand Forks, North Dakota, when Governor Orval Faubus defied a Supreme Court order and used armed troops to bar black children from entering a previously all-white school in Little Rock. When the news media learned of his cancellation of the tour, Louis said, "The way they are treating my people in the South, the government can go to hell. It's getting' so bad, a colored man hasn't got any country." He called Faubus an "uneducated plowboy" and said that President Eisenhower had "no guts." When his road manager, Pierre Tallerie, tried to make light of the incident by telling reporters that his boss "was sorry he spouted off," Louis fired him (but later welcomed him back).

Louis received a call from the State Department asking him to reconsider, but he refused. (Benny Goodman eventually went in his place.) When a reporter asked for an explanation, he replied:

> They've been ignoring the Constitution, although they're taught it in school, but when they go home, their parents tell them different — say, "You don't have to abide by it, because we've been getting away with it for a hundred years." ... So if they ask me what's happenin', if I go now, I can't tell a lie.

Among those who initially denounced him, Sammy Davis, Jr., later said in a television interview that, although Louis wasn't the spokesperson for the Negro people, he was "a great credit to his race." Davis added that he did agree with his stand but not "his choice of words." Those who supported Pops included Lena Horne, Eartha Kitt and Jackie Robinson.

After Eisenhower sent National Guard troops to Little Rock, Louis sent a wire to the White House, thanking the President: "If you decide to walk into the schools with the little colored kids, take me along, Daddy. God bless you." In October, the student body at Arkansas University voted to cancel his scheduled concert there. Louis said he'd rather play a gig in the Soviet Union than in Arkansas, because Governor Faubus "might hear a couple of notes— and he don't deserve that."

Though he received some bad publicity over the ordeal, Pops continued to make guest appearances on television, including a rather unorthodox duet with Rex Harrison on "Crescendo," the September 29 *Dupont Show of the Month*. He again teamed with Frank Sinatra and Bing Crosby, for the October 13 broadcast of *The Ford Edsel Show*, during which they were joined by another superb vocalist, Rosemary Clooney.

Crosby opened the *Edsel Show* solo, singing the introduction to "Now You Has Jazz," with each member of the All Stars lit by a separate spotlight as the lyric pertained to him: Hall, Young, Kyle, Gersh, Deems and, finally, Pops, as the song swung into high gear.

Sinatra, accompanied by Crosby's banter, sang brief excerpts from "All the Way," "Love and Marriage" and "Baby, Won't You Please Come Home?" before the duo took a musical "tour around the world" to Mexico, Paris, Hawaii and Morocco, where Bob Hope paid a surprise visit to sing along on the title song from *The Road to Morocco* (1942). Improvising as much as possible, Sinatra deliberately made a mess out of Eugene Loring's choreography, fiddling about, a la Charlie Chaplin, with a cane, which he actually dropped at one point.

Clooney's solo spot, and another production number featuring Sinatra and Crosby, were followed by Louis' second performance, a duet with Frank on "The Birth of the Blues." After Sinatra called him "Professor A.," Pops returned the favor, referring to Frank as "Professor S." The interplay between Frank's phrasing and Louis' scat, soloing and commentary (of course, he calls Sinatra "Daddy" at one point) was the highlight of the program, with them hitting a unison "Oh, yeahhhh!" on the ending. The most smoothly integrated number, it culminated with Frank giving Louis some skin.

The remainder of the show featured a lengthy vocal jam between Frank, Rosie and Bing, with them singing a line or two from three dozen standards before Pops returned to blow them into the finale, "On the Sunny Side of the Street." The four vocal greats were all onstage together for about one minute. On the eve of the Edsel

The Ford Edsel Show (October 13, 1957; hosted by Bing Crosby). **Satchmo sends Sinatra while swinging "The Birth of the Blues."**

show, Louis and Lucille celebrated their 15th wedding anniversary. Among the Hollywood guests were Pops' good friends Nat Cole and Peggy Lee.

Musical parochialists viewed Louis' collaborations with Oscar Peterson as unsuitable to both performers. Hardcore Armstrong fans couldn't understand why the traditionalist was working with an exponent of modern jazz; and Peterson admirers believed their main man was backsliding by accompanying an old-timer. Open-minded music lovers knew that the material would showcase the tasteful talents of both jazz titans. For the Verve album *Louis Armstrong Meets Oscar Peterson*, Norman Granz selected 12 more standards to be recorded with the musicians from the *Ella and Louis Again* sessions, immediately after the final *Porgy and Bess* takes were completed on October 14.

The Peterson Trio–Louis Bellson pairing provides the same elegant accompaniment for Pops' vocals and occasional solos. Highlights include Harold Arlen and Ted Koehler's "Let's Fall in Love," the Gershwins' "I Was Doing All Right," Cole Porter's "Just One of Those Things" and the romantic "You Go to My Head," featuring a lovely, airy-toned solo and one of Louis' most accomplished ballad vocals. Pops also sings an intimate "There's No You," accompanied only by Herb Ellis' guitar. "Moon Song," featuring some marvelous trumpet inventions, low-register scat, and a bouncy groove by the combo, is as good as it gets.

In late 1957, Louis signed a contract to appear on four jazz-filled installments of the *Timex All-Star Show*. Broadcast from New York on December 30, the first swinging program featured him to good effect, alongside Gene Krupa, Woody Herman, June Christy and Dave Brubeck, whose band had opened the 1956 Lewisohn Stadium concert. "I played with him on different shows," Brubeck recalled. "Quite a few times."[9] On "Rockin' Chair," Jack Teagarden and Pops shared the vocals, backed by the All Stars, featuring Young, Shaw, Cole, Peanuts Hucko (clarinet) and Marty Napoleon (back on piano).

On January 15, 1958, Louise Morgan of Boston's WNAC-TV hosted a discussion of the *Satchmo: A Musical Biography* album. The second *Timex* show, broadcast April 30, 1958, also featuring Teagarden and Krupa, added Gerry Mulligan, George Shearing and Lionel Hampton. The All Stars—Napoleon, Cole, Tony Parenti (clarinet) and Chubby Jackson (bass)—played "Basin Street Blues" sans Louis, substituting Ruby Braff on trumpet, and Teagarden, who sang and played trombone. Following a brief introduction by Braff on "Jeepers Creepers," Pops could be heard blowing off-camera just before he strutted into the shot to trade off-vocal riffs with Teagarden, and solos with Big Tea and Napoleon.

At its annual meeting, called to order by Leigh Whipper at New York's Grand Street Boys Association on February 2, 1958, NAG re-elected Louis and Duke Ellington as vice presidents. That week Pops spent four days recording another concept album for Milt Gabler at Decca.

"A jazzman performing spirituals?" Martin Williams asked in his original liner notes to *Louis and the Good Book*. "In a sense, that is what he has been doing all along."[10] A man who was open-minded about various theologies, Pops was far more spiritual than religious. On February 4–7 he recorded twelve gospel songs with the All Stars and the Sy Oliver Choir. Mort Herbert took over on bass, and additional musicians included George Barnes and Everett Barksdale (guitar), Dave McRae (clarinet) and Nickie Tragg (organ). The selections about "the Good Book" equally cover the Old Testament and the New, reflecting Pops' respect for Judaism as well as Christianity, and mix good-natured humor with reverence.

"Nobody Knows the Trouble I've Seen" is a lightly swinging opening for the album, with Louis rapping two brief sermons about "looking up to the Big Boss." Though backed by Oliver's angelic choir, "Shadrack" is funkier than ever, with Pops working his rhythmic magic on multi-syllabic names like Abednigo and Nebuchadnezzar. The choir provides a powerful introduction for the bluesy spiritual "Go Down, Moses": "Tell ol' Pharoahs to let my people go," sings Louis, before ripping into a high-register solo during the final chorus.

"Rock My Soul" is a 16-bar gospel blues written by Richard Huey. The choir sets "Ezekiel Saw de Wheel" in motion—the "Negroest" of the arrangements—as Pops tells the tale of "ol' Zeke—my man, Zeke—ol' Zeke was wailin' that time!" "On My Way" is a blues with a train-like locomotion and a smokin' solo section featuring Louis and Trummy. "Down by the Riverside" gets a traditional treatment until Pops, Trummy and Dave McRae swing into a Dixieland instrumental. Vocalist Lillian Clark opens "Swing Low, Sweet Chariot," which Louis reverently takes up on the trumpet before singing the familiar lyrics, including some improvisation during stop-time breaks ("Yeah, man; get me out of here!" he tells the Creator).

He opens "Sometimes I Feel Like a Motherless Child" with a bluesy solo, then has a hip conversation with a choir member. "Jonah and the Whale" is the album's most lighthearted romp, followed by the spiritual about Noah and the Flood, "Didn't It Rain?" Rosetta Tharpe's "This Train" also gets the locomotive treatment, stop-time vocal breaks and a powerhouse solo. A fast-moving program, *Louis and the Good Book* is one of his most unusual and satisfying concept albums.

After spending time in Africa, hinting at his roots in *Satchmo the Great*, and speaking out for civil rights, this grandson of slaves put his own take on the music his ancestors sang in the killing fields of the Old South. Proving that these "historical" pieces could always be a balm for current ills, he characteristically included his natural message of hope and happiness: As he concludes "Motherless Child," he raps, "I dig. I am a long ways from home. But things could be worse. Sure could."

In *Jazz Singing*, Will Friedwald refers to *Louis and the Good Book* as "his ultimate religious statement," noting Pops' true spiritual essence: "Louis' relationship with God superceded Sunday visits, and as extreme as it may sound, I like to think that he gave us Louis Armstrong as the ultimate proof of Divine existence."[11]

Pops again followed a classical musician on the small screen, this time young Van Cliburn on the Sunday, May 25, 1958, broadcast of *The Steve Allen Show*. In an unorthodox merging of symphonic and swing music, the finale of Tchaikovsky's "Piano Concerto No. 1" was conducted by none other than Skitch Henderson. Called "one of the great humorists of this era" by *Variety*'s "Jose,"[12] Louis sang a swinging version of "Mack the Knife" and then contributed to the strange brew by reciting a poem by the great Scottish bard, Robert Burns. Van Cliburn's manager had refused to allow his client to perform with Pops, but the two musicians pleased the unbiased, jazz-loving Allen by jamming "My Melancholy Baby" after the show.

On July 7, Louis appeared at the 1958 Newport Jazz Festival, playing with the All Stars, Jack Teagarden and the International Youth Band. Filmmaker Bert Stern was on hand during the festival, which, for the first time, included popular rock 'n' rollers like Chuck Berry. (Stern's experimental opus would be released more than two years later.)

In October, Pops filmed scenes for two major Hollywood productions—*The Five Pennies* and *The Beat Generation*—for release during the coming year. While in tinsel town, he and the All Stars also recorded three numbers, "I Love Jazz," "Basin Street Blues" and "Otchi-Tchor-Ni-Ya," which were included on the Decca album *I Love Jazz* with five songs recorded at earlier sessions. The lineup on the October 8 date included Eddie Miller (tenor saxophone), Al Hendrickson (guitar) and Danny Barcelona (drums).

Though Melville Shavelson and Jack Rose's screenplay is sentimental at times, *The Five Pennies* is one of the finest films featuring either Louis or Danny Kaye, and perhaps the only picture costarring Pops that can be considered a classic jazz lover's treat. (It also provided a financial windfall for Louis, who received $50,000 for 11 days' work.)

Opening in 1924, this excellent VistaVision production (directed by Shavelson and photographed by widescreen master Daniel L. Fapp) focuses on cornetist Loring ("Red") Nichols' (Kaye) determination to play true New Orleans–style jazz (or, as one scene demonstrates, "too loud"). After leaving a band led by Wil Paradise (Bob Crosby), Nichols becomes a Dixieland dynamo, but when his career adversely affects the relationships with his wife Bobbie (Barbara Bel Geddes) and young daughter Dorothy (Susan Gordon), who is stricken with polio, he abandons music for a blue-collar job in a shipyard. As a teenager, Dorothy (Tuesday Weld) encourages her father to begin blowing again. Staging a comeback, Nichols also is delighted by his daughter's improved health.

Moreso than in his other films, Louis plays an important role throughout *The Five Pennies*, and his performance is even more warm and dynamic than usual. He first is seen on stage, after Fapp's camera tracks out from the bell of his trumpet, which resembles an old-style iris used during the silent era. Pops and Danny share some impressive duets: one has them trading off beautifully phrased names of classical composers; and another features young Susan Gordon and Kaye laying down two separate obbligati over Louis' melody. At one point Kaye calls Pops "the Supreme Court of Cats" and "the Mahatma of Jazz."

Krin Gabbard wrote:

> [O]nce again the white musician gains sexual maturity after he plays with the black master. Armstrong's brazen treatment of Nichols ... is especially remarkable in light

The Five Pennies (1959). Danny Kaye, Susan Gordon and Louis clown during rehearsal (photograph courtesy of Susan Gordon).

of his 1957 attacks on Eisenhower and Faubus. It is as if his outspoken political statement had spilled over into *The Five Pennies*, the first film he made after his highly publicized remarks on integration.[13]

The polio subplot adds some sentiment, but is handled evenly by Shavelson. When Susan dances to the singing of Bel Geddes (dubbed by Eileen Wilson) and the blowing of Pops during the final scene, everyone plays it with utter believability. Bel Geddes gives one of her very attractive, down-to-earth performances, and the presence of Bob Crosby—together with depictions of Jimmy Dorsey (Ray Anthony), Dave Tough (Shelley Manne), Arthur Schutt (Bobby Troup) and Glenn Miller (Ray Daly)—adds to the realistic atmosphere. As with most of his cinematic characters, there is a lot of Kaye's own personality in Red Nichols, but he balances his comic flights with a serious quality only occasionally glimpsed in other roles (such as in *The Secret Life of Walter Mitty* [1947] and *The Court Jester* [1956]). Kaye also proves adept at miming the cornet solos by the actual Loring Nichols, who, according to Mezz Mezzrow,

> was very tough and guttural ... giving you a kind of Southern-gangster impression because he tried to use Negro colloquialisms. ... It took somebody like Red or Eddie (Condon) to make sure there was money coming in at the end of the week ... the history of our music might have been changed some if Red ... had been closer to the spirit of the music that obsessed us all. ... We had always thought Nichols stunk, with or without his corny Dixieland Five Pennies...[14]

Susan Gordon, then nine years old, had made her acting debut in the B-horror film *Attack of the Puppet People* (1958), directed by her father, Bert I. Gordon. Attending a "cattle-call" audition for *The Five Pennies*, she was one of 500 young girls who were interviewed. After narrowing the field to five youngsters, Paramount, using the late-night poker scene, screen tested only two. "They apparently liked my performance," Gordon recalled, "for they gave me the part."[15]

The role of Dorothy was a rigorous one, requiring a multi-talented child. "I was perhaps too young to make any serious observations about what was going on around me," Gordon admitted, "but working on the film was definitely one of the most memorable experiences of my life, and one of the most memorable roles I have ever had."[16] She said:

> The most challenging part about making *The Five Pennies* was to sing in it. Singing professionally was a totally new experience for me. They had a professional singer lined up to do my songs, but the voice teacher at Paramount, on listening to me sing, thought he could train me sufficiently to do the songs myself. With two weeks training, I was ready to perform. I loved the recording sessions. I loved later performing the songs in the scenes.[17]

Of her big scene with Louis, she remembered:

> The filming of the nightclub scene has to be one of my favorite scenes in the whole movie. Not only did I get to perform with both Danny and Louis, but I got to wit-

The Five Pennies (1959). Susan Gordon, Louis and Danny Kaye on the nightclub set (photograph courtesy of Susan Gordon).

ness their wonderful singing of "When the Saints Go Marching In." To watch the two of them in action was awe inspiring.

For the trio with Danny and Louis, we each recorded our part separately in the recording studio. They then combined the three parts together, and, on the day of the shoot, when we did the scene, we sang along with the tape. It was a magical experience, and one that I will never forget.[18]

Gordon also had some pleasant experiences on the set with Pops:

Louis Armstrong was so wonderful to work with; such a fine actor and a real gentleman, on camera and off. He was always very nice to me and had told my mother, "You have a very talented little daughter." Coming from the great Louis Armstrong, it was indeed a great compliment.[19]

The musical score is impressive, including swinging renditions of "When It's Sleepy Time Down South," "My Blue Heaven," "Indiana" and "When the Saints Go Marching In." Kaye's wife, Sylvia Fine, who served as associate to Jack Rose (who also produced), wrote four new songs for the film: "Lullaby in Ragtime," "Follow the Leader," "Good Night, Sleep Tight" and "Five Pennies."

The *New York Times'* A. H. Weiler wrote:

[W]ith Danny Kaye playing the dedicated cornetist as though to the jam session born, and with such sidemen as Satchmo Armstrong himself to come up with the proper riffs at the right time, the slightly damp and obvious portions of this saga, which wilts considerably near the end, can easily be overlooked ... the team of Kaye and Armstrong, using their masterful brand of scat-singing, do wonders...[20]

The Beat Generation features the most unpleasant content of any of Louis' films. Also known as *This Rebel Age*, this Albert P. Zugsmith exploitation production deals with the efforts of Dave Culloran (Steve Cochran), a corrupt policeman, to nab Stan Hess (Ray Danton), a serial rapist whose victims are all married women. MGM released the film with a title attracting patrons who had no idea what the film depicted. Cowritten by Lewis Meltzer and science-fiction specialist Richard Matheson, the screenplay pits a group of beatniks against the establishment, and becomes absurd when Hess runs amok, maniacally "spout[ing] excessive coffee-house jargon."[21]

The film boasts an impressive supporting cast, including Fay Spain (as Culloran's wife, who is attacked by the rapist), Jackie Coogan (Jake Baron, a cop), Cathy Crosby (a singer), Charles Chaplin, Jr. ("Loverboy"), "Slapsie" Maxie Rosenbloom (an imbecilic wrestler), and Fifties camp icons Irish McCalla, Mamie Van Doren and Vampira (who also appeared in Edward D. Wood, Jr.'s, infamous *Plan 9 from Outer Space* that year). Louis and the All Stars add a strange element to scenes in which the beatniks dig their swing, which is antithetical to the bebop one would expect to hear in the film.

Variety reported:

> The beatniks ... are not angry young men, at all, but Freudian cases who impersonate statues and gaze moronically at Vampira reading a jingle on how to loathe one's parents. ... There's a man-size portion of sex in this production which is geared mainly to the wish-they-were market. Both its hero and its villain are woman-haters, a point that's made none too subtly. ... Even to the person who feels the beatnik is a pseudo-intellectual living in a fake Bohemia, this depiction is a ludicrous one. ... Louis Armstrong and his All-Stars add a brief, but notable, scene or two...[22]

After completing his scenes for the two films, Pops made his third appearance on the *Timex All-Star Show* on November 10, guesting with Hoagy Carmichael, Jane Morgan, Anita O'Day and Bob Crosby. During a jam session he was backed by Gene Krupa, Lionel Hampton and Chico Hamilton. The fourth and final installment, broadcast on January 7, 1959, featured an even more powerhouse lineup and a major event in the history of jazz. After sharing a scene with Jackie Gleason, Pops was paired with Dizzy Gillespie in what was described as a musical "peace summit," and jammed "Perdido" with Diz, Krupa, Coleman Hawkins, Roy Eldridge, and the Duke Ellington band. (Pops and Diz initially ended their "rivalry" by teaming up during the rehearsal with Gleason.) Joining the All Stars—Young, Hucko, Kyle, Herbert and Barcelona—Louis played a rousing rendition of "Tiger Rag," creating some instrumental excitement while "jousting" with Young during their solos.

Louis and the All Stars appeared on camera several times during their 1959 European tour. On January 26 they were captured in Copenhagen for the Danish film *Kaerlighedens Melodi*. A February 7 television broadcast from Amsterdam's Con-

The Beat Generation (1959). Original advertisement for the oddball Albert Zugsmith production about beatnik culture.

certgebouw was followed by a German show shot eight days later at Stuttgart's Liederhalle. In between live shows on the small screen, they performed for two German films, *Die Nacht vor der Premiere*, shot in Hamburg on February 23, and *Auf Wiedersehen*, in Berlin two days later.

A broadcast of their March show at Antwerp's Ancienne Belgigue was followed

The Beat Generation (1959). Satchmo blows for the beatniks.

by a program titled *Louis Armstrong— Il Musichiere* shot in Rome on April 25. On May 7, Italy's Eurovision broadcast a live transmission to the BBC in London. For 30 minutes, Pops, Velma and the band were seen performing in a small venue, the La Bussola nitery, in Viareggio. Called a "socko half-hour" by *Variety*'s "Erni," the set included "Tiger Rag," "Now You Has Jazz" and "When the Saints Go Marching

In." Erni added, "Where the show scored most ... was in its close-shot studies of Satchmo. This was standout stuff, conveying the man's artistry, application and show-manship."[23]

On May 20, Louis and the cats were back in Berlin to perform in the film *La Paloma* (1959). While in Spoleto, Italy, on June 23, Pops fell ill in his hotel room and was admitted to the hospital with a temperature of 104 degrees. Though Louis said he was "fine," and a press release claimed he had pneumonia, he actually had suffered a heart attack. Undaunted, he flew back to New York two days later and — partly to dispel rumors that he had died — appeared at a Lewisohn Stadium concert on July 4, blasting his way through a brief 15-minute set including "When It's Sleepy Time Down South." The All Stars had gone on without him in Spoleto, and a portion of the performance was included on the July 19 *Ed Sullivan Show*.

In Chicago for the Playboy Jazz Festival, Louis recorded 13 numbers with the Dukes of Dixieland on August 3–5. Most of the selections were favorites from his early career, including "Dipper Mouth Blues," "Struttin' with Some Barbecue," "Cornet Chop Suey" and "Muskrat Ramble."

By September he was back on the road. Ed Sullivan opened the autumn 1959 television season with a 90-minute special from Las Vegas on Sunday, September 20, welcoming Rosemary Clooney, Jose Ferrer, Alan King, Eileen Farrell and Pops, who, "always a delight, got time to be a fullblown hit."[24] Following a swinging set with the All Stars, Pops and the gang backed up Farrell's classical soprano on the Gershwins' "S'Wonderful." *Variety*'s "Jose" wrote, "Satch trotted out some of his standards, and endowed them with his traditional style and good humor, scoring heavily during this event."[25]

On September 29, Louis helped create a once-in-a-lifetime musical summit on an outstanding *Bing Crosby Show* sponsored by Oldsmobile, who used the historic occasion to advertise its new 1960 models. Louis had appeared on television with each of his costars before, but not with all of them on the same program. The formidable quartet of Bing, Frank Sinatra, Peggy Lee and Pops, a veritable Mount Olympus of vocalists, opened the 60-minute show, strolling arm-in-arm as they sang "I'm Glad We're Not Young Anymore."

Each artist excelled on solo performances: Bing on "Looking at the World Through Rose-Colored Glasses," Frank on a rendition of "Willow Weep for Me" that resembled the matchless version from his 1958 album *Only the Lonely*, Peggy on "Baubles, Bangles and Beads," and Pops on "Mack the Knife."

Referring to Lee's trademark controlled sensuality, Sinatra told Crosby, "She cast a spell, she sure do," before they introduced an unforgettable collaboration between all three — among the very best and most influential singers of the 20th century, all of whom adapted their styles from that of their other guest, *the* jazz singer. Welcoming three great jazz pianists to the stage, each vocalist paired off with one — Sinatra with Los Angeles swinger Paul Smith, Lee with George Shearing (with whom she had collaborated on the Capitol album *Beauty and the Beat!* earlier that year), and Crosby with Joe Bushkin.

Lee demonstrated her effortless way of delivering a great melody with flawless diction on "Lullaby of Birdland," before Sinatra proved how it's *really* done on "The

One I Love Belongs to Somebody Else," unleashing his miles-behind-the beat phrasing and adding some Satch-style scat on the end. Crosby then concluded the jam with his classic "When the Blue of the Night Meets the Gold of the Day." Each pianist benefited from a hard-swinging solo spot.

Several collaborations filled the remainder of the program. Bing and Peggy collaborated on a beatnik parody, "Too Neat to Be a Beatnik, Too Round to Be a Square," which followed the show's low point (the only scene that didn't feature any of the vocalists), a dance revue called "Cool Fairy Tales: Cinderella, or If the Shoe Fits, Swing It." Louis and Bing sang "Basin Street Blues" ("The ol' French Quarter still swings!" Pops tells him), "Everybody Loves My Baby" and "Lazy Bones." The swingin' Gate nearly cracked up the cool Cros when he improvised, "I just want to *annihilate* myself in the good old shade!"

Bing ripped into an "Ohhhhhhhh!" as the number ended, then landed, "Yeahhhhh" perfectly with Pops, really bringing it home. Of course, Louis laid him some skin.

Pops launched into "Them There Eyes," Peggy sauntered in with "Some of These Days," and then all four again were shown on stage together. (Although his actual on-screen contact with his good friend Peggy was nearly nonexistent, it was a major accomplishment for Pops to appear in the same shots with her.) Sinatra crooned "If I Could Be with You," then went "(Up the) Lazy River" with Lee, who joined Crosby on "High Society." Louis again performed "When It's Sleepy Time Down South," and "Now You Has Jazz" with Bing, Frank and Peggy, bringing to a close one of the finest television broadcasts in the history of popular music.

The Bing Crosby Show (September 29, 1959). Louis and Frank Sinatra sing a duet during the "Oldsmobile Show," which also featured Peggy Lee.

Director Bill Colleran also co-produced the show with Sammy Cahn for Bing Crosby Productions and ABC. Cahn and his partner Jimmy Van Heusen contributed special lyrics and music, and Sinatra's erstwhile collaborator Axel Stordahl conducted the orchestra.

The day after the show, Pops and the All Stars began recording another "tribute" album, *Satchmo Plays King Oliver*, at Radio Recorders in Hollywood. Over the next three days they cut 13 numbers from the Joe Oliver catalog, plus an additional song, "I Ain't Got Nobody," which the King didn't actually wax. Most of the musicians didn't know the tunes, so Louis had to spend some time in teacher mode.

Peanuts Hucko unleashes his beautiful clarinet tone on "St. James Infirmary," featuring a powerful Pops solo that provides a dynamic contrast to the funereal style of the ensemble. On "(I Want a) Big Butter and Egg Man," Louis gave the May Alix vocal part to Danny Barcelona, marking the first time solo drums were used in this manner on a recording. Barcelona rolls up a storm — and Pops and Trummy tear up the ending — on the Spanish-American War favorite "There'll Be a Hot Time in the Old Town Tonight."

"Frankie and Johnny" is a highlight, with Billy Kyle providing atmospheric, honky-tonk accompaniment for Pops' impeccable vocal. "Jelly Roll Blues," at low-down tempo, features Kyle on several piano breaks, Hucko in brilliant low register, and Louis simply soaring. Stephen Foster minstrelsy is swung into submission on "My Old Kentucky Home," with Kyle playing an Ellingtonian solo before the band joins together for a gang vocal. On the fabulous "Chimes Blues," Kyle chords the chimes, while the horn players blow the blues, with Hucko playing Louis' original cornet part before his boss rips into the Oliver solo. "In New Orleans — my home town, you know," Pops informs during "New Orleans Stomp" — "the land of the red beans…" Later that month they were back in blues land, playing Keesler Air Force Base in Biloxi, Mississippi.

6

Wild Man and Duke

[O]ne guy who was interested said, "This will never work on Broadway, because you cannot try to educate the people. They want to be entertained." That was such a disappointment. And I've done a lot of things—Iola and I—that had a message. People are afraid sometimes.

— Dave Brubeck[1]

Louis' first screen performance of the 1960s occurred on "Our Musical Ambassadors," a special New Year's Day version of the Friday evening *Bell Telephone Hour*. Appealing to nearly every musical taste, the program featured soprano Jane Froman singing selections from *Porgy and Bess*, Shirley Jones and Jack Cassidy presenting a special "Music of the Movies" segment, and Pops, as reported by *Variety*'s "Tube":

> To top it all off, the viewer was treated to a generous helping of Louis Armstrong's artistry. It was an usually warm and personal showcase for this venerable giant of jazz, and the moving way in which he played "Nobody Knows the Trouble I've Seen" was alone ample demonstration of his great versatility and feeling.[2]

Massachusetts Public Television featured Pops on a May 4, 1960, broadcast of *Dateline Boston — The Jazz Scene*. Later that month, he, the All Stars and vocalist Jewell Brown were televised in a performance at Madison Square Garden. Back on the road, Pops— the most famous living American musician — was shocked to be denied access to a public restroom after the bus driver pulled over for a break. He also was having difficulties with Southern promoters, who refused to book his integrated band.

When pianist Dave Brubeck, who also led an integrated band, heard of Louis' problems, he and his wife Iola proposed to Joe Glaser the possibility of starring Pops in a Broadway show presenting jazz as a true force for civil rights. The Brubecks were aware of Louis' globetrotting tours; and after Dave led his own State Department–sponsored foray into Europe and the Middle East, the couple wanted to document the importance of these "cultural exchanges," which had been made possible by President Eisenhower's "People to People" program. Iola thought of having jazz

153

musicians portray themselves in "some kind of story" that dramatized an actual tour. She recalled:

> At about the same time, there was a series of jazz concerts in Central Park. I remember coming away from the Central Park concert — after hearing Joe Williams with the Basie band — saying, "There was more drama and more story told in *that* than almost anything we had seen on Broadway. So that underlined the idea that something could be done in a jazz style, with a jazz personality as big as Armstrong. That would be something that could actually work on Broadway.[3]

Glaser, who also represented the Brubecks, didn't want to take his top client off the road to act in a lengthy stage production, but did approve of recording the project as an LP release, telling Dave to meet up with Louis in Chicago, where the All Stars were playing a hotel gig. At first, Brubeck was snubbed by the Armstrong retinue, managing only to contact Pierre Tallerie and others who refused to give him Louis' room number. He remembered:

> I finally managed to get the room number, but they told me not to bother Louis. So I sat on the floor outside his door, across the narrow hall. Room service came up and knocked on the door. And Louis, when he let them in, said, "Dave! What are you doin' sittin' on the floor?"
>
> I said, "Well, they won't give me your number. This is the only way I could figure out to see you."
>
> He said, "Well, why didn't you knock on the door?"
>
> I said, "They told me not to."
>
> He said, "Well, come on in! Unfortunately, they've just brought me a big meal — a steak." To the waiter, he said, "Get Dave the same thing I'm eatin'. Bring it right up as soon as you can."[4]

Pops thought that *The Real Ambassadors* was a terrific idea, and asked Brubeck to send him piano recordings of the tunes and lyrics printed in bold type so he could learn the material while on the road. He also asked Dave to sit in with the All Stars at the hotel:

> Billy Kyle was the first great jazz pianist I ever heard. That was in about 1938 or earlier, '36. The Billy Kyle Trio. A friend of mine had those records. And I just thought Billy was great. Now, here I'm going downstairs, and asking Billy to leave the stage, and I'll sit in. Although I think it's a great honor to play with Louis, I hate to have Billy Kyle get up and walk off the stage. So we said, "Hello," and he was smiling and said, "Yeah, Dave, please sit in."
>
> So I did, and then we all had a talk afterwards. It was all very friendly.[5]

Two thousand radio and 57 television stations broadcast the 1960 Newport Jazz Festival on July 1, when Louis' 60th birthday was celebrated — though he actually was a mere 58. After including rock 'n' roll performers at two previous festivals, the Newporters, hoping to eliminate the hell raising that had troubled those events, returned to a jazz-only program, only to be inundated with riffraff on Saturday night.

But the night before, after Dizzy Gillespie and Gerry Mulligan played in the pouring rain, Mammy was still fallin' on her knees and the Southland was still dear as the All Stars—with Barney Bigard back on clarinet—cooked up a storm, swinging more freely and wildly than they had in many months. "Jesus, boy! What do you think you're doin'?" Pops asked Danny Barcelona after the drummer deliberately slopped through a solo on "Now You Has Jazz," still including the reference to "Bing Crosby in Technicolor." "Mr. Crosby and them cats" were again honored on "High Society Calypso"; W. C. Handy was swingingly revered on "Ole Miss" and "St. Louis Blues"; and Bigard led the Armstrong band in another attempt at Ellington on "C-Jam Blues." Mort Herbert was turned loose on the Ellington–Johnny Hodges classic "I'm Beginning to See the Light," then provided the pulse on the requisite "Mack the Knife." Velma had emerged for "St. Louis Blues," then sang a duet with Pops on "Ko Ko Mo." "We had a wonderful time, even in the rain!" he announced just before the band broke into "The Star Spangled Banner."

On the day following his ceremonial nativity, Satch joined Cros for the recording of an album, *Bing and Louis*, in New York. Billy May arranged 10 songs, blending one man who had influenced the other — merging black and white —creating pop magic by merely *orchestrating Louis.*

Bing, backed by a chorus, opens the opus with "Muskrat Ramble," doing his usual black-inspired riffing before joining with Pops on the perfectly poised "Sugar." If the listener doesn't hear the "Preacher," Pops' dynamically quiet, yet rhythmically groovy, solo will lift up those unbelievers.

The two voices flawlessly fuse on "Dardanella," before they trade off on "Let's Sing Like a Dixieland Band," during which the crooner calls the growler "Gate" and they end up as "ol' Bing an' Lou." "Way Down Yonder in New Orleans" gets a bouncy, new Billy May groove, surprisingly stripped down as Crosby smoothly responds to Pops' hip improvisations. The utterly pale, gay '90s introduction to "Little Ol' Tune" is rescued by the vocal interplay, though May's arrangement is remarkably pallid, even for 1960.

Crosby effortlessly swings "At the Jazz Band Ball," setting up the groove for Louis, who demonstrates his vocal influence on Bing before blowing a supremely economical solo. Pops plays a bit of "Sleepy Time" on the introduction of "Rocky Mountain Moon," reminding the listener just who is driving Bing's stylistic bus, before they vocally intertwine on a duet ending with Satchmo scat and a harmonic coda.

By the time *Jazz on a Summer's Day* (1960), Bert Stern's cinematic interpretation of the 1958 Newport Festival, was released, its maker had revolutionized American advertising, captured famous color images of Marilyn Monroe that have saturated popular culture, and amassed a fortune as an innovative commercial still photographer. He had never made a motion picture, but was intrigued by the Newport scene.

"It amused me, at first," Stern recalled in 1999, "when I first heard they were going to have a jazz festival in Newport, where all the rich people lived." He elaborated:

> I was just ... basically a photographer who wanted to make a movie before he was 30. This idea came along that I felt I could handle, 'cause it wasn't a real movie, like

a script. It was a form of documentary and it had a lot to do with photography. And it wasn't something that I had ever seen before and it just intrigued me. ... I don't know if you want to call the movie directed. It's more of a happening ... interpretive, happening.[6]

During a visit with his friend Jean Stein, daughter of MCA owner Jules Stein, in Newport, Stern met Elaine Lorillard, who founded the jazz festival. Planning to produce a short film, Stern scouted the location and was disappointed with what he saw. The venue was unimpressive, he thought — too small, with a tacky stage and seats. Having decided to finance the film himself, he dropped the project; but, inspired by the comments of Charlie McWater, an attorney he met on the flight home, he changed his mind.

Stern wrote a script, but then shifted toward an "improvisational" approach, filming the musicians, the diverse crowds at the four-day event, locations in and around Newport, and footage of the 1958 America's Cup yacht trials, held that same weekend. Before the cameras rolled, Stern asked Columbia Records if they would record the audio, and company head George Avakian agreed to act as consultant, particularly to determine which artists and songs could be cleared for use in the film. During the performances, Stern would await the high sign from Avakian before calling action. Avakian's brother, Aram, a talented film editor, also assisted Stern.

Realizing that the light levels at the venue were too low to expose the Eastman-color film in his Arriflex cameras, Stern told festival organizer George Wein that he would foot the bill if he could light the performances himself. He began shooting without a budget, paying expenses with the profits from his still photography projects. Stern filmed only those musicians and singers approved by Avakian, leaving out such giants as Duke Ellington, Benny Goodman, Miles Davis, John Coltrane, Dave Brubeck, Teddy Wilson, Willie ("the Lion") Smith and Ray Charles. He revealed:

As far as Duke Ellington ... if George said we couldn't clear it, we didn't shoot it. So that's why Duke Ellington is not in the film. We didn't shoot anything with Duke Ellington or Miles Davis. Personally, I didn't like Miles Davis. He's too far-out for me.[7]

The finished 84-minute film opens with the sounds of the Jimmy Giuffre Trio (Giuffre [tenor sax], Joe Brookmeyer [trombone] and Jim Hall [guitar]) accompanying the title and credits superimposed over images of Newport Harbor. Shots of the America's Cup trials (filmed from a Piper Cub by Stern) are intercut with the initial performances. Giuffre is followed by Thelonious Monk (playing the fabulous "Blue Monk"), Sonny Stitt, Anita O'Day, George Shearing and Dinah Washington, Gerry Mulligan, Big Maybelle, Chuck Berry (a curious inclusion, playing "Sweet Little Sixteen") and Chico Hamilton, before Louis and the All Stars hit the stage.

A brief interview with Pops prefaces his performance. Discussing his recent trip to Italy, he describes eating in the dining room of a trumpet player and looking up at the ceiling to see paintings of "Marc Antony and Cleo and all them cats." He also mentions the tale of the Pope asking him if he and Lucille had any children.

"No, Daddy, but we're still wailing."

Jazz on a Summer's Day (1960). Louis and Jack Teagarden, featured in Ben Stern's landmark documentary filmed at the 1958 Newport Jazz Festival.

From Louis' set, Stern included "(Up the) Lazy River," a breakneck "Tiger Rag," Pops and Teagarden's duet on "Rockin' Chair," and "When the Saints Go Marching In." The film then concludes with Mahalia Jackson, whose closing number is an incomparable version of "The Lord's Prayer," which holds the entire audience in stunned silence. Though Avakian had told Stern not to roll the cameras during this song, the filmmaker said to his cameramen, "Let's roll it!"[8]

The copyright clearances had to be obtained before editing could begin. The footage of Louis was previewed for Joe Glaser, who deemed it "great"; but when the hardnosed agent quoted $25,000 as their fee, Stern, whose entire budget topped out at $115,000, considered dropping him from the final cut. Later, Stern recalled that Louis' status as a movie personality "must have" helped Galaxy Films sell it at the box office:

> He's probably the biggest known star in the movie. And even though we were having a hard time trying to figure out how to pay the $25,000 that they asked, I do think he's very important as part of the film because he's the most important jazz artist there is, in history.[9]

Though the Avakian brothers and Stern had a falling out over who really "directed" *Jazz on a Summer's Day* (Stern has stressed that it "is not directed; it was produced and filmed"[10]), and others have criticized him for neglecting important artists and making the festival look more attractive than it was, the picture has been lauded for creating a lasting, unique impression of a significant cultural event. In 1999 the Library of Congress placed it on the National Film Registry.

After *Jazz on a Summer's Day* was screened at the Venice Film Festival in August 1960, *Variety*'s "Hawk" wrote:

> Pic is undoubtedly one of the greatest films on jazz ever made. But it is more than that. ... It's Americana ... a stylist's delight and a rich emotional experience.... There have been few if any films which have so impressively mirrored the impact of jazz, or even other forms of music, on spectators and on the musicians themselves.[11]

After finishing *Jazz on a Summer's Day*, Stern, having realized that filmmaking was a "very painful and difficult process," returned to still photography. In 1999 he speculated on the significance of his movie:

> 1958 was a very "up" period in which things were on a very positive note, certainly very different than today. And one of the things in the movie was the mixture of black and white people in the audience, which at the time was controversial. In fact, we were told that this movie could never be released in the South at that time, because that's before a lot of things. This movie was made before the Beatles. It was ten years before Woodstock. And maybe, even before the desegregation in the South. ... We just felt it was a very positive period and certainly in Newport it was very progressive in the way people thought.[12]

While Louis and the All Stars were on a State Department–sponsored tour of Africa, a prerecorded installment of *An Hour with Danny Kaye* was televised on October 30. Having appeared in two films with Kaye, Louis had greatly enjoyed shooting his small-screen guest spot with the multitalented entertainer. However, during the impromptu jam of their "When the Saints Go Marching In" scat duet from *The Five Pennies*, Pops was often overwhelmed by Kaye's incessant scene stealing. In films, directors could reign in Kaye, shoot retakes and edit footage, but live-in-the-studio performances allowed him to run rampant. Though Kaye launched into a gibberish onslaught, during which Louis could only simultaneously scat a few riffs, the genuine friendship of the two men — singing, arm in arm — was a rare sight on a prime-time television show in 1960. Of course, Pops laid Kaye some skin, going one better by following the usual palm gesture with a "pinkie" version.

In Ghana, Louis enjoyed visiting his friend Prime Minister Nkrumah before playing concerts in Nigeria; the Congo (now Zaire), where he stayed with Moise Tshombe (who would become leader of the nation and then a convicted murderer after assassinating his political rival, Patrice Lumumba); and Beirut, Lebanon. While in Katanga, the All Stars — with Barney Bigard on clarinet and Arvell Shaw back on bass — played the usual high-energy set.

During the tour, Velma Middleton suffered a stroke and, after Louis and the All Stars continued without her, passed away in a small African hospital. Underrated (and often condescendingly criticized by jazz historians as a "rotund comedienne-

An Hour with Danny Kaye (October 30, 1960). During a re-creation of the "When the Saints Go Marching In" scat duet from *The Five Pennies*, Kaye characteristically launched into a gibberish onslaught, but Pops still dug the scene.

blues singer"), she was, at times, a very capable vocalist, and, regardless of the bizarre nature of her "choreography," an amusing entertainer.

In Paris on December 14, Louis played "Wild Man" Moore in the Martin Ritt–directed *Paris Blues* (1961), a well-intentioned but heavy-handed film saved by good performances and a terrific Duke Ellington score. Two American expatriots, trombonist Ram Bowen (Paul Newman) and saxophonist Eddie Cook (Sidney Poitier) are living and working in Paris—the former to study and compose classical music, and the latter to escape racism at home. While working in a nightclub run by Bowen's girlfriend, Marie (Barbara Laage), they become involved with Lillian Corning (Joanne Woodward) and Connie Lampson (Diahann Carroll), two tourists from the States, and briefly toy with the idea of moving back across the Atlantic. At the last minute, Bowen cannot leave the possibility of musical success to marry Lillian, so Cook stays with him in Paris.

The film's character development is hampered by too much talk — particularly scenes in which Cook preaches about discrimination — but the choice selection of tunes, including "Mood Indigo," "Take the 'A' Train" and "Sophisticated Lady"— consistently swing the narrative out if its philosophical miasma. Louis first appears on a Paris billboard and then shares an exciting Montmartre "Battle Royal" scene with Newman (whose trombone playing was dubbed by Murray MacEachern, who had recorded with Pops and the Casa Loma Orchestra in 1939) that builds from the first moment to the last — one of the few times a jazz cutting contest has been depicted in a theatrical feature. The film ends at the train station: As the two women depart and the musicians walk away from the platform, workers begin to cover up the huge poster of the "Wild Man."

Though on screen for just a few minutes, Pops' presence permeates the film — the first since *New Orleans* to suggest the scope of his popularity in Europe. While shooting his scenes, he enjoyed hanging out on the set with Ellington, who had been in Paris since November. On Duke's first evening in the French capital, a party in his honor was hosted by Newman and Woodward, whose guests included Ingrid Bergman, Anthony Perkins, Yves Montand, flautist Claude Bolling and composer George Auric. Ellington discussed his cinematic contribution:

> I [had] to write for specific artists — specific sounds. The visual music was to be recorded in Paris, principally by French musicians, and the underscore, which amounted to half of the music, was to be done in New York with my band. One thing in advance was that there was a lot of Louis in the picture so I knew I had to write Louis to sound like Louis.[13]

Newman, fresh from his triumph in *The Hustler* (1961), is in top form. Poitier wavers between disinterest and preachiness, and Woodward and Carroll are pleasantly naturalistic. Bosley Crowther considered the film "contrived," "weak" and "aimless," but appreciated Pops' participation: "Best number ... is a thing called "Battle Royal," in which Louis Armstrong is involved. ... That is jazz, man. That is good."[14]

In Hollywood on January 19, 1961, Louis played a "Delegate to the UMN (United Musical Nations)" in one of the finest television productions of his career. Filling in for the absent Dinah Shore, pop singer Kay Starr hosted a special "Swingin' at the Summit" version of *The Chevy Show*, depicting the message that, "Music is still the language that enables all people everywhere to communicate with each other."

Opening with the "Convention of Delegates," the show introduced Louis and Starr's colleagues — Tony Bennett, George Shearing and Harpo Marx — as they all performed "The Music Makers." (Of course, Harpo honked his horn while the others sang.) From the very first scene, "Swingin' at the Summit" demonstrated that, for once, Louis was given equal footing with his fellow performers; and for one solid hour, he enjoyed a filmed performance devoid of racial stereotypes.

Each performer then took a solo spot. Bennett sang a ballad arrangement of "I've Got the World on a String" and a moderately swinging version of "Takin' a Chance on Love," before Starr, mentioning Pops' recent State Department–sponsored tour, announced, "The Ambassador of Jazz requests that he be heard." Louis then delivered "Mack the Knife" and "Blueberry Hill," during which Starr joined in to close the song, offering her own Satchmo impression — to which he responded with a thumbs-up. "Ambassador at Large" Harpo used pantomime to help Starr introduce Shearing, whose pianistic virtuosity was followed by the Marx Brother's own, which began with his attempt to tune the squeak on the piano seat.

Back at the convention, Pops embarrassed Starr by endowing her with several epithets. "Just wait a minute, Louis!" she responded. "If you give me any more titles,

I'll have to have my calling cards printed in Cinemascope." She then sang "Lonely Nights" and "I Only Wanted a Buddy, Not a Sweetheart." Louis then joined Starr and Bennett on "That's What the Good Book Says."

The program's extended production number was described by Starr as a "hop-scotch" around the world to "inaugurate that new musical foreign policy we talked about." Dissolving from a graphic of the globe and maps of specific nations to the performers in a hot-air balloon (and Harpo floating with a small balloon he inflated himself), the sequence included Bennett singing "One for My Baby" in Italian to a Roman bartender, and Pops performing "C'est Ci Bon" at the Ecole de Jazz in Paris. Offering to "lay a little translation" on the Parisians, Louis exchanged French terms for jive, with *le maison* becoming "a pad!" Ending the song, Louis substituted, "Oui, Oui!" for his "Oh, yeahhhh!" After Harpo fell out of the sky into the Scottish Highlands, he met a bizarre scarecrow and, attired in tartan plaid, played some Celtic melodies on a harp he discovered in some bracken. The scene ended with Starr singing an Israeli song.

The show concluded with the delegates performing "The Man Upstairs," first with Starr and chorus, then Shearing on piano, Harpo on harp and Pops on trumpet. Starr was joined by Bennett and Louis on the vocals, during which Pops worked in a little scat. After the curtain fell, all five appeared side by side to close with the Chevrolet theme song, a fitting tribute to a corporation that sponsored a considerate, truly democratic program.

On March 5 and July 2, 1961, Pops paid more visits to his old friend on *The Ed Sullivan Show*. In between, a historic collaboration between the founding fathers of jazz occurred in New York during an April 3–4 session at RCA Victor's Studio One on East 24th Street, when Louis and Duke Ellington recorded together for the second time in their four-decade careers. (Their only previous meeting was the *Esquire* Award track "Long, Long Journey," cut 15 years earlier.) Attempting to make the two giants comfortable, Roulette Records producer Bob Thiele asked Louis to perform numbers written by Duke, who temporarily became pianist for the All Stars, including Young, Bigard, Herbert and Barcelona. Though they had a mere 12 hours to collaborate, enough takes were recorded to fill two album releases.

Bigard had re-joined Pops just in time to play with his "other" boss, the Duke. "It was fun to be recording with the two most important bandleaders in my career at one session," he recalled, "but the main thing was that Louis got along so great with Duke … two prominent leaders on one date could have been rough, but we had no problems."[15] The initial session ran from 6 P.M. until 1:30 A.M.; but everyone was back by 2 P.M., as Louis nursed his ravaged lips with nitrate-soaked cotton balls.

Ten tracks were released on the Roulette LP *Together for the First Time*. Bob Thiele wrote lyrics for "C-Jam Blues," transforming it into "Duke's Place," on which the maestro's piano literally swings the All Stars into Ellington space. From the beginning, the juxtaposition of the two unique rhythmic styles is a miraculous thing. Any listener — who should realize, "I'm Just a Lucky So and So" — will enjoy living when "Cottontail" arrives: Barcelona and Herbert swing away behind Ellington as the horn players solo and Pops scats up a storm, his "chops flying everywhere." Bigard lays down ravishing tonality on "Mood Indigo," a tune he cowrote with Ellington, as Pops floats his scat over Young's sensual muted trombone.

Ellington's rhythmic and harmonic wizardry on "Do Nothin' Till You Hear from Me" is solid evidence of his influence on Thelonious Monk — and Pops' vocal isn't bad, either. Due to the tight schedule, Thiele somewhat rudely ruled from the recording booth, as Duke directed from the piano bench.

"The Beautiful American" was written by Ellington during the first session. He sang the melody to Bigard and then scored it as the clarinetist played it back to him. After stuffing Barney's beret into Trummy's trombone, he kicked the ensemble into gear. On the released take, Louis blows a solo as melodically inventive as anything in bebop — and *rhythmically* untouchable.

Duke and Bubber Miley's "Black and Tan Fantasy" gets a supreme shot of spirituality when Duke, Barney and Louis converge, creating one of the finest jazz — make that *musical* — performances ever recorded. First, Pops sprays happiness across Ellington's ominous mood, then tears into a goosebump-raising high-note solo that stands among his greatest achievements.

Pops declares, "All the cats are still ... beatin' out those riffs ... yeah, man ... you'll get red beans and rice — it's very nice" during "'Drop Me Off in Harlem' — *Daddy*." Not surprisingly, Ellington smoothly swings "The Mooche," allowing Bigard, Young and Pops room to stretch out. The *Together* LP ends with an in-the-pocket "In a Mellow Tone," featuring buoyant blowing by Barney and Louis.

The second LP release, *The Great Reunion*, features seven Ellington standards. The first, "It Don't Mean a Thing (If It Ain't Got That Swing)," opens with Pops improvising over Duke's vamp before he settles into the first verse, then scatting his way toward solos by Young, Bigard, Ellington and *himself*. Louis' balladry on "My Solitude" is caressed by Trummy and Barney's obbligati before he soars into a solo. Bigard weaves a mesmerizing clarinet spell around Pops' vocal on "Don't Get Around Much Anymore"; then Duke displaces enough rhythm for Pops to swing it back into place with a flaming trumpet finale.

During the recording of "Don't Get Around," Pops attempted to blow one of his trademark riffs at the end of take two. When it went awry, he announced, "Duke! I was just figuring to make an ending there. I don't know," and blew an example to get the maestro's approval before they launched another quickly aborted take. "Duke — he made a mistake," Pops told the band. Take four barely got started; then the cats swung through an entire fifth shot at the song, but the ending proved another washout. "He's conductin' it!" Pops said of Ellington to Thiele, still trying to nail down the closing riff.

"I'm Beginning to See the Light" also necessitated several takes. On the released version, Louis glides above the ensemble, then sings two verses — "Now that your *chops* are burnin' mine" — before soaring once again. On take four, Pops started blowing in the wrong key, then toyed with the lyrics during the next attempt. After Ellington slowed the tempo on takes six and seven, the band finally got in the groove.

"Just Squeeze Me" features Bigard in all his sustained glory, and Pops bouncing the melody off Trummy's trombone riffs. "I Got It Bad (and That Ain't Good)" gets some sexy soloing from Louis, before the album ends with "Azalea," a number

Duke actually wrote 20 years earlier, with ol' Satchmo as inspiration. Though two previous Ellington recordings of the song had remained on the shelf, this off-the-cuff version is a musical revelation, with Louis sight reading, first blowing the melody, then singing the lyrics about the New Orleanian atmosphere he always treasured. The recording required many takes to complete a composite version, however; on the ninth time through, Duke became frustrated after hitting a wrong chord.

In September, Louis and the All Stars joined Dave and Iola Brubeck, Carmen MacRae, Dave Lambert, Jon Hendricks and Annie Ross to record *The Real Ambassadors* at Columbia's 30th Street studio in New York. Dave had asked Paul Desmond to join his regular bandmates (Gene Wright [bass] and Joe Morello [drums]), but the virtuoso alto sax man replied, "Oh, you've got Louis Armstrong. Why do you need me?"[16]

Iola, who wrote the album's civil rights–oriented lyrics, said:

> It was an opportunity for Louis to really make a statement about the whole racial issue, and he put his heart and soul in it. He had made some statements, but they were contradicted by people, saying, "Well, he didn't really mean that" or "He didn't actually say that." So, although he had made statements, I think that the African American community just felt that he hadn't made a bold enough statement."[17]

Prior to the sessions, Dave's brother, Howard Brubeck, went over the music with Louis. Iola added:

> I think they must have discussed the concept at that time. And then, when we actually got into the recording, everybody was too busy, trying to get the recording done. But Louis *knew*. I think he was acting on very strong instincts and intelligence. He just knew what was expected of him.
>
> Nothing much *verbally* ever happened — but every piece of music that he tackled ended up being *his*. So it was his own interpretation, his own feeling about the song, and that sort of thing. So, at times, it was rather transformed from what you originally thought it might sound like.[18]

Louis recorded his contributions on September 12–13 and 19 — and had no time for proper rehearsals, as Dave recalled:

> We went into the studio, and my brother had written out the lyrics very large, that was on the music stand for Louis. And I had recorded on tape, so that Louis could listen to the tunes on the road. Now, that's not much of a rehearsal, and yet, he *knew*— just by ear, from the tapes— how the tunes went.[19]

All the tracks were recorded on a tight schedule devised by Howard Brubeck, with Carmen McRae returning for an additional session in December. Her first-ever meeting with Pops was during their initial session together, and they cut all their duets in real time. Dave said, "Everybody just loved the idea," with Iola emphasizing, "They really jumped into it with great enthusiasm. Carmen had never met Louis. It was amazing."[20]

"Everybody's Comin'" opens the album, with Lambert, Hendricks and Ross announcing the arrival of the performers, and Pops interjecting, "Yess! Yess!" The swinging harmony continues on "Cultural Exchange," and Louis proclaims, "The State Department has discovered jazz," explaining the value of the music in international relations. A stylistic musical exchange reinforces the lyrical content, with the bebop of Brubeck alternating with the New Orleanian swing of the All Stars and a soaring Pops solo.

Carmen McRae sings "Good Reviews," another oscillation between Dave and Dixieland. Pops then advises, "Remember Who You Are" to those swinging ambassadors, with Trummy enjoying a solo. Carmen has "My One Bad Habit" all to herself; and Louis gets "Lonesome," on which he dubbed a vocal over his trumpet-piano duet with Brubeck. The poignant "Summer Song" is a perfect vehicle for Pops' positive outlook (and predated "What a Wonderful World" by several years). Dave said, "It's Billy Kyle and me on two pianos, playing behind Louis. Here it had gone full circle for me."[21]

Trummy inquires what the boss would do if he was "King for a Day," during which Pops replies that he'd call a "basement" session, bringing harmony and blues that would overpower "Khrushchev poundin' both his shoes." The vocal trio combines furious bop and rap on "Blow Satchmo," then smoothly swings "The Real Ambassadors," during which Louis, referring to segregation, reveals, "Though I represent the government, the government don't represent some of the policies I'm for."

"Man, there's really something happening here tonight!" Pops declares on the Arabic-influenced "Nomad." Carmen finds herself "In the Lurch," then shares "One Moment Worth Years" with Louis, who slips in his famous scat riff on the end. They sound fabulous while sharing another duet, on "You Swing Baby (The Duke)," during which Pops blows a beautifully syncopated solo.

Louis sings Iola's powerful lyric, speculating whether God might be black, while introducing "They Say I Look Like God?" repeating, "Set man free" and "*really* free" on this sacred-style song using the call-and-response structure of a traditional spiritual. He then harmonizes with Carmen on the ballad "I Didn't Know Until You Told Me." Iola said:

> The original idea was for him to sing the melody, and Carmen was to sing the harmony — and they switched.
> She said, "You can do this better than I can." So she sang the melody.[22]

Louis was particularly impressed with the composer's style on the song "Since Love Had Its Way," another of the album's masterful fusions of traditional and modern jazz, during which Pops blows a delightfully rhythmic, sensitive solo. Dave explained:

> He said, "You've got the feeling of a dance we used to do in New Orleans," and he imitated some shoulder movements and dancing. That really made me feel *great*, because I wanted to be in that idiom somewhat.[23]

Carmen briefly advises "Easy as You Go" before the concluding medley, "Swing Bells/Blow Satchmo/Finale." During the last section, Pops blows some of his legendary high notes — his own improvised addition that startled the Brubecks. Dave enthused, "The high F! We couldn't believe it — at his age — he kept going up there, and he never missed one once. He banged out that high F above high C. That was a surprise."[24]

Iola said:

> I think the phenomenal thing was his ear. He picked up everything so fast. Over and over again, we were just amazed at how quick and, really, just so musically gifted — that wonderful, natural talent that was there.[25]

The album was praised by critics, but sales proved disappointing. Dave explained:

> You know, you think it would have been a big record, but I don't think it was. You can never figure the record business, or how something is going to go. I expected it to be bigger than it was. Serious people loved it, but I don't know about the public, whether they ever latched onto it.[26]

Iola added:

> It just seems that the record-buying public buys from habit, a lot. We have, over the years, noticed that, if the record is the Dave Brubeck Quartet, it seems to have better sales than if it's the Dave Brubeck Trio with Gerry Mulligan, or with somebody else. The music is just as good — almost the same, as far as the genre is concerned — but it's like a trademark name or something. And I think that, often, albums that have a number of different people, like this one did, do not sell as well as an individual Armstrong record, or an individual McRae record, or an individual Dave Brubeck record.[27]

Though the album sold poorly, the group performed the material live at the 1962 Monterey Jazz Festival. Organizer Jimmy Lyons was aware of the record and phoned Brubeck to ask if the work could be presented by the full lineup in September. A year had passed since the material was recorded, and Brubeck needed to get all the performers together for rehearsals at San Francisco's St. Francis Hotel prior to driving down to Monterey.

Lyons had built a separate stage for Iola's narration of a storyline that tied the songs together. She explained:

> Some time that summer, Lucille Armstrong had telephoned. She said, "I've heard about this production in Monterey. You know, that's far too much work for Louis to do. He's never going to be able to do all of that, because he's on tour." She was just sort of saying, "You should forget this whole idea."
>
> So it was with some trepidation that we went to that first rehearsal, because I thought it may be that he'd say. "Well, I'll do one or two songs, but I'm not going to go through with this whole production idea."
>
> But that was not it at all. He was right with it, and did the rehearsals and cooperated fully with everything. So, I think that he was eager to do it.[28]

Dave recalled:

The Real Ambassadors (1962). The groundbreaking civil-rights concept album, signed by Dave and Iola Brubeck.

Louis was supposed to wear a top hat and carry an attaché case at rehearsal — working out entrances, and where the band would sit. We asked him to enter with a top hat and the attaché case, and he said, "No, I won't do that."

And I said, "Okay. Just come in from the side of the stage."

When the curtains opened, and we were playing the first music, in comes Louis, and he has on the top hat, and the attaché case. And when he walked by the piano, he said, "Am I hammin' it up enough to suit you, Pops?"[29]

Dave remembered a request that Louis made prior to the performance:

He said that he had to have the words bigger than what he'd had in New York; so my brother wrote everything on huge pieces of cardboard. And Louis followed those, when he wanted to look down, and it wasn't too obvious to the audience.[30]

"They were not like huge cue cards," added Iola. "And it was very subtle, and he didn't have to look down very much, but he just wanted that for a little assurance."[31]

Dave also remembered the audience response:

> The reviews were fantastic. Hardened critics were crying—tears in their eyes. People like Dizzy Gillespie were just overjoyed. All the musicians that were playing at the festival were there at the performance, and just threw their arms around Louis afterwards. It was really joyful.[32]

Referring to the whole "bebop feud," Dave clarified, "Dizzy used to go by Louis' house all the time, and talk with him — while they were saying that they weren't getting along. It wasn't true at all."[33]

Brubeck was particularly impressed by the gravity Louis displayed during the performance of "They Say I Look Like God": "The lines that Iola and I had written to make the audience *laugh* about segregation — he delivered with such seriousness that they didn't get a laugh. He went the opposite of what we told him to do."[34]

Unfortunately, Glaser asked them not to allow a local television crew to broadcast the performance. Aside from Brubeck not having the $750 to pay them —"we were rarely with $75"[35]— Glaser said that perhaps a Broadway version could be filmed at a later date. Dave explained:

> Joe said, "Oh, those people out there won't know how to do a good job. Wait until you get to New York. Don't let them televise this." I would have gone to people like my attorney from San Francisco. He was going to be there that night. I could have gone to a few people for money, but he said, "Don't you dare televise this."
>
> And, I tell you, we missed one of the great documents on Louis that probably has ever been done. Louis told everybody, "The Brubecks have written me an opera."
>
> He loved opera — and he thought that this was an opera. Iola and I told him that it was more of a Broadway show, and he said, "Well, yeah, but what about these songs that I'm singin'? Sounds like opera to me!"[36]

But the Broadway *Real Ambassadors* never came to pass. Dave concluded:

> I took it to the leading guys—and the one who loved it, was going to make me a big famous writer—he didn't come back. And one guy who was interested said, "This will never work on Broadway, because you cannot try to *educate* the people. They want to be entertained." That was such a disappointment. And I've done a lot of things—Iola and I—that had a message. People are afraid sometimes.[37]

On September 24, 1961, John S. Wilson published an article titled, "Jazz Film Maestro" in the *New York Times*, describing the efforts of a private collector to "gather ... neglected films before they are irretrievably lost." Noting the "scornful attitude [of aficionados] toward what they consider Hollywood's warped treatment of jazz," Wilson wrote:

> In the last few years ... it has occurred to a few jazz collectors that invaluable pictorial records of jazz stars at work have turned up in even the shoddiest Hollywood musicals and long forgotten short subjects. ... Ernest R. Smith has recently been

showing some early jazz films at meetings of such groups as the Jazz Arts Society and the Duke Ellington Jazz Society. His program included the only known film appearance of the great blues singer, Bessie Smith [and] several shorts made by Louis Armstrong and Duke Ellington between 1929 and 1935 that catch these musicians at the height of their youthful vigor...[38]

Smith was not impressed with most of the Hollywood films, but considered *New Orleans*, "despite its historical inaccuracies and its stereotyped jazz vs. classics basis, the movies' best effort at tracing the spread of jazz in the United States."[39] His top titles were two Ellington shorts, *Black and Tan Fantasy* (1929, with Fredi Washington) and *Symphony in Black* (1934, with Billie Holiday), Gjon Mili's *Jammin' the Blues* (1944, with Lester Young) and *Jazz on a Summer's Day*.

Louis again shared the stage with Ed Sullivan, this time at West Berlin's Sportspalast in a special U.S. Army show for the 40th Armored Berlin Command broadcast by CBS on Sunday, October 8, 1961. Pops and the All Stars opened the program with "When It's Sleepy Time Down South" and, according to *Variety*, "a hot instrumental which featured [his] tip-top trumpeting."[40] Interspersed with performances by Maureen O'Hara, Connie Francis, Van Cliburn, and Rowan and Martin, Louis returned with "The Faithful Hussar" and "When the Saints Go Marching In," another fine swinger "marred only by the fact that the camera strayed away from the tootlers for an overlong runthrough of the show's credits."[41] Sullivan broadcast a second show from West Berlin the following Sunday, capturing a performance by Pops at McNair Barracks, as well as Sid Caesar, Shari Lewis, Roberta Peters and Janet Blair, who appeared at various venues across the city.

Louis and Duke Ellington repeated their historic summit for the December 21, 1961, broadcast of *The Ed Sullivan Show*, the only time the jazz giants performed a small-screen duet. Pops sang "Nobody Knows the Trouble I've Seen" and jammed with Ellington on "Duke's Place" and "In a Mellow Tone." Other guests lucky enough to be on hand for the gathering of the musical gods were Paul Anka, Barbara Cook, Walter Chiari, Corbett Monica, and Wayne and Shuster.

On April 2, 1962, Pops, along with Young, Kyle, Barcelona, Joe Darensbourg (clarinet), Billy Cronck (bass) and Jewell Brown, appeared in *The Louis Armstrong All Stars*, a 25-minute concert film commissioned by the Goodyear Tire Company, who had planned a series, to include the Eddie Condon All Stars and the Bobby Hackett Sextet. Shot at Pathé's New York studio in 35mm color by director Bernard Rubin, it was the finest visual representation of the "real" Pops to date, providing a longer and more inclusive look at the band than their segment in *Jazz on a Summer's Day*. Though the audio was recorded in stereo, the films were released in 16mm with a mono soundtrack.

Depicting the worldwide appeal of Louis' music, the set includes a large globe in the background and a smaller one on a pedestal in the foreground. Opening with "When It's Sleepy Time Down South," the band moves on to "C'est Si Bon," "Someday," "Jerry" (featuring Brown), "Nobody Knows the Trouble I've Seen" and "When the Saints Go Marching In." Each of Pops' song preambles is framed in a medium close-up, as are his introductions of the band members, who each get a good tight shot.

"We've got Satchmo Armstrong," announced Walt Disney during his introduc-

The Ed Sullivan Show (December 21, 1961). The historic television summit of Louis and Duke Ellington.

tion to the April 15, 1962, broadcast of *Disneyland After Dark*, a one-hour program intended to orient television viewers (and filmgoers in Europe, where the show was released in theaters) with the goings-on at the Anaheim, California, theme park after the sun went down.

Directed by Hamilton S. Luske and William Beaudine (who helmed the 1926 silent masterpiece *Sparrows* and dozens of golden-age potboilers), this fast-paced color film opens with shots of the park entrance, the famous monorail and several rides. Disney enters, "buying" popcorn and signing autographs for visitors (the show's running gag). Park performers, including a barbershop quartet, are followed by

The Louis Armstrong All Stars (April 2, 1962). *Top:* Louis, backed by Billy Kyle (piano), Danny Barcelona (drums), Trummy Young (trombone), Billy Cronck (bass) and Joe Darensbourg (clarinet), during the concert film commissioned by the Goodyear Tire Company. *Bottom:* Pops blows "When It's Sleepy Time Down South."

Annette Funicello and Bobby Burgess, Bobby Rydell (singing "Around the World"), a glimpse at the nightly fireworks show, and the Royal Tahitians (three grass-skirted dancers baring more skin than one expects from 1962 Disney, a "fire knife" dancer and a "firewalker") before "the ol' *Mark Twain*" rounds a bend in the river.

"The Young Men from New Orleans," including Kid Ory (trombone), Johnny St. Cyr (banjo) and Harvey Brooks (piano), are heard aboard the riverboat as a vocal quartet performs on the nearby dock. Blues growler Monette Moore sings a rousing "Kansas City" before the sequence cuts to Pops in the audience. "That's my kind of music," he announces before launching into a laid-back "(Up the) Lazy River," which shifts into a medium-tempo swinger, his scatting a pure pleasure as he acts out each nonsense syllable.

Introducing St. Cyr and Ory, Pops points out that they "played with me in one of my swingin' groups called The Hot Five."

Discussing the early days in New Orleans, Johnny St. Cyr tells Pops, "We didn't make much money, but we sure had fun."

"Yeah, but the rent was cheap, too, Daddy," Pops adds.

Brooks then remarks that St. Cyr was "playing banjo in New Orleans when the blues were born," and Pops amends, "I was there to help deliver it. Since all the cats are here, let's re-create," before breaking into "Muskrat Ramble."

"That tune was really a gasser," Louis says after blowing the final high note. "And you know one thing folks? Kid Ory wrote that tune."

Brooks then requests, "How about doing some 'Parade Down Ol' Bourbon Street'?"

"Let's all take some," Louis replies, "Yeah! We're gonna rock this ol' *Mark Twain* right on down to New Orleans," and then sings a duet with Moore. Here (and during the entire sequence), the passengers are genuinely delighted.

At this point, the program musically shifts 180 degrees, to the tiny Osmond Brothers—Alan, Wayne, Merrill and Jay—who, at their youthful ages (six to twelve), demonstrate incredible vocal control and phrasing on "Side by Side." The show closes with a musical mess when singer Tony Paris attempts to perform "Twilight Time" and "Yakety Yak" as the audience is encouraged to "back him up."

During the 1962 All Stars European tour, an April 24 concert at the Paris Olympia was broadcast on Europe 1 radio. Three W. C. Handy numbers—"Ole Miss," "Yellow Dog Blues" and "St. Louis Blues," with vocals by Jewell Brown—were included in the set. Back in the States on August 1, they recorded a Chicago gig, deviating little from the established set.

During NAG's campaign to sell advertising space in its 1962 yearbook, Jackie Robinson wrote a letter to Joe Glaser, who responded with $500 for a back-cover ad. Performing at Guantanamo Naval Base in Cuba on December 23, Louis wished a Merry Christmas to U.S. troops during yet another guest spot on *The Ed Sullivan Show*. Though Connie Francis, Carol Lawrence, Jack Carter, Frank Fontaine and George Carl also appeared, Pops received substantial screen time during a set that included "Blueberry Hill," "Mack the Knife," "Indiana," "Nobody Knows the Trouble I've Seen" and "Sleepy Time Gal." NBC later repeated the program on August 11, 1963.

In early 1963, Louis appeared on Ralph Gleason's public-television show *Jazz Casual*, broadcast by San Francisco's KQED. A half-hour program featuring the host "kicking back" with his legendary guests (which, during its run, included Count Basie, John Coltrane, Dizzy Gillespie, Dave Brubeck, Carmen McRae and B. B. King), this installment, directed by Richard Moore, offered Pops commenting on specific recordings, including "When It's Sleepy Time Down South," "Snake Rag," "Courtin' the Blues," "Skid-Dat-De-Dat" and "Mack the Knife."

On May 23, 1963, Louis was a featured performer at the New York birthday party for President John F. Kennedy. On June 18, Kennedy wrote to thank Pops:

> Dear Louis:
>   I want you to know how much I appreciated all the efforts you made and time you spent in making my birthday party ... such a success. It was delightful and I am very grateful to you for the part you played in making it so enjoyable.[42]

On December 3, 1963, Louis recorded two Broadway songs in a New York recording studio. Producer David Merrick was preparing to stage *Hello, Dolly!* and wanted the title number on the airwaves to promote the show. Journalist Jack Bradley, who was covering the session, witnessed Pops' disappointment when seeing the sheet music for the two-minute song, thinking that the second number, "A Lot of Livin' to Do" from *Bye Bye Birdie*, might be radio-friendly. A surprise to everyone involved, Kapp Records' single release of "Hello, Dolly!" stayed on the *Billboard* chart for 22 weeks during 1964, reaching number one in May. The greatest shocker of all occurred when the song knocked the Beatles' "Can't Buy Me Love" from the top chart position. All told, the record remained in the top 100 longer than any other pop song that year, also reaching number one on the Adult Contemporary chart. Furthermore, it contributed heavily to the success of the show, which became the longest-running Broadway musical to date. Gary Giddins noted, "'Hello, Dolly!' was a triumph for him, for his generation, for jazz. It was also a class record."[43]

In early March 1964, Louis, feeling under the weather, was pleased to hear from actor Jose Ferrer, who mentioned his friend's favorite laxative: "Sorry to hear you're laid up. Have you tried Swiss Kriss? Rosie and I send you our love. I'll keep in touch and come in and see you. Your man —" (Instead of signing his name, Ferrer drew a caricature of his famous profile.)[44]

Soon Louis was back in the spotlight, plugging "Hello, Dolly" on television talk shows. On March 22 he was persuaded to sing it a cappella when he was a "surprise guest" on *What's My Line?* hosted by Ross Hunter. Wanting to capitalize on the single, Michael ("Mickey") Kapp arranged with Joe Glaser for Louis to record 10 more songs, during a month-long engagement in Las Vegas, to add to "Hello, Dolly!" and "A Lot of Livin' to Do" for an album release.

Also titled *Hello, Dolly*, the LP, including Satchmo favorites, Broadway numbers and current pop fare, was an even bigger hit, remaining on the chart for 74 weeks, including six weeks at number one. The jazz icon had become a recognized worldwide pop star. By this time, Trummy Young, at the insistence of his wife, had left the road to settle into his Hawaiian home, and was succeeded by Russell ("Big Chief") Moore, a member of Arizona's Pima tribe who first recorded with Pops in 1944. The All Stars also welcomed Arvell Shaw back on bass. Two guitar-banjoists, Glen Thompson and Tony Gottuso, also play on the album.

"This is Lou*is*, Dolly!" Pops announces at the beginning of "Hello, Dolly!" perhaps wanting listeners to pronounce his name correctly. He not only offers a masterful pop vocal, but a fine solo as well. Jule Styne and Sammy Cahn's "It's Been a Long, Long Time" is a bridge between the single and its B side, before the familiar "A Kiss to Build a Dream On" has Pops again requesting, "Babe! Lend me your chops for just a moment." His own "Someday" is followed by the show tune "Hey, Look Me Over" and another Styne-Cahn number, "I Still Get Jealous," which was released as a follow-up single. Though Kapp had Pops ask, "Hey, Dolly?" to open the song, which is similar in structure, tempo and duration to its predecessor, the new record only reached number 45 on the pop chart.

Johnny Mercer and Henry Mancini's lovely ballad "Moon River," eventually recorded by nearly every 1960s pop singer, is sensitively sung and played by Pops, though the trite trombone accompaniment is distracting. "Be My Life's Companion" is an upbeat throwaway, "Blueberry Hill" plods along, and "You Are Woman, I Am Man" is another arrangement in the "Hello, Dolly!" mold. The album concludes with a cookin' version of "Jeepers Creepers," featuring Pops' jazziest vocal and solo spots for all.

On September 3, 1964, Louis and the All Stars recorded two numbers, "So Long, Dearie" and "Pretty Little Missy" for Mercury in New York. Pops sang "Hello, Dolly!" to great applause on *The Ed Sullivan Show* on October 4, following up with "So Long, Dearie" and sharing the stage with Sid Caesar, Pat Boone and Abbe Lane. On November 3 they cut two more Mercury songs, "Bye 'n' Bye" and "Faith."

7

Richer Than Rockefeller

Who wants to be sitting and looking at four walls just because they got a whole lot of money and they're scared they're going to lose it? Like I told Bing, he says, "Don't you think you should slow up now? You're pretty well straight, aren't you?" I'd say, "Bing, always remember, you can't have bread and loaf." ... I figure as long as my stomach feels good and I feel good period, I feel more rich than Rockefeller. You can't even show him a pork chop.

— Louis Armstrong[1]

Louis was in Copenhagen when Martin Luther King led a civil rights march from Selma to Montgomery, Alabama, in March 1965. Recently, civil rights workers had been murdered in Selma, where the sheriff had authorized the use of tear gas, whips and clubs on demonstrators. After hearing about the riots, Pops remarked, "They would beat Jesus if he was black and marched."

The violence went beyond color to anyone threatening the Old South. On the final night of the march, snipers shot to death a white woman who was driving demonstrators back to Selma from Montgomery. President Lyndon Johnson responded by sending a right-to-vote law to Congress, authorizing federal authorities to register African American voters in 11 states, half of them in the deep South, where various methods, including "literacy tests," had been used to prevent blacks from voting.

Though he was wealthy enough to afford a lavish home, Pops preferred to stay in Corona, "right out here with the rest of the colored folk and the Puerto Ricans and Italians and the Hebrew cats. ... The Frigidaire is full of food. What more do we need?"[2] Three decades had passed since he became the first African American performer to receive star billing in a major Hollywood film, but he had absolutely no intention of ever moving there — nor of hanging out with his fellow actors: "Even though I've played with a lot of them — Danny Kaye, Sinatra — I don't even know where they live. In fact, I've never been invited to the home of a movie star, not even Bing's."[3] Pops still dug all the children who came by to learn about the trumpet or watch Westerns on television — and the jazz aficionados and musicians, like Dizzy Gillespie and Clark Terry, who dropped in.

174

On May 1, 1965, ABC broadcast a special episode of *The Hollywood Palace* celebrating Louis' 50th year in show business. Featuring tributes by the erudite Edward G. Robinson, the ever-friendly Jimmy Durante, and a congratulatory wire sent by President Johnson, the program was hosted by Satchmo himself.

Diahann Carroll sang "Outskirts of Town," "Porgy" and "Nobody Knows You When You're Down and Out," while Rowan and Martin directed some satirical shtick at Pops, which he responded to by singing "Hello, Dolly!" "When the Saints Go Marching In," "Mack the Knife," "Blueberry Hill" and, with Jimmy D., a charming "Old Father Time," after which Durante expressed a wish that his partner "defy the Old Boy for 'another 50 years.'" *Variety*'s "Abel" reported:

> Whether it was the genuine warmth of … Robinson … the infectious camaraderie that … Durante portrayed, and the generally contagious esprit evidenced by the entire cast of this Saturday night [show], there was no doubt about Louis Armstrong's niche in the American scene.
>
> The smiling, roly-poly virtuoso of the horn handled all his charges, and seemed genuinely pleased … that his professional colleagues were as cheery about his 50th anniversary … as seemingly, also, was the case of the studio audience. Closeups on the latter mirrored empathy and affection for Satchmo.[4]

Once again it was off to Europe for the All Stars. BBC-TV broadcast their June 3, 1965, concert from London in its entirety as "Back o' Town Blues," then repeated it, edited into two "Satchmo" installments of *Show of the Week*, on October 7 and 16. English jazz musician Humphrey Lyttelton wrote and narrated the episodes, alternating Louis' reminiscences with performances of "Muskrat Ramble," "Black and Blue" and "My Bucket's Got a Hole in It". The initial 45-minute program was called "a neat blend of documentary and jazz" by *Variety*'s "Otta":

> Armstrong came across strongly as a personality, seeming relaxed and compensated with sincere vigor and expression for a certain lack of anecdote. … The only musical disappointment was that Armstrong was sparing of solos, though his vocal in "Bucket's Got a Hole" was a potent reminder of his stature.[5]

Louis was back in Hollywood during the summer, combining live dates with recording sessions and more television guest appearances. In July, three new All Stars— Tyree Glenn (trombone), Buster Bailey (clarinet) and Buddy Catlett (bass)— joined for a Mercury date that yielded "Short but Sweet." The following month, the new lineup cut another Mercury number, "The Circle of Your Arms," and two songs for Fontana, "I Like This Kind of Party" and "The Three of Us," released only in Europe.

On September 24, Louis wrote a letter to Lucille from the Disneyland Hotel:

> We opened at Disneyland tonight and with great success. They had an after hours party as they always do. But this time "Tommy Walker," "Our Boy," gave out a lot of presents to All the Stars and Leaders of all the Festival including me.
>
> Well, Darling, it's about time for me to throw my "Black Ass" into the bed. I have three hard days in front of me. Especially Disneyland. Of course you already

know. So there is nothing left to say other than — I have lifelong love for you — even if you should divorce me. P.S. Trying to be "funny again." MY HEART BELONGS TO YOU. FROM YOUR HUSBAND — Louis NUTS (ABOUT YOOO).[6]

The letters he wrote to Lucille during 1965 often include references to "everybody" and "his public" still "loving him all the way." In closing the missives, he always used one of his nicknames, including "Satch" and "Pops."

He returned to *The Hollywood Palace* on September 25, guesting on one of the 28 episodes hosted by his buddy Bing. Crosby sang "My Blue Heaven" and collaborated on "Dardenella" with Louis, who also performed "Way Down Yonder in New Orleans." Phil Harris and the Young Americans then joined the duo for "South Rampart Street Parade."

Pops also guested on *The Dean Martin Show*, singing a duet with Dino during the inaugural season of the hugely popular, innovative variety hour. On November 4 and 11, Louis paid visits to the popular music program *Shindig*, performing lengthy sets that included "When It's Sleepy Time Down South," "Indiana," "My Bucket's Got a Hole in It," "Blueberry Hill," "Hello, Dolly!" "When the Saints Go Marching In," "Struttin' with Some Barbecue," "Mack the Knife," "Avalon," "Ole Miss" and "I've Got a Lot of Living to Do." Jewell Brown also was featured, singing "I Left My Heart in San Francisco" and "My Man."

The following month the German television program *Schlager, Stars und Schnulzen* (*Pop Hits, Stars and Corny Ditties*) focused on how the culture of "decadent Western civilization" was encroaching on the Communist East. Much of this influence, according to writer Gottfried Kludas, was due to broadcasts by RIAS (the U.S.–sponsored West Berlin radio station), the American Armed Forces Radio Network, and Radio Luxembourg. More recently, television also had brought Western entertainers behind the Iron Curtain, where a few — including the Glenn Miller Orchestra and Louis and the All Stars — also had performed live concerts.

Two truly cool cats: Dino and Satchmo team up during the inaugural season of *The Dean Martin Show* (1965).

Pops' spring 1965 tour of Eastern Europe was noted as having "enthus[ed] even party stalwarts."[7]

In his January 20, 1966, *New York Times* review, Howard Thompson wrote, "If the music of the Gershwin brothers can survive a terrible little musical such as *When the Boys Meet the Girls*, as happened yesterday, chances are it could outlast atomic annihilation."[8] Surrounded by more mediocrity than in any of his preceding cinematic efforts, Pops, on screen for less than three minutes, is a redeeming feature in this Sam Katzman production, adapted from the 1930 Broadway musical *Girl Crazy* by screenwriter Robert E. Kent. "Thank heaven, at least, for Louis Armstrong," Thompson added, "and, again, the brothers Gershwin, whose gold shines through all the cardboard and tin."[9] Top-billed Connie Francis personally asked MGM to include Pops, and he received third billing in the credits.

When the Boys Meet the Girls (previously filmed as *Girl Crazy* [1943] with Judy Garland and Mickey Rooney) costars Francis as Ginger, a mail carrier from a Nevada backwater, and Harve Presnell as Denny, an urban playboy hiding out in the boonies to escape a breach-of-promise suit filed by Tess (Sue Ann Langdon), a chorus girl. When country meets big city, Ginger takes Denny's advice and transforms the family home into a dude ranch for divorcees! After the narrative is tidied up, Louis reemerges to close the show with the famous line from "I Got Rhythm": "Who could ask for anything more?" His other musical contribution is a performance of "Throw It Out of Your Mind," which he cowrote with Billy Kyle.

Whenever Francis and Presnell aren't struggling with such Gershwin standards as "Embraceable You" and "But Not for Me," hugely inappropriate acts like Herman's Hermits, Sam the Sham and the Pharoahs, and Liberace fill in wretchedly. The presence of Louis is the only musical casting that makes any sense. His two numbers were recorded at MGM on July 26, 1965. Though the version of "I Got Rhythm" used in the film is primarily instrumental, he also cut a swinging alternate version that included an entire vocal verse — the first time he had waxed the number since 1931.

After his lengthy tenure with the All Stars, Billy Kyle was succeeded by pianist Marty Napoleon, who returned to record with Pops during a New York session in April 1966. Three numbers, "When the Saints Go Marchin' In," "Tyree's Blues" and the novelty song "Cheesecake," were cut for Mercury. The following month, "Mame" was recorded for a new single, featuring "Saints" as the B-side. Two other tunes, "Tin Roof Blues" and an unknown title, also were laid down. In July, Louis recorded two numbers with the Guy Lombardo Orchestra, "Mumbo Jumbo" and "Come Along Down," for release as a Capitol single. On August 25 he was back with the All Stars to cut a single for Columbia, "Canal Street Blues," backed with "Cabaret."

When the jazz drama *A Man Called Adam* was released by Embassy Pictures during the summer of 1966, Ike Jones, who co-produced with James Waters, became the first African American to receive such a credit in a major Hollywood film. Sammy Davis, Jr., stars as the title character, Adam Johnson, a trumpeter racked with guilt over an auto accident that killed his family. Unable to cope with his inner demons and the pervasive prejudice around him, he ditches a gig at a Cincinnati club and watches his opportunities disappear. Rebuffed by Claudia Ferguson (Cicely Tyson),

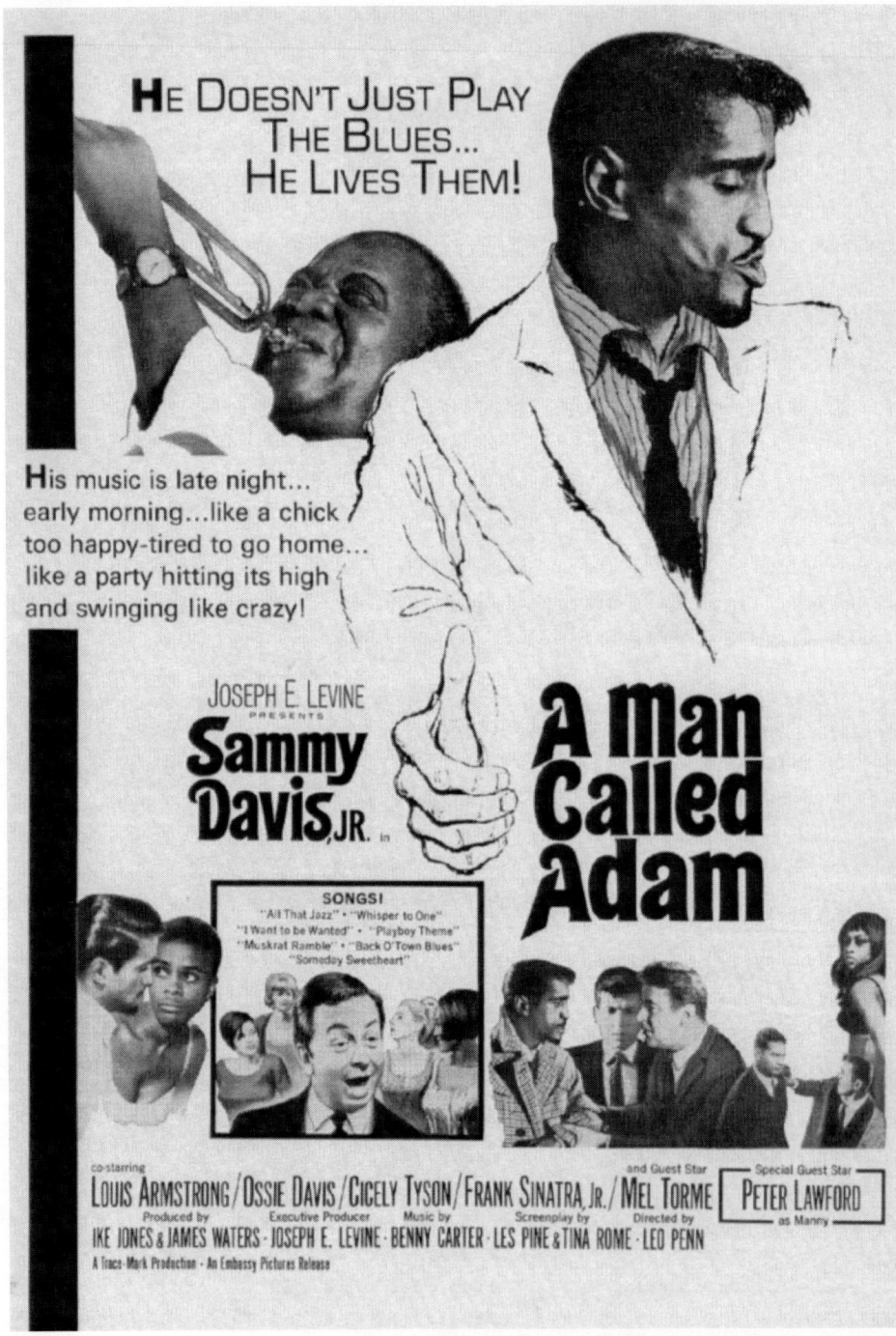

A Man Called Adam (1966). Louis played a rare character role in this downbeat jazz drama starring Sammy Davis, Jr., Ossie Davis, Cicely Tyson and Frank Sinatra, Jr.

a civil rights activist, he then agrees with his agent, Manny (Peter Lawford), to tour the South, where Vincent (Frank Sinatra, Jr.), a white member of his band, is badly beaten by three rednecks. One evening Adam joins Claudia's grandfather, struggling trumpeter Willie ("Sweet Daddy") Ferguson (Louis), at a gig, but collapses and dies backstage.

Restricted by a low budget, director Leo Penn and cinematographer Jack Priestly used black and white to create a cinema verité atmosphere in scenes set in smoky nightclubs and hotel rooms filmed on location in New York. Produced by Sammy Davis, Jr.'s, own company, Trace-Mark Productions, the project originally was planned by Nat Cole, who passed away in 1965.

Leo Penn, who previously had directed Davis in a *Ben Casey* television episode, recalled the improvisational skills of the versatile entertainer:

> Sammy is a very creative, spontaneous performer, and I took advantage of this wonderful spontaneity of his. We would rehearse a scene as it was written, and suddenly, almost instinctively, he might come up with a bit of business that would enhance the action or add to the illumination of the character. ... Literally, we inspired each other. He certainly brought out the best in me, and I hope I did the same for him. It was a sheer joy to direct Sammy.[10]

Embassy Pictures' official pressbook claimed, "For the first time in his long and illustrious career, Louis Armstrong is given the chance to portray on screen an honestly conceived dramatic character."[11] To fashion a screenplay with believable characters, Ike Jones and writer Les Pine went on the road with different groups of musicians. Jones explained:

> We have tried to show these musicians as they really are. Most pictures of jazz players are cliché-ridden. I cannot recall a single one which dealt with these people in other than stereotypical fashion. The men emerged as cardboard figures. ... We try to be authentic in our language. Traveling in buses for a series of one-nighters is a hard life, and in our picture the men do not suddenly break out in a gay theme song of the joys of the road as they journey from one job to another.[12]

When the struggling Sweet Daddy can't get enough bread together to pay for a hotel room, jazz club owner Nelson Davis (Ossie Davis) moves him into Adam's apartment. Here he receives the brunt of the tormented man's angst, including being sent packing when the uninformed, drunken Adam is angered by his presence. Making the most of a rare dramatic opportunity, Louis effectively conveys the disillusionment of a hot jazzman in the era of cool. Many years later Ossie Davis recalled, "Louis Armstrong, to me, is a smile, a handkerchief, and sweat, and the capacity to move me above and beyond tears."[13] On the *Adam* set in 1965, Davis' preconceptions about Pops were challenged one day after the rest of the cast and crew had gone to lunch:

> The set was quiet. As I came back toward the set, I looked up and there was Louis Armstrong sitting in a chair, with a handkerchief tied around his head, looking up with the saddest expression I've ever seen on a man's face. I looked, and I was startled, and I started to back away because it seemed such a private moment.

But he heard me backing away, and he broke out of it right away: "Hey, Pops! Hey, looks like these cats got to starve ol' Louis to death. Hey, man. Wow!" and everything, you know.

I went into it with him, but I never forgot that look, and it changed my concept of Louis Armstrong, because I, too, as a boy had objected to a lot of what Louis was doing. I figured all them teeth and the handkerchief—we called it "Ooftah," by which we meant, "You do that to please the white folks, don't you?" You know, you make them happy and all that stuff. You make us look like fools.

But only then I began to understand something about Louis. You know, he could put on that show—he could do that whole thing, because, in that horn of his, you know, he had the *power*—to kill. That horn could kill a man. So there was where the truth of Louis Armstrong resided. Whatever he was, the moment he put the trumpet to his lips, a new truth emerged, a new man emerged, a new power emerged. And I looked on Louis for what he truly was, after that—an angelic presence, to me, after that moment.[14]

Louis' songs include "Ole Miss," "Back o' Town Blues," "Muskrat Ramble" and "Some Day Sweetheart." Swinging alongside him are Nat Adderley (who dubbed Sammy's trumpet solos), Bill Berry, Junior Mance, Kai Winding, and All Stars Glenn, Bailey, Kyle, Catlett and Barcelona.

Variety's "Murf" found the film "a downbeat, somewhat uneven programmer":

The empathy of jazzmen, their music and their simpatico friends (not hangers-on) has yet to receive adequate exposition in any pic, "Adam" included, although periodic attempts have been made. Perhaps it can never be done. In any case, the usual result is a bunch of cats making with the hip jive talk, and interacting with stereotyped squares who snap their fingers on "one" and "three."

Impressed with both Davises, Cicely Tyson, and a cameo by Mel Torme, Murf referred to Pops' performance as "an unusually effective offbeat character."[15]

The *New York Times*' Howard Thompson reported:

Almost as provocative as the theme ... is the heartening fact that the movie not only stars a Negro artist but also has both Negro and white players in key roles, another rarity. ... The best single moment occurs when Mr. Davis and young Frank Sinatra, Jr. ... aim their trumpets straight up at a cheering balcony in a segregated theater.[16]

Praising Tyson for the best acting in the film, Donald Bogle also offered his most balanced perception of Pops: "[I]t was fascinating to see the great Louis Armstrong cast as the old musician Sweet Daddy. Still not an actor, Armstrong nonetheless endowed the film with pathos and feeling."[17] Making his screen debut, future star Morgan Freeman has a bit part in the film.*

On August 21, 1966, Howard Thompson was back, this time with a *New York Times* article titled "Movies: Out of Tune with the World of Jazz," claiming:

The following year, Freeman landed a Broadway role in the all-black Pearl Bailey version of Hello, Dolly!*; but he wouldn't see his career take off until 1971, when he began playing "Easy Reader" on the children's television show* The Electric Company. *One of the most naturalistic, tasteful character actors in film history, his love of African American music led him to open the Ground Zero Blues Club, an authentic juke joint, in Clarksdale, Mississippi.*

The screen has yet to yield a rounded, first-rate drama on the world of jazz. After all these years, and with a gold mine of talent and material, two indigenous, American art forms—jazz and movies—continue to collide in passing. The recent opening of the new Sammy Davis, Jr., vehicle, "A Man Called Adam," revives the old question: Why?[18]

Using a discussion of *Adam* to preface a brief history of African American screen depictions, Thompson noted that, in the new film, "smoke swirls, ice cubes rattle and music throbs sweet, cool or red-hot, in a racial intermingling of black and white as right as the rain." In a section headlined, "The Awful Truth," he wrote:

In the comparative handful of previous movies delving into jazz, the Negro has generally been denied what amounts to an artistic birthright, being relegated to "guest" specialties or a line or two of "proper" dialogue. The screen's early image of the typical Negro singer, as projected in whimsical "blackface" by such entertainers as Al Jolson, patly persisted for decades.[19]

Thompson covered William Gillespie in *Blues in the Night* (1941), Dooley Wilson in *Casablanca* (1942) and Ella Fitzgerald in *Pete Kelly's Blues* (1955), then noted, "The plain truth is that the screen has hardly done better by white jazz proponents in terms of flesh-and-blood characterization than it has been by the Negro talent allotted fringe benefits,"[20] citing *Young Man with a Horn* (1951), based on Dorothy Baker's novel about Bix Beiderbecke, whose career really began after he heard Louis playing on a riverboat near Davenport, Iowa.

Decrying the Hollywood tendency to dilute jazz stories with subplots involving romance, gambling and gangsterism, Thompson concluded, "Even an ideal blueprint for a jazz movie can die aborning. Such was the case several seasons ago with 'Paris Blues'... What happened? Nothing, absolutely nothing, except a stunning earful of Duke Ellington music."[21]

"Entertainment out of *Who's Who*" was offered by the 1966 season premiere of the *Ed Sullivan Show* on Sunday, September 12.[22] In full CBS color, Red Skelton provided a dynamic opening before Louis performed "Cabaret" and the Rolling Stones rocked the screaming teenagers with two numbers. In classic variety-show fashion, the Stones were followed by Robert Goulet and a young, relatively unknown Joan Rivers, who had become a coffeehouse favorite. On November 16, Pops provided "a joy to the eye and ear" during the *Danny Kaye Show*, performing solo and in a trio with his old friend Kaye and Caterina Valente.[23]

In March 1967, Louis and the All Stars joined Gerald Sims' Orchestra for a Brunswick session in New York. Four numbers—"Day Dream," "Step Down, Brother, Next Case," "Louis' Dream" and "Northern Boulevard Blues"—were recorded.

On April 1, Bing Crosby again hosted *The Hollywood Palace*. After crooning "This Is the Life," he announced:

Tonight, we are extremely fortunate, because we have with us a most famous singer. This fella—his dulcet voice has been described as having the rich, full sound of a thousand violins, the texture of thick velvet, and the crystal purity of a mountain brook. It's not Mario del Monaco of *La Scala*, no. It's not Robert Merrill of the Metropolitan Opera Company.

"April Fool!" shouted a voice from a smiling face emerging from behind the stage curtain. "It's me!" laughed Louis as he walked out to greet Cros, giving him some skin. "Well, Pops," he told Bing. "I gotta keep workin'. You can't have bread and loaf."

The highlight of the program, this introduction prefaced a declining series of acts, including acrobats; a dreadful "hick" group called the Good Time Washboard Three; Red Buttons doing stand-up; a magician called the Electrifying Marvin Roy; Nanette Fabray enacting a ballet parody that destroyed the set; and the "famous Czechoslovakian mimes," the Black Theatre of Prague. This hodgepodge of talent contributed to one of the worst television shows ever graced by ol' Gate.

Touted as "America's Ambassador of Music to the Whole Wide World," Louis finally was allowed to sing a number, the ridiculous "Cheesecake," during which Bing crooned a little and the trombonist hammed it to the hilt. Backed by Napoleon and Barcelona, Pops improved the performance as soon as the trumpet hit his lips, then segued into a medley of "Like a Dixieland Band" and "Muskrat Ramble" with Bing.

Recalling the success of "Hello, Dolly!" Bob Thiele contacted Louis about cutting a single, a ballad titled "What a Wonderful World," which only required him to sing. Agreeing to record it on August 16, 1967, for the scale fee of $250, Louis allowed Thiele to lavish the remainder of the ABC Records budget on other musicians, including a string section conducted by Tommy Goodman. A second number, "The Sunshine of Love," also was completed, featuring Clark Terry (trumpet), Urbie Green (trombone) and Hank Jones (piano). At the same session, Pops and the All Stars (now with Joe Muranyi on clarinet) cut versions of "Hellzapoppin'" and "Cabaret."

When he heard "What a Wonderful World," ABC president Larry Newton despised it, but, rather than allow Joe Glaser to buy it, released the record sans promotion. Though it tanked in the United States, the song sold over 600,000 copies in Great Britain, causing Newton to do a quick about-face. After much profane haggling, Glaser wrenched $25,000 out of the executive to record an entire *What a Wonderful World* album the following summer.

The Kraft Music Hall welcomed Louis, and Herb Alpert and the Tijuana Brass, on September 13, 1967. On October 9 and November 1, Pops and members of the All Stars joined the Dick Jacobs Orchestra to cut seven numbers for Brunswick, including "You'll Never Walk Alone," "I Believe" and "The Gypsy in My Soul." He and the All Stars then recorded several songs for the Company Discografica Italiana on December 11 and 12. Clark Terry again played trumpet on some Satchmo sides, "Mi Va Di Cantare" and "Dimi Dimi Dimi." The following week, Terry was back with Pops and the band to cut "No Time" and "We're a Home" for United Artists.

On December 20 and 21, Louis joined director Jack Shea, host Dick Cavett and the Terry Gibbs Orchestra to film a special *Operation Entertainment* Christmas program for troops at the Ft. Hood Army Base in Killeen, Texas. Featuring his performances of "What a Wonderful World," "Hello, Dolly!" and "When It's Sleepy Time Down South," the show, executive produced by Chuck Barris, was broadcast by ABC on January 19, 1968.

On February 20, 1968, Pops recorded "Life of the Party" and "Kinda Love Song" with Dick Jacobs. He then made a final visit to *The Hollywood Palace* on the last day of the month, performing "Willkommen" and "No Time Is a Good Goodbye Time." Host Milton Berle also welcomed the Lettermen and Phyllis Diller.

The day prior to guesting on *Hollywood Palace*, Louis began a series of sessions to record an LP combining music and motion picture material, *Disney Songs the Satchmo Way*. Ten familiar songs from eight classic Walt Disney films were arranged by Maxwell Davies and produced by Tutti Camarata. Though the initial session was held in New York on February 27, the remaining two were completed at Hollywood's Sunset Sound Recorders. Clark Terry again joined the All Stars, who received additional support from a studio orchestra.

Pops opens the album with some enthusiastic scat on "Zip-a-Dee-Doo-Dah" from *Song of the South*. Particular highlights include a fine vocal and swinging solo on *Snow White and the Seven Dwarfs*' "Whistle While You Work," and a laid-back, grooving "Chim Chim Cher-Ee" from *Mary Poppins*, laden with ominous atmosphere, peerless vocals and two fat-toned, beautiful solos. The lyrics of "Chim" are perfect for Pops. "Chimee, Chimee, Chimee!" he scats, breaking himself up.

"Bibbidi-Bobbidi-Boo" is the album's silliest song, but the nonsense lyrics by Jerry Livingston, as phrased effortlessly by ol' Pops, sound similar to Satchmo scat. "But you put them together, *Gate*, and what have you got?" he asks. The listener has yet another example of Louis' ability to make any kind of material his own, even managing to add a superbly swinging solo to "The Ballad of Davy Crockett." The great film composer Leigh Harline wrote the music for *Pinocchio*'s "When You Wish Upon a Star," allowing Pops to close the album with a warm vocal, singing, "*Mama*, when you wish upon a star," and an equally engaging solo.

On March 26, Louis and the All Stars recorded three Brunswick numbers, "Sunrise, Sunset," "I Will Wait for You" and "Talk to the Animals" (from the 1967 film *Dr. Dolittle*). Two days later he was one of Johnny Carson's guests on *The Tonight Show*.

Louis also was scheduled to perform the Oscar-nominated "Talk to the Animals" on the 40th Annual Academy Awards program broadcast from the Santa Monica Civic Auditorium on April 10. He even attended a rehearsal, where he sustained an injury:

> At the Academy Awards, this guy was fixing the stage, I'm standing there when we did this bit with the animals, there wasn't nobody there but the people that were there that afternoon. Still, the guy said, "Move aside, we're going to trim them leaves behind the stage," so when they got ready to trim the trees, he snatched it, and bam, I made one of them falls, and I got up right away because I didn't want nobody to know. But, I suffered almost the two weeks I was at the Latin Quarter from that. ... And I kept turning to this bear, and I didn't figure his distance, and I had one word I had to say at a time, and every time I turned, his nose was right at my cheek. Boom. Dr. Gottlieb saw it, Lucille saw it, said, "That man poked you in the jaw," and I said, "That ain't the first time. He's been doing it all day long." I believed in it; I knew it was going to pass over.[28]

However, following the April 4 assassination of Martin Luther King in Memphis, Louis joined Sidney Poitier, Diahann Carroll and Sammy Davis, Jr., in refusing to appear on the show.

Louis, Dave Brubeck, Dizzy Gillespie and Charles Lloyd were the featured artists on "Jazz: The Intimate Art," a special episode of *Bell Telephone Hour*, broadcast in color by NBC on Friday, April 26. In an attempt to explain the different styles of popular jazz, producers Robert Drew and Mike Jackson chose these four seminal musicians, "relating each to the mainstream of jazz, but at the same time pointing out their unique contributions."[24] *Variety*'s "Mor" praised the show for not "indulging in a great deal of psychological and/or sociological speculation" and managing to be "informative without being pedantic and entertaining without being hokey." Finding Gillespie "touching" in his explanation of "the dark devils of his past that drove him to create bop," he also was particularly impressed with Pops:

> There were scenes of extraordinary poignancy in the show. Armstrong looking back with shy triumph to 1923 when Joe Oliver brought him up from New Orleans to play second cornet at the old Lincoln Gardens in Chicago only to have Satchmo dethrone him as King within a year. Armstrong in a recording studio looking for a new "Hello, Dolly!" a crackerjack studio band making much of a songwriter's tentative effort.[25]

While playing another engagement in Las Vegas, Louis and the All Stars joined Bob Thiele on July 23 and 24 to record seven more numbers for the *What a Wonderful World* album. Already in the can were "The Sunshine of Love," "Cabaret," "Hellzapoppin'" and the title track. In his original liner notes, John F. Szwed wrote:

> [T]he most striking quality of Armstrong's singing is the sense of confidence he expresses with every song. It's as if no melody or verse is not suited to his approach. Armstrong has not only saved many a fine song ... but he has also rescued lesser material from the stock pile of bad songwriting.[26]

"The top echelon was looking for another 'Hello, Dolly!,'" recalled Bob Thiele, "not a ballad with a 16-piece string section!"[27] Louis' vocal on "What a Wonderful World" is one of his finest ballad performances. The unique resonance, emotional warmth and natural rhythmic dexterity of his voice blend into two minutes of perfection as he sings lyrics representing the world view he always had advocated. And it ends with an enthusiastic yet gentle, "Oh, yeaaahhhh."

Pops proves he could still blow up a storm on the All Stars' swinging version of "Cabaret," then sings the contemporary ballad "The Home Fire," backed by an orchestra conducted by Art Butler. Louis sings and solos on "Dream a Little Dream of Me" and "Give Me Your Kisses," both recorded with the All Stars. "The Sunshine of Love," with its wall-of-sound harpsichord, strings and chorus, is a typically overproduced late 1960s pop song, but is made palatable by some Satchmo scat.

Two more Art Butler–backed ballads, "Hello Brother" and "Fantastic, That's You" (both featuring solos by Tyree Glenn), bracket the All Stars' light swinger "There Must Be a Way," during which Pops, Glenn and Joe Muranyi trade off sensitive solo licks. "I Guess I'll Get the Papers and Go Home," concluding with an ensemble version of Pops' most famous riff, is the last of the All Stars tracks, followed by the cookin' "Hellzapoppin!" cut the previous summer.

Hello, Dolly! (1969). Director Gene Kelly gave Louis star billing, though he is on screen just long enough to sing the song to Barbra Streisand.

David Merrick and Gene Kelly gave Louis star billing in *Hello, Dolly!* (1969), although he is on screen just long enough to sing the song to Barbra Streisand. Prior to shooting this two-minute-and-thirty-second number, he had seen two versions of the stage show: the mainstream ("with Carol Channing") and the all-black production ("with Pearl Bailey").[29]

As turn-of-the century New York matchmaker Dolly Levi, Streisand, at 26, is too young to be convincing in the role, and her performance is not aided by the workmanlike direction of Gene Kelly, who was unhappy with being the hired hand of producer-writer Ernest Lehman, rather than enjoying his accustomed *auteur* status. After raking in huge profits from the release of *The Sound of Music* in 1965, Twentieth Century–Fox lavished huge budgets on this film ($24 million) and two other musicals—*Star* and *Dr. Dolittle*—all of which bombed at the box office. In a cast including Michael Crawford and Tommy Tune, Walter Matthau is miscast, clumsily singing and dancing.

As he had done so often, Pops' ebullient performance (added to the screenplay following the success of the single) again rose above the material, here a pretentious and overlong film. During its initial release, audiences frequently applauded when Louis appeared. Pops recalled:

> [T]he finale ... I'm singing with Barbra Streisand in that tune, and we've got a nice little jazz thing going there. ... As I come in, then she fills in, then I have a few

innings with the horn, then that throws it back into the chorus, which works out nice.[30]

Louis and Lucille attended the Broadway premiere of the film, elegantly dressed in black tie and tails, and fur coat and white gloves, respectively. Gary Giddins— who met Louis when he played a gig at Iowa's Grinnell College the previous year —called the film "godawful."[31] Thirty-five years after its release, *Hello, Dolly!* is remembered by many solely for its teaming of Barbra and Louis.

Pops was back on the BBC in August 1968 for a special broadcast of *Louis Armstrong and His All Stars*, taped during a show at the end of his recent tour. Viewers were "startl[ed by] the sight of the new slimline Satch ... still a formidable and unique entertainer, who doesn't sing or play a note which isn't jazz."[32] Affording solo spots to Tyree Glenn and Jewell Brown, Pops performed "Indiana," "Rockin' Chair," "A Kiss to Build a Dream On" and "What a Wonderful World."

While recuperating from an illness that autumn, Louis received a get-well letter from Bing Crosby:

> Dear Pops:
>   I've been keeping tabs on your physical progress. I'm happy to hear that you're home now, and definitely on the mend, and that you're going to start to work pretty soon on firming up your chops.
>   We got to get you back into the scene, because the months that elapsed since you've been ill, have left quite a void, when we don't hear your horn regularly.
>   Of course, we've got your records— and you made some good ones just before you were ill. They're playing them now a lot, but I mean those personal appearances on TV. They're always classics.
>   I just did a couple of shows for the Hollywood Palace, and all the boys around there were inquiring about how you're coming along. [A]nd they're pleased to learn that you are improving daily.
>
>   Your old friend,
>   Bing[33]

In February 1969, during a two-month stretch in Beth Israel Hospital fighting serious heart and kidney ailments, Louis learned that Joe Glaser had suffered a stroke in the elevator of his office building. While penning more autobiographical musings, Louis mentioned his beloved "boss," referring to himself as "his boy and disciple who loved him dearly."[34] After languishing in a coma, Glaser died on June 6. Two months later, Glaser's will, filed on June 3 of the previous year, was read in the Circuit Court of Cook County, Illinois. From an estate consisting of $2 million in personal wealth, $250,000 in real estate, and a $30,000 annual income from real estate, Louis was bequeathed "all ... right, title and interest, legal and equitable, in and to all shares of stock of INTERNATIONAL MUSIC, INC ... and in the event of his death to his wife, LUCILLE."[35]

On September 1, 1969, the A.B. Corporation renewed three of Louis' contracts, securing 10 percent agent fees for all payments received under the terms outlined by the Standard AFTRA Exclusive Agency Contract, the Theatrical Motion Picture Artists' Manager Contract, and the Television Motion Picture Artists' Manager

Contract. Louis signed the agreements, mailed to him by A.B.'s Donald Gold, on August 11.

In late October, Pops flew to London to record "We Have All the Time in the World," the theme song for the James Bond film *On Her Majesty's Secret Service* (1969). Conducted by John Barry, the United Artists session, featuring Louis on vocals and trumpet, also yielded another version of "Pretty Little Missy." Back in the States two months later, he landed a lucrative deal with Midas Muffler Shops, who paid him $25,000 to sing and record voice-overs for 60-second television and radio commercials.

Johnny Carson welcomed Pops, Jerry Stiller and Anne Meara to *The Tonight Show* on February 13, 1970. On April 16, Lucille agreed to guest on *The Mike Douglas Show*, broadcast by Philadelphia's KYW-TV. Listed as a "performer" on the Mike Douglas Entertainments, Inc., contract, she was paid $265 for her appearance.[36]

In New York on May 26–29, Louis was joined by a gang of heavyweights to record the *Louis Armstrong and Friends* album, another Bob Thiele–produced project. Several of the 10 (primarily pop) songs—both classic and contemporary—focus on themes of peace and universal brotherhood, a fitting concept for what would be Pops' final LP. Forced by doctor's orders to set the trumpet aside, he focused exclusively on singing.

The album opens with the civil rights anthem "We Shall Overcome," on which Louis is supported by a chorus that includes Eddie Condon, Miles Davis, Ornette Coleman, Tony Bennett, Bobby Hackett and Ruby Braff, and an orchestra conducted by Oliver Nelson. "Oh, my, my—what a beautiful song," Pops raps. "*Our* song. I want every sister and brother up there to sing like they never sang before—for ol' Satchmo. Let's go!" With Pops and Miles on the same recording, this unusual album gets off to an interesting start.

Louis mostly raps through the somewhat funky *Midnight Cowboy* number "Everybody's Talkin' (Echoes)," then provides a monologue for a new, Latin-tinged arrangement of "What a Wonderful World," mentioning societal ills such as walls, hunger and pollution, before countering with positive vibes about giving the world a chance and the true secret of it all: love. "And man, this world would be a *gassuh*," he concludes. "That's what ol' Pops keeps sayin'."

"Boy from New Orleans" is an "autobiographical" swinger written by Ruth Roberts, William Katz and Bob Thiele. Pops sings his own story, mentioning his Fourth of July "birthday," Back o' Town, Bunk Johnson, Bing Crosby and Grace Kelly, and his European trips as Ambassador. The original take of "The Creator Has a Master Plan (Peace)" featured only Louis' singing—some of which was deemed unsatisfactory—so an additional "pygmy-inspired" vocal by flautist Leon Thomas was overdubbed onto the released version. Unfortunately, the edited version excised some of Pops' most joyous, jazzy rapping, including such beloved jive as "chops," "Gate," "wailin'" and comments on how the drummer looks like Count Basie!

"Give Peace a Chance" is the John Lennon–Paul McCartney hippie anthem, here featuring Pops and six backing vocalists. "Give peace a chance—oh, yessss!" Pops growls, scatting away; like a preacher, he adds, "Give 'em peace! Give 'em peace!"

Duke Ellington and Barney Bigard's "Mood Indigo" gets another vocal treatment by Pops, supported by Oliver Nelson's orchestra, including Frank Owens (piano), Kenny Burrell (guitar) and James Spaulding (flute). "His Father Wore Long Hair" is another Bob Thiele original (with "What a Wonderful World" writer George David Weiss and Pauline Rivelli), followed by the album's one pop standard, "My One and Only Love." The closer, "This Black Cat Has Nine Lives," is a biographical number, with Pops tagging "Meowwwww" onto the ending.

Louis Armstrong and His Friends was a noble effort by Thiele to create a project of substance for an ailing Pops. The trumpet-less Louis gave the material all he had, but his improvisatory jazz spirit only sporadically breaks through the studio production techniques. Overdubbing and editing is rampant on the record, and Thiele's decision to over-produce the songs detracts considerably from Pops' performances, particularly his pleasant improvisations on "The Creator Has a Master Plan." Louis had lived into the era of the rock concept album, the meticulously planned, performed and produced audio *product* made possible by multi-track recording and electronic processing. Very little real jazz ensemble playing could survive this approach; and if Satchmo had been able to swing much further into the 1970s, he may have been saddled with increasingly frustrating projects. But Pops, as always, probably would have grinned and scatted through it.

During the May 26 *Friends* session, Louis also recorded a Yuletide number for Philips, "Here Is My Heart for Christmas," a 6/8 country-pop song with strings. On July 1–2 he was back at NBC Studios in Burbank, rehearsing with Johnny Carson for the "Sun City Scandals" television special. Guaranteed that his taping would be completed by 8 P.M. on July 3, so he could "attend a show in his honor," Pops was paid $7,500 plus expenses, and asked to perform "Hello, Dolly!" "On the Sunny Side of the Street," "The Bare Necessities" or "Someday."

The tribute to Pops on the eve of July 4 marked what everyone assumed was his 70th birthday. As rain poured down on Hollywood, 6,700 fans surrounded the outdoor stage at the Shrine Auditorium, waiting for him to play his set. Considering this event one of the *Freedom Days: 365 Inspired Moments in Civil Rights History*, African American historian Janus Adams noted:

> As he walked on the covered stage of his birthday tribute, his fans were drenched by rain, and yet they refused to leave the amphitheater. Pops hurried through a medley to spare his guests undue exposure. It put the grin in context. Here was a man who had found his way in out of the rain and knew there were still others on the outside looking to him for joy and relief. Obliging them with everything he had to give, he made things better for a time, and somehow lessened the chill.[37]

In the July 9 issue of *Down Beat*, jazz critic Martin Williams included his tribute "For Louis Armstrong at 70":

> Of how many American artists can it truly be said that they have changed the world in their lifetimes? ... Armstrong's music has affected all our music, concert hall to barroom. ... Armstrong has shown that brass instruments, and the trumpet in particular, are capable of things that no one thought them capable of before he came along. ... We are likely to subdivide our popular music into a multitude of ill-defined categories—jazz, rock, soul—but Armstrong has affected them all. ... Our most

Salute to Louis Armstrong, filmed at the Newport Jazz Festival (July 10, 1970). Unable to play his trumpet, Pops collaborated with his friend Mahalia Jackson, who fed him gospel lyrics as he delivered them in his inimitable style.

everyday rock-and-roll groups and our simplest rhythm-and-blues bands use his ideas constantly and probably unknowingly. Wherever his music has touched down in any part of the world, it has had its effect.[38]

Another elaborate Armstrong celebration was staged by George Wein at the Newport Jazz Festival. On July 10, Pops, unable to play his trumpet, sang "Mack the Knife" to rousing applause, and collaborated with his friend Mahalia Jackson, who fed him gospel lyrics as he delivered them in his inimitable style. His performance was filmed for release in a series of 45-minute documentaries—*Anatomy of a Performance, The Antiquarians, Trumpet Players' Tribute* and *Finale*—which were then edited into a 26-minute compilation, *Salute to Louis Armstrong*. Louis provided producer-directors George Wein and Sidney J. Stiver with narration for all five.

Bob Phillips of the A.B. Corporation wrote to Lucille on July 16, regarding Louis' request that Screen Gems provide a "token payment of $10,000" for their use of 45 seconds of *Satchmo the Great* in the television series *And Beautiful*. Eventually, a compromise of $5,000 was reached.[39] On July 23, Lucille received a letter from A.B.'s Oscar Cohen, informing her that Louis' Screen Actors Guild contract would expire on August 31 and asking that he sign the new agreement, to begin on September 1, 1970.[40]

New York Governor Nelson Rockefeller wrote to Pops on July 28, thanking him for attending a recent meeting of the state's Arts and Entertainment Committee:

> Dear Louis:
>
> Again, may I say how delighted I am that you have agreed to serve as a co-chairman of the ... Committee, and that you were able to be on hand for the Committee's announcement.
>
> As I said to you at the time, one of the more positive dimensions open to government as far as I am concerned is the fostering of the arts that give pleasure and meaning to our lives.
>
> As a person who has devoted so much of your life and energies to doing just that, and to improving the quality of life in general, I am enormously pleased and grateful for your support now through the Arts and Entertainment Committee.
>
> Thank you again.
>
> Sincerely,
> Nelson[41]

During August, Pops became involved with another project geared toward current musical trends. Teaming with a Nashville-style combo in New York, he recorded 12 songs for *Louis "Country and Western" Armstrong*, again leaving the trumpet at home. The master takes included "You Can Have Her," "Wolverton Mountain," "Ramblin' Rose" and "Crazy Arms." On the final day of the month he began rehearsing for a September 4 taping of the groundbreaking *Flip Wilson Show*, to be broadcast by NBC on October 22. For his guest appearance he received his standard $7,500, $2,500 for expenses, and a residual scale for reruns.[42] After singing "Mack the Knife," he (Leroy) joined Wilson's "Rev. LeRoy" on "When the Saints Go Marching In." During a closing medley, Pops told Flip, "The devil made me do it, Daddy!"

In return for the use of his name and permission to depict him "as a boy," Louis received $2,000 from Barney's Men's Store of New York, a deal brokered by Oscar Cohen and Jack Byrne of J.B. Advertising on September 8.[43] On October 29, writer-producer-directors Finley Hunt and Phil Schultz shot eight hours of rehearsal and concert footage during Louis' London benefit performance for the National Playing Field Association of England. Bing Crosby narrated the resulting 53-minute color documentary, *The Boy from New Orleans — A Tribute to Louis Armstrong*, broadcast by CBS.

The following day, Louis signed a contract with the William Morris Agency to rehearse and tape an episode of *The Pearl Bailey Show* on November 2–5, for a broadcast in January 1971. He received $7,500, expenses, and a residual scale.[44] Pops also rehearsed and taped an *Andy Williams Show* at NBC on November 2–6, for a December 12 broadcast. Performing for both programs simultaneously ensured fine accommodations — not only did he grab another $7,500, but also an additional $2,500 for expenses and four New York–Los Angeles round-trip airline tickets.[45] In one final television guest spot that month, Pops also paid a visit to *The Johnny Cash Show* at ABC, where he got low-down with the inimitable Man in Black on Jimmie Rodgers' "Blue Yodel No. 9" — marking the only time the single greatest icons of jazz and country music stood on the same stage.

Louis donated his $15,000 fee as a yuletide gift to UNICEF after appearing on the International Paper/CBS-TV benefit *Christmas Cavalcade for Children of the World*

Actress and occasional chanteuse Marlene Dietrich always dug Satchmo's singing. They were first teamed in the homefront short *Show Business at War* in May 1943. Late in their careers they were featured in *Christmas Cavalcade for Children of the World*, a CBS television benefit for UNICEF broadcast on December 22, 1970.

on December 22. Featuring footage filmed at the United Nations, White House, Empire State Building and Statue of Liberty, this 60-minute special also featured guest performances by Julie Andrews, Leonard Bernstein, Carol Burnett, Richard Burton, Marlene Dietrich, Rex Harrison, Danny Kaye, Steve McQueen, Dean Martin, Liza Minnelli, Paul Newman and Elizabeth Taylor.

The Motion Picture and Television Section of the United States Information Service also produced a short documentary, *Louis Armstrong*, during 1970. Running eight minutes, the film includes clips from *Jam Session* (1944), the October 5, 1964, *Ed Sullivan* performance, and the March 28, 1968, *Tonight Show*.

Pops was back on television in February 1971, resurrecting "Pennies from Heaven" with Bing, and he recorded narration at his Corona home for a Continental 45-rpm release of "The Night Before Christmas." The next month he played a two-week gig at the Waldorf-Astoria, where his physician, Dr. Gary Zucker, warned him that blowing his horn could kill him. Indeed, it nearly did, as yet another heart attack sent him back to Beth Israel Hospital, where he remained for several weeks. On June 7, President Richard Nixon sent him a warm get-well letter:

> Dear Satchmo:
>   I just wanted to tell you how pleased Mrs. Nixon and I were to learn that you are out of the hospital and now well on the way to better health. I know all your friends, both here and abroad, are looking forward, as we are, to hearing the sounds of your trumpet and sharing in the happiness which you give so freely to everyone.[46]

After he moved into the White House in 1969, Nixon — an apparent admirer of jazz who hosted an all-star tribute to Duke Ellington and later coaxed Frank Sinatra out of retirement — had asked Louis to perform at the presidential home. Pops' private response was, "Fuck that shit. Why didn't they do it before? The only reason he would want me to play there now is to make some niggers happy."[47]

On July 4, television reporters and cameramen converged on Corona, where a convalescing Pops informed them that he would blow again as soon as possible. The next day he called an All Stars rehearsal.

The following morning, at 5:30 A.M. on July 6, 1971, Louis slipped into his final sleep, peacefully in his bed. The man who had revolutionized music was planning yet another gig as death claimed him. He would have blown that horn just one more time — scatted that gravelly voice just a few more nonsense syllables — but nearly 70 years of very hard living had worn him out. The cigarettes, the 40 years of marijuana use, the constant flushing of his digestive system with powerful laxatives, and the workaholic pace of life on the road, in recording studios, and on motion picture and television soundstages had converged finally to still the live sound of Satchmo; but he'd never really die, thanks to the phenomenal, unfathomable legacy he left behind.

At the Seventh Regiment Armory on Park Avenue and 66th Street, Louis lay in state as 25,000 mourners filed past to pay their final respects. His New York funeral, at which no music was played, was held at the Corona Congregational Church on July 9. Bing Crosby was one of the pallbearers. Louis' mortal remains were laid to rest at Flushing Cemetery.

A traditional jazz funeral — the kind Pops expected — was waged in New Orleans two days later. The lavish parade included a performance by the Onward Brass Band, playing some of the same numbers Louis had blown more than 50 years earlier. Lucille received over 20,000 sympathy cards and letters, including one from a Connecticut man who wrote, "My wife and I ... cried real tears when we heard of the passing of your husband, one of the greatest people who ever walked the face of the earth ... the human race has lost a fabulous human being."[48]

The African American phenomenon was still touching the souls of people, of all ages, persuasions and backgrounds, worldwide. Far away from Queens, in a small Midwestern town in Iowa, a 10-year-old boy had walked over to the neighbors' with tears in his eyes. "Louis Armstrong died," he told his friends.

Louis' passing was briefly noted by NAG in the "Final Curtain" section of its July-August 1971 newsletter. On August 28, Lil Hardin, while playing "St. Louis Blues" during a televised tribute concert at Chicago's Civic Center, fell from the piano bench to the stage, the victim of a massive heart attack. She had died while performing one of the familiar numbers she had shared with her ex-husband during the glory days of the Hot Five—ironically adding another unforgettable screen appearance to the Armstrong canon.

8

Dead Man Blues

To those who had come of age in the movement years of the 1960s, haunted and conflicted by the dapper elder grinning at the Ed Sullivan Show *camera, handkerchief in hand, Armstrong was strutting off the beat of that revolutionary time. … What this generation didn't know was the man every knowledgeable black musician called "Pops" in deference not to his age but to his extraordinary abilities with a cornet. Lost also was Armstrong's prowess as a prolific writer and diarist. As the sound of his incredible "Hot Five" horn and the volumes he had written would attest, Pops had reason to smile.*

— Janus Adams[1]

Since Louis' demise, he has been recognized as many things — among them, *the greatest* "jazz musician," "American musician," "20th-century musician" and, occasionally, "musician, *period*." Thanks to the efforts of historians, educators, filmmakers, and modern trumpet masters like Wynton Marsalis — another New Orleans musical powerhouse — his reputation has soared.

The prodigious trumpeter Nicholas Payton, also born in the Crescent City (in 1973), has recorded *Dear Louis*, a tribute album to Pops. Mentored by Marsalis, "Doc" Cheatham and Clark Terry, Payton cut his own arrangements — "with a different twist" — of such Satchmo standards as "Potato Head Blues," "Tight Like This," "Tiger Rag" and "West End Blues." He also completed the homage by singing "I'll Be Glad When You're Dead, You Rascal You" and "I'll Never Be the Same." Another New Orleanian, Dr. John, also was on hand to lay down vocals on "Mack the Knife."

In his liner notes, Payton wrote:

Some of his accomplishments … are still baffling. … When Louis Armstrong is playing, it's as if he's speaking a language to us in a manner that we've never heard before, yet it sounds so familiar. He spoke a language that was universal, one that had no boundaries — whether racial, cultural, or otherwise.[2]

Since the early 1970s, Pops has been represented in various ways on the American screen. He briefly returned in 1974, when cinema verité pioneer Robert Drew released *On the Road with Duke Ellington*, a groundbreaking documentary filmed six

On the Road with Duke Ellington (1974). Filmed during the maestro's 1968 tour, this ground-breaking documentary briefly shows a rare convergence of America's musical marvels, here sharing a warm moment backstage.

years before the maestro's death. Candid footage of Ellington in hotel rooms (eating his standard breakfast of a steak and baked potato), backstage, in airports and on the telephone—checking on the health of the beloved Billy Strayhorn, who passed away during the shooting of the film—are only a few of the highlights. One back-stage scene shows Pops dropping in to see his old friend, who tells him he should come on stage and blow. When Louis declines, explaining that he has bought a ticket and "*always* comes backstage," Duke gently kisses him twice on each cheek.

Made by Charles Fries Productions in 1975, the television movie *Louis Armstrong, Chicago Style* was broadcast by ABC on January 25, 1976. Loosely based on Louis' stint in Hollywood in 1931 and his subsequent return to Chicago before hiding out in Europe three years later, James Lee's teleplay whitewashes most of the facts, but Ben Vereen's impersonation of Pops is occasionally warm and charming.

Vereen, at 29, was nearly the same age as Louis when the actual events took place; and though he is more conventionally handsome than Pops, his mannerisms, particularly his recreations of certain facial expressions and the trademark Louis laugh, look convincing in some of director Lee Philips' medium and long shots. Prior to shooting this movie, Vereen had appeared in only three feature films and two TV series, and was a little more than a year away from his powerful breakout performance as "Chicken" George Moore in ABC's miniseries adaptation of Alex Haley's *Roots* (1977).

Chicago Style opens with a montage of tinsel town sites, culminating with an image of a "nightclub on the outskirts of Hollywood, 1931" as "When the Saints Go Marching In" fills the soundtrack. After Louis turns down his manager, "Red" Cleveland's (Red Buttons), bid to return to Chicago, the mob-connected hustler frames him on a marijuana rap. In a fictionalization of the true incident, Louis is shown standing in the street during a break, conversing with an acquaintance who is found with shuzzit in his pocket. This is only one of the liberties James Lee takes with Pops' behavior and actions.

On the way back to Chicago, when some shotgun-totin' rednecks surround Cleveland's car at a gas station, Louis, sitting in the back, goes into a "coon" act, pretending that he is the driver. One of the rubes refers to Louis as a "Nigra," a common Southern pronunciation of Negro.

Back in the Windy City, Louis visits "Alma" (Margaret Avery), who is working as a maid. During an argument with her, Vereen displays his best acting in the film, subtly capturing some of Louis' downbeat facial expressions. He also drops in on Lil (Janet MacLachlan), who is giving piano lessons while practicing to be a classical performer.

The remainder of the teleplay focuses on a fictionalized version of Louis' problems with local gangsters, and ends with him telling Cleveland, "I'm not your nigger anymore" and sailing for Europe with Alma. Scenes set at the Okeh recording studio (including one featuring Jack Teagarden [Jerry Fogel]) add a bit of realism, but sequences in a Chicago jail (where Louis serenades his cellmates with "When It's Sleepy Time Down South") and on the streets, where inept tough guys chase his taxi as silent-movie style music plays on the soundtrack, are ridiculous. Also, having several characters refer to Louis as "Satch," and his use of songs not heard until later in his career, are two of the script's more glaring anachronisms.

Benny Carter provided special music, but Vereen's unconvincing miming of Pops' trumpet playing mars the overall effect. (He does, however, do a respectable job with the vocals.) Though Leonard Feather acted as "technical adviser," whatever facts he contributed played second chair to the television-movie tendency to champion melodramatic sensationalism.

Traditional jazz aficionado (and part-time musician) Woody Allen included a reference to Pops in his 1979 masterpiece *Manhattan*. In a scene late in the film, while tape-recording a list of reasons for living, would-be novelist Isaac Davis (Allen) mentions, "Groucho Marx, Willie Mays, Louis Armstrong's recording of 'Potato Head Blues'... Marlon Brando, Frank Sinatra..."

An early scene in Francis Ford Coppola's *The Cotton Club* (1984) features white cornet man Dixie Dwyer (Richard Gere) jamming with a black counterpart. Observing the performance, Dutch Schultz (James Remar) praises Dixie's blowing, claiming his competitor "boosted those riffs from King Oliver." Late in the film, Gere — who did his own cornet work — blows Louis' "Big Butter and Egg Man" as Dwyer becomes the first ofay musician to play Owney Madden's (Bob Hoskins) joint.

In 1988 the success of the film *Good Morning, Vietnam*, starring Robin Williams as an Armed Services Radio disc jockey, finally made "What a Wonderful World" a major hit in the United States. A new generation was introduced to Louis; and though the song gave young listeners no idea of Pops' true significance, they gained some inkling of the positive philosophy permeating his music.

Louis was briefly impersonated by actor Byron Stripling in the March 13, 1993, "Mystery of the Blues" episode of the television series *The Young Indiana Jones Chronicles*, which starred Sean Patrick Flanery as the young Jones, Harrison Ford as the elder Indy, Frederick Weller as Eliot Ness, Nicholas Turturro as Al Capone, Keith David as King Oliver and Jeffrey Wright as Sidney Bechet. Set in 1920s Chicago, the program was a disjointed hodgepodge of jazz and Jones', Ness', Ernest Hemingway's and Ben Hecht's attempts to deal with gangland corruption. The scenes involving Bechet's efforts to teach Jones how to "jazz on soprano sax" were entertaining. At one point, Pops, leaving the bandstand to speak to Bechet, was introduced to Indiana. A stuporous Bix Beiderbecke also appeared in a few sequences.

Archival footage of Pops also has appeared in a number of excellent documentaries aired on PBS and released on video, including Gary Giddins' *Satchmo* (1986), Charlotte Zwerin's *Ella Fitzgerald: Something to Live For* (1999), Ken Burns' 10-episode series *Jazz* (2000), and *Sinatra: The Classic Duets* (2003).

In September 2002, Dave and Iola Brubeck restaged *The Real Ambassadors* at the Monterey Jazz Festival. Combining images of the 1962 Louis on a large video screen with the current Brubeck band and guest singers and musicians, the composers proved the timelessness of their work. Discussing the title song, Iola said, "The lyric, 'I represent the policies of the government, but the government doesn't represent some of the policies I'm for'—of course, that really applied to nowadays."[3] Dave added:

> They went to this blackout, and Louis was on this big screen, and said, "Now I leave you. Now I go. Now I think you know as much as ol' Satchmo." And that's the way it ended. And that audience paused, and then broke into huge applause. I think it was better than the original, to be back there, like that.[4]

Just as the ultimate biography of Louis Armstrong remains to be written, filmmakers will always have the opportunity to adapt the phenomenal, true life of Satchmo for the silver screen. During 2004, *Saint Louis Blues*, a new feature film starring Sean Patrick Thomas as Pops, was announced.) Does his classic story possess the elements for commercial Hollywood success in an era of disposable, online, instant gratification culture?

Well, Daddy, just try beatin' out one of the good ol' good ones...

Louis Armstrong helped open the door for performers of color, both as a musician and a film and television actor. Even if he was only infrequently outspoken in a rhetorical way, he consistently used his unparalleled talent to contribute a unique, profound African American influence to popular *and* "high" culture in the United States.

Could an "Uncle Tom" accomplish what Louis Armstrong inadvertently, *naturally* achieved?

> I think that I have always done *great* things about uplifting my race ... but *wasn't appreciated*. I am *just* a musician and *still* remember the time, as an *American* Citizen I *Spoke* up for my people during a *big* Integration *riot* in Little Rock (Remem-

ber?). ... I was trying to stop that unnecessary *Head whippings* at the time — that's all ... do *things* the *right* way. *Force* and *brute strength* is *no* good.... There isn't anything nicer to know and feel deep down in your heart that you have something — *anything*— that you've *worked* and *strived* for honestly — rather than to do a *lot* of *ungodly things* to get it. *Yes*— you *appreciate* it better. ... I may not profess to be the *smartest Negro* in the *world*. But I was *taught* to *Respect* a *man* or *woman* until they *prove* in my *estimation* that they *don't* deserve it. I came up the *Hard* way, the same as lots of people. But I always *help* the *other* fellow if *there's Anyways* possible.[5]

Swing it, Gate...

Appendix A:
Swingin' Satchmo Sides

Many of the recordings discussed in this book are available on the following compact-disc editions. They are highly recommended listening.

Bessie Smith: The Complete Recordings, Volume 2. Columbia Legacy (C2K 47471), 1991.

The Complete Ella Fitzgerald and Louis Armstrong on Verve. Verve (314 537 284-2), 1997.

Disney Songs the Satchmo Way. Walt Disney Records (60920-7), 1996.

Louis Armstrong: Louis and the Good Book. Verve Master Edition (314 549 593-2), 2001.

Louis Armstrong: Portrait of the Artist as a Young Man, 1923–1934. Columbia Legacy (C4K 85670), 1994.

Louis Armstrong: Satchmo Serenades. Verve by Request (314 543 792-2), 2000.

Louis Armstrong: The California Concerts. Decca Jazz (GRD-4-613), 1992.

Louis Armstrong: The Complete Hot Five and Hot Seven Recordings. Columbia Legacy (C4K 63527), 2000.

Louis Armstrong: The Complete RCA Victor Recordings. BMG Classics (09026-68682-2), 1997.

Louis Armstrong: The Great Chicago Concert, 1956, Complete. Columbia Legacy (C2K 65119), 1997.

Louis Armstrong and Duke Ellington: The Great Summit/Complete Sessions/Deluxe Edition. Roulette Jazz/Blue Note/EMI (7243 5 24547 2 2/3), 2000.

Louis Armstrong and His Band, Dave Brubeck, Lambert, Hendricks and Ross, and Carmen McRae: The Real Ambassadors. Columbia (CK 65119), 1994.

Louis Armstrong Meets Oscar Peterson. Verve Master Edition (314 539 060-2), 1997.

Louis Armstrong Plays W. C. Handy. Columbia Legacy (CK 64925), 1997.

Satch Plays Fats: A Tribute to the Immortal Fats Waller by Louis Armstrong and His All Stars. Columbia Legacy (CK 64927), 2000.

Satchmo the Great. Columbia Legacy (CK 62170), 2000.

Appendix B:
Satchmo in Hollywood

Louis Armstrong appears in the following Hollywood feature films.

Ex-Flame (November 19, 1930)

Liberty Productions; Running Time: 74 minutes

    Credits *Director:* Victor Halperin; *Screenplay:* George Draney; *Story:* Victor Halperin; Based on the novel *East Lynne* by Mrs. Henry Wood; *Director of Photography:* Ernest Miller; *Editor:* W. Donn Hayes; *Art Director:* Charles Cadwallader; *Production Manager:* George Bertholon; *Assistant Director:* J. Gordon Cooper; *Sound:* Harold Hobson; *Dialogue Director:* Herbert Farjeon; *Supervisors:* Edward Halperin, M.H. Hoffman.

    Cast Neil Hamilton (Sir Carlisle Austin), Marian Nixon (Lady Catherine), Judith Barrie (Barbara Lacey), Norman Kerry (Beaumont Winthrop), "Snub" Pollard (Boggins), Roland Drew (Umberto), Jose Bohr (Argentinian), Joan Standing (Kilmer), Cornelius Keefe (Keith), May Beatty (Lady Harriett), Lorimer Johnston (Colonel Lacey), Joseph North (Wilkins), Charles Crockett (Parson), Billy Haggerty (Master Stuart Austin), Louis Armstrong (Himself).

Pennies from Heaven (November 16, 1936)

Major Pictures/Columbia Pictures; Running Time: 80 minutes

    Credits *Director:* Norman Z. McLeod; *Producer:* Emanuel Cohen; *Screenplay:* Jo Swerling; Based on the novel *The Peacock's Feather* by Katherine Leslie Moore; *Director of Photography:* Robert Pittack; *Editor:* John Rawlins; *Musical Score:* Johnny Burke, Harold Jackson, Arthur Johnston, Louis Silvers, William Grant Still; *Musical Arranger:* John Scott Trotter; *Musical Director:* George E. Stoll; *Art Director:* Stephen Gooson; *Sound:* Glenn Rominger; *Makeup:* Robert J. Schiffer; *Production Manager:* Earl Rettig.

    Cast Bing Crosby (Larry Poole), Madge Evans (Susan), Edith Fellows (Patsy), Donald Meek (Gramps), John Gallaudet (Hart), Louis Armstrong (Henry), Tom Dugan (Crowbar), Nana Bryant (Miss Howard), Charles C. Wilson (Warden), Harry Tyler (Concessionaire), William Stack (Carmichael), Tom Ricketts (Briggs), Lionel Hampton (Himself), Stanley Andrews, Stanley Blystone, George Chandler, Arthur Hoyt, Nydia Westman.

Artists and Models (August 13, 1937)

Paramount Pictures; Running Time: 97 minutes

    Credits *Director:* Raoul Walsh; *Producer:* Lewis E. Gensler; *Screenplay:* Walter DeLeon, Francis Martin; *Story Adaptation:* Eve Greene, Harlan Ware; *Story:* Sig Herzig, Eugene

Thackrey; *Director of Photography:* Victor Milner; *Editor:* Ellsworth Hoagland; *Songs:* Frederick Hollander, Burton Lane, Ralph Rainger, Leo Robin, Ted Koehler; *Musical Arranger:* Victor Young.

Cast Jack Benny (Mac Brewster), Ida Lupino (Paula Sewell), Richard Arlen (Alan Townsend), Gail Patrick (Cynthia), Ben Blue (Jupiter Pluvius), Judy Canova (Toots), Cecil Cunningham (Stella), Donald Meek (Doctor Zimmer), Hedda Hopper (Mrs. Townsend), Martha Raye (Specialty), Andre Kostelanetz (Orchestra Conductor), Louis Armstrong (Bandleader), Russell Patterson, Peter Arno, McClelland Barclay, Arthur William Brown, Rube Goldberg, John LaGatta (Artists), Anne Canova, Zeke Canova, Connee Boswell (Specialties), Sandra Storme (Model), Jerry Bergen (Bartender), Alan Birmingham (Craig Sheldon), Virginia Brissac (Seamstress), Edward Earle (Flunky), Madelon Gray (Marjorie), Dell Henderson (Lord), Howard C. Hickman (Mr. Currie), Harry C. Johnson, Henry Johnson (Jugglers), Kathryn Kay (Lois), Pat Moran (Tumbler), David Newell (Romeo), Harvey Porier (Sharpshooter), Mary Shepherd, Gloria Wheeden (Water Waltzers), Jack Starry, Jack Trevor (Cycling Stars), Jane Weir (Miss Gordon), Ethel Clayton, Virginia Dabney, Harry Hayden, Dorothy McHugh.

Every Day's a Holiday (December 18, 1937)

Paramount Pictures; Running Time: 80 minutes

Credits *Director:* A. Edward Sutherland; *Producer:* Emanuel Cohen; *Screenplay:* Mae West; *Director of Photography:* Karl Struss; *Editor:* Ray Curtiss; *Musical Score:* Leo Shuken; *Original Songs:* Hoagy Carmichael, Sam Coslow; *Musical Director:* George E. Stoll; *Art Director:* Wiard Ihnen; *Production Manager:* Joseph H. Nadel; *Sound:* Hugo Grenzbach; *Costume Designer:* Sciaparelli; *Wardrobe:* Basia Bassett; *Assistant Director:* Earl Rettig; *Special Effects:* Gordon Jennings; *Choreographer:* Leroy Prinz.

Cast Mae West (Peaches O'Day), Edmund Lowe (Captain McCarey), Charles Butterworth (Larmadou Graves), Charles

Winninger (Van Reighle Van Pelter Van Doon), Walter Catlett (Nifty Bailey), Lloyd Nolan (John Quade), Louis Armstrong (Himself), George Rector (Himself), Herman Bing (Fritz Krausmeyer), Roger Imhof (Trigger Mike), Chester Conklin (Cabby), Lucien Prival (Danny the Dip), Adrian Morris, Francis McDonald, John Indrisano (Henchmen), Irving Bacon, Allen Rogers, John "Skins" Miller, Otto Fries (Quartet Members), Ron Moody, Johnny Arthur, William Austin (Bits), Edgar Dearing (Cop), Dick Elliot (Bar Patron), Weldon Heyburn, Ferdinand Munier, Herbert Rawlinson (Guests at Party), James C. Morton (Bartender), Maude Eburne.

Doctor Rhythm (May 18, 1938)

Major Pictures; Paramount Pictures; Running Time: 80 minutes

Credits *Director:* Frank Tuttle; *Producer:* Emanuel Cohen; *Associate Producer:* Herbert Polesie; *Screenplay:* Richard Connell, Jo Swerling; Based on the story "The Badge of Policeman O'Roon" by O. Henry; *Directors of Photography:* Floyd Crosby, Charles Lang; *Original Songs:* Johnny Burke, James V. Monaco; *Orchestrator:* John Scott Trotter; *Musical Director:* George E. Stoll; *Costume Designer:* Ernest Dryden; *Assistant Director:* Russell Matthews; *Choreographer:* Jack Crosby.

Cast Bing Crosby (Bill Remson), William Austin (Mr. Martingale), Mary Carlisle (Judy Marlow), Dolores Casey (Nurse), Gino Corrado (Cazzata), Laura Hope Crews (Mrs. Minerva Twombling), Rufe Davis (Al), Andy Devine (Officer Lawrence O'Roon), Frank Elliott (Lorelei's Butler), Desmond Gallagher (Stage Manager), John Hamilton (Inspector Bryce), Sterling Holloway (Luke), Fred Keating (Chris LeRoy), Beatrice Lillie (Mrs. Lorelei Dodge-Blodgett), Alphonse Martell (Marvelous Marko), Allen Mathews (LeRoy's Henchman), Harold Minjir (Mr. Coldwater), Charles R. Moore (Chauffeur), Franklin Pangborn (Mr. Stenchfield), Emory Parnell (Sgt. Olson), Harry Stubbs (Police Captain), Henry Wadsworth (Otis Eaton), Louis Armstrong (Trumpet Player/scenes cut from released version).

Going Places (December 31, 1938)

Cosmopolitan Productions/First National Pictures/Warner Bros. Pictures; Running Time: 84 minutes

    Credits   *Director:* Ray Enright; *Producer:* Hal B. Wallis; *Screenplay:* Sid Herzig, Maurice Leo, Jerry Wald; Based on the play *The Hottentot* by William Collier, Sr., and Victor Mapes; *Director of Photography:* Arthur L. Todd; *Editor:* Clarence Kolster; *Original Songs:* Harry Warren, Johnny Mercer; *Musical Score:* Sam Perry, Heinz Roemheld; *Musical Arrangers:* Ray Heindorf, Frank Perkins; *Musical Director:* Leo F. Forbstein; *Art Director:* Hugh Reticker; *Costume Designer:* Howard Shoup; *Sound:* Robert B. Lee; *Director:* Hugh Cummings.

    Cast   Dick Powell (Peter Mason/Peter Randall), Anita Louise (Ellen Parker), Allen Jenkins (Droopy), Ronald Reagan (Jack Withering), Walter Catlett (Franklin Dexter), Harold Huber (Maxie Miller), Larry Williams (Frank Kendall), Thurston Hall (Colonel Harvey ["Poopsie"] Withering), Minna Gombell (Cora Withering), Joyce Compton (Joan ["Mousey"], the Colonel's Mistress), Walter Warwick (Walter Frome), John Ridgely (Mayfield Inn Desk Clerk), Joe Cunningham (Hotel Night Clerk), Eddie ("Rochester") Anderson (George, a Groom), George Reed (Sam, Withering's Butler), Louis Armstrong (Gabriel ["Gabe"], the Black Hostler), Maxine Sullivan (Withering's Singing Maid), Brooks Benedict (Man at Party), Ward Bond (Clarence, a Policeman), Eddy Chandler (Second Policeman), Jesse Graves (Butler at Party), John Harron (Man at Party), Ferdinand Munier (Man on Electric Horse), Jack Richardson, Leo White (Men at Track), Janet Shaw, Rosella Towne (Young Ladies at Party).

Cabin in the Sky (April 9, 1943)

Metro-Goldwyn-Mayer Pictures; Running Time: 98 minutes

    Credits   *Directors:* Vincente Minnelli, Busby Berkeley; *Producer:* Arthur Freed; *Associate Producer:* Albert Lewis; *Screenplay:* Joseph Schrank, Marc Connelly; Based on the play by Lynn Root; *Director of Photography:* Sidney Wagner; *Editor:* Harold F. Kress;

Musical Score and Original Songs: Harold Arlen, E. Y. Harburg, Vernon Duke, John Latouche, Duke Ellington; *Musical Arranger:* Hall Johnson; *Musical Adapter:* Roger Edens; *Orchestrator:* George Bassman; *Musical Director:* George E. Stoll; *Art Directors:* Cedric Gibbons, Leonid Vasian; *Set Decorators:* Hugh Hunt, Edwin B. Willis; *Costume Designers:* Irene, Howard Shoup, Gile Steele; *Assistant Director:* Al Shenberg; *Sound:* Douglas Shearer, William Steinkamp.

    Cast   Ethel Waters (Petunia Jackson), Eddie "Rochester" Anderson (Joseph ["Little Joe"] Jackson), Lena Horne (Georgia Brown), Louis Armstrong (the Trumpeter), Rex Ingram (Lucifer, Jr./Lucius), Kenneth Spencer (the General/Rev. Greene), John "Bubbles" Sublett (Domino Johnson), Oscar Polk (the Deacon/Fleetfoot), Mantan Moreland (First Idea Man), Willie Best (Second Idea Man), Fletcher "Moke" Rivers (Third Idea Man), Leon "Poke" James (Fourth Idea Man), Ford "Buck" Washington Lee (Cablegram Messenger), Bill Bailey (Bill), Butterfly McQueen (Lily), Ruby Dandridge (Mrs. Kelso), Nicodemus Stewart (Dude), Ernest Whitman (Jim Henry), Duke Ellington and His Orchestra (Themselves), Archie Savage, Carmencita Romero (Dancers), Aranelle Harris.

Jam Session (April 13, 1944)

Columbia Pictures Corporation; Running Time: 77 minutes

    Credits   *Director:* Charles T. Barton; *Producer:* Irving Briskin; *Screenplay:* Manuel Seff; *Story:* Patterson McNutt; *Director of Photography:* L. William O'Connell; *Editor:* Richard Fantl; *Original Songs:* Jule Styne, Sammy Cahn; *Musical Director:* Morris Stoloff; *Art Directors:* Lionel Banks, Paul Murphy; *Set Decorator:* William Kiernan; *Assistant Director:* Earl Bellamy; *Sound:* Paul Holly.

    Cast   Ann Miller (Terry Baxter), Jess Barker (George Carter Haven), Louis Armstrong (Himself), Charlie Barnet (Himself), Charles D. Brown (Raymond Stuart), Pauline Drake (Evelyn), George Eldredge (Bell Berkley), Jan Garber (Himself), Glen Gray (Himself), Eddie Kane (Lloyd Marley),

Charles La Torre (Coletti), Anna Loos (Nene Canendish), Clarence Muse (Henry), Teddy Powell (Himself), Alvino Rey (Himself), Renie Riano (Miss Tobin), Ray Walker (Fred Wylie), Nan Wynn (Herself), Hank Bell (Driver), Eddie Bruce (Guide), Marguerite Campbell (Girl Jitterbug), George M. Carleton (Cop), Vernon Dent (Butler), John Dilson (Man), Jay Eaton (Designer), Margaret Fealy (Old Lady), Allen Fox (Cutter), Joanne Frank (Girl), Terry Frost (Assistant Director), Charles Haefeli (Rostler), Eddie Hall (Smart Young Man), Marilyn Johnson (Stenographer), Tom Kingston (Sound Engineer), Ethan Laidlaw (Jackson), Eddie Laughton (2nd Assistant Director), Nelson Leigh (Blake), Ted Mapes (Guard), George McKay (Policeman), Bill Shawn (Dancer), Ben Taggart (Willie), J. Reilly Thompson (Boy Jitterbug), Victor Travers (Actor), John Tyrrell (Actor), Robert Williams (Taxi Driver), Constance Worth (Miss Dooley), Paul Zaramba (Rip).

Atlantic City (August 3, 1944)

Republic Pictures Corporation; Running Time: 87 minutes

Credits *Director:* Ray McCarey; *Associate Producer:* Albert J. Cohen; *Screenplay:* George Carleton Brown; *Story:* Arthur Caesar; *Director of Photography:* John Alton; *Editor:* Richard Van Enger; *Songs:* Clarence Gaskill, Walter Scharf, Ernie Erdman; *Musical Director:* Alfred Newman; *Orchestrator:* Joseph Dubin; *Art Director:* Russell Kimball; *Costume Designer:* Adele; *Assistant Director:* R. G. Spingsteen; *Sound:* Richard Tyler; *Choreography:* Seymour Felix, Dave Gould.

Cast Constance Moore (Marilyn Whitaker), Stanley Brown (Brad Taylor), Charley Grapewin (Jake Taylor), Jerry Colonna (Professor), Paul Whiteman (Himself), Louis Armstrong (Himself), Robert Castaine (Carter Graham), Adele Mara (Barmaid), Pierre Watkin (Senator), Harry Tyler (Sherman), Stanley Andrews (Rogers), Donald Kerr (Oaks), Charles Williams (Man on the Street), Daisy Lee Mothershed (the Maid), Ford Washington Lee (Buck), John William Sublett (Bubbles), Dorothy Dandridge (Herself), Belle Baker (Himself), Joe Frisco

(Himself), Jack Kenney (Ed Gallagher), Gus Van (Himself), Charles Marsh (Joe Schenk), Louise Franklin, Al Shean, Alma Carroll, Bill Chaney, Pat Hogan, Stubby Kruger, Wilbur Mack, Howard M. Mitchell, Barbara Slater, Larry Steers, Robert Thom, Ricki Van Dusen.

Pillow to Post (May 17, 1945)

Warner Bros. Pictures; Running Time: 92 minutes

Credits *Director:* Vincent Sherman; *Producer:* Alex Gottlieb; *Executive Producer:* Jack L. Warner; *Screenplay:* Charles Hoffman; Based on the play *Pillar to Post* by Rose Simon Kohn; *Director of Photography:* Wesley Anderson; *Editor:* Alan Crosland, Jr.; *Musical Score:* Frederick Hollander; *Musical Director:* Leo F. Forbstein; *Orchestrator:* Jerome Moross; *Art Director:* Leo Kuter; *Set Decorator:* Walter F. Tilford; *Costume Designer:* Milo Anderson; *Makeup:* Perc Westmore; *Assistant Director:* Jesse Hibbs; *Sound:* Charles Lang; *Special Effects:* Warren Lynch; *Montage:* James Leicester.

Cast Ida Lupino (Jean Howard), Sydney Greenstreet (Colonel Michael Otley), William Prince (Lieutenant Don Mallory), Stuart Erwin (Captain Jack Ross), Johnny Mitchell (Earl ["Slim"] Clark), Ruth Donnelly (Mrs. Grace Wingate), Barbara Brown (Mrs. Kate Otley), Frank Orth (Clayfield Taxi Driver), Regina Wallace (Mrs. Mallory), Willie Best (Lucille, Colonial Auto Court Porter), Louis Armstrong (Himself), Marie Blake (Wilbur's Mother), Bob Crosby (Clarence Wilson), Dorothy Dandridge (Herself), Ferdinand Munier (Traveling Salesman), Leah Baird (Archie's Mother), Robert Blake (Wilbur), Eddy Chandler (Oil Engineer), Joyce Compton (Army Wife on Bus), William Conrad (First Motorcycle Cop), Joe Devlin, James Flavin (Army Sergeants in Jeep), Diane Dorsay (Mildred Henning), William Haade (Big Joe, Loolie's Date), Paul Harvey (J. R. Howard), Victoria Horne (Mildred), Carol Hughes (Loolie Fisher), Charles Jordan (Cpl. Chuck Corliss), Anna Loos (Mrs. Pudge Corliss), Don McGuire (Sailor at Bus Station), Johnny Miles (Marine at the Tavern), Sue Moore (Doris Wilson), Anne O'Neal (USO Housing Clerk), Bunny Sunshine (Celeste Corliss), Grady Sutton (Alex, Coast Oil Flunky), Lelah Tyler (Jerry Martin).

New Orleans (April 18, 1947)

Majestic Productions, Inc.; United Artists Pictures; Running Time: 90 minutes

Credits *Director:* Arthur Lubin; *Producer:* Jules Levy; *Associate Producer:* Herbert J. Biberman; *Screenplay:* Elliot Paul, Dick Irving Hyland; *Director of Photography:* Lucien Andriot; *Supervising Editor:* Bernard V. Burton; *Original Music:* Louis Alter, Bob Carleton, Edgar De Lange, Cliff Dixon, Nat W. Finston, Woody Herman; *Non-Original Music:* Frederic Chopin, W. C. Handy, Nick La Rocca, Meade "Lux" Lewis, Paul Mares, Walter Melrose, Theo A. Metz, "Jelly Roll" Morton, Joe Oliver, the Original Dixieland Jazz Band, Leon Rappolo, Spencer Williams; *Art Director:* Rudi Feld; *Costume Designer:* Teddi Barri; *Makeup:* Karl Herlinger; *Hair Stylist:* Peggy Shannon; *Production Manager:* Joseph H. Nadel; *Assistant Director:* Maurie Suess; *Music Editor:* Leon Klatzkin; *Sound:* Roy Meadows, Elmer Raguse; *Special Effects:* Nick Carmona; *Wardrobe:* Elmer Ellsworth; *Musical Director:* Nat W. Finston.

Cast Arturo de Cordova (Nick Duquesne), Dorothy Patrick (Miralee Smith), Marjorie Lord (Grace Voiselle), Irene Rich (Mrs. Rutledge Smith), John Alexander (Colonel McArdle), Richard Hageman (Henry Ferber), Jack Lambert (Biff Lewis), Bert Conway (Tommy Lake), Joan Blair (Columnist Constance Vigil), Louis Armstrong (Himself), Billie Holiday (Endie, Miralee's Maid), Woody Herman and His Orchestra (Themselves), Zutty Singleton, Barney Bigard, Kid Ory, Bud Scott, George "Red" Callender, Charlie Beal, Meade "Lux" Lewis (Themselves), Brooks Benedict (Croupier), Papa Mutt Carey, Lucky Thompson (Themselves), Pat Flaherty (Moving Man), Jesse Graves (Smith's Butler), Josh Hamilton (Police Chief), Ralph Montgomery, Bert Stevens (Men in Audience), Jeffrey Sayre (Drunk), Shelley Winters (Miss Holmbright), John Canady, Sammy Davis, Jr., Bill Walker, Ethel Waters.

A Song Is Born (October 19, 1948)

Goldwyn Pictures Corporation; RKO-Radio Pictures; Running Time: 113 minutes

Credits *Director:* Howard Hawks; *Producer:* Samuel Goldwyn; *Screenplay:* Harry Tugend; *Director of Photography:* Gregg Toland; *Editor:* Daniel Mandell; *Musical Directors:* Hugo Friedhofer, Emil Newman; *Songs:* Don Raye, Gene de Paul; *Orchestrator:* Sonny Burke; *Art Directors:* Perry Ferguson, George Jenkins; *Set Decorator:* Julia Heron; *Costume Designer:* Irene Sharaff; *Makeup:* Robert Stephanoff; *Hair Stylist:* Marie Clark; *Production Manager:* Raoul Pagel; *Executive in Charge of Production:* Leon Fromkess; *Assistant Director:* Joseph Boyle; *Sound:* Fred Lau; *Special Effects:* Harry Redmond, Jr.; *Special Photographic Effects:* John P. Fulton; *Script Supervisors:* Sam Freedle, Anita Speer; *Grip:* Ralph Hoge; *Still Photographer:* Hal McAlpin; *Camera Operator:* Hal Shipham.

Cast Danny Kaye (Professor Hobart Frisbee); Virginia Mayo (Honey Swanson); Benny Goodman (Professor Magenbruch), Tommy Dorsey, Louis Armstrong, Lionel Hampton, Charlie Barnet, Mel Powell (Themselves), Hugh Herbert (Professor Twingle), Steve Cochran (Tony Crow), J. Edward Bromberg (Dr. Elfini), Felix Bressart (Professor Gerkikoff), Ludwig Stossel (Professor Traumer), O. Z. Whitehead (Professor Oddly), Esther Dale (Miss Bragg), Mary Field (Miss Totten), Howland Chamberlain (Mr. Settler), Paul Langton (Joe), Sidney Blackmer (Adams), Ben Weldon (Monte), Ben Chasen (Ben), Peter Virgo (Louis), Harry Babasin (Bass), Louie Bellson (Drums), Alton Hendrickson (Guitar), Page Cavanaugh and His Trio (Themselves), Lane Chandler (Policeman at Inn), Joseph Crehan (District Attorney), Joe Devlin (Gangster), Robert Dudley (Justice of the Peace), Jack Gargan (Stenotypist), Norma Gentner (Girl with Samba Kings), Sue George (Cigarette Girl), Barbara Hamilton, Jill Meredith, Janie New (Women at Dorsey Club), Ford Washington Lee (Buck), John William Sublett (Bubbles), the Samba Kings (Themselves), Will Lee (Waiter), Gene Morgan, Jeffrey Sayre (Men at Dorsey Club), Pat Walker (Photographer at Dorsey Club), Karen X.

Gaylord, William Haade, John Impolito, Marjorie Jackson, Martha Montgomery, Diana Mumby, Milicent Patrick, Irene Vernon, Alice Wallace, Don Wilmot.

The Strip (August 1951)

Metro-Goldwyn-Mayer Pictures; Running Time: 85 minutes

Credits *Director:* Laszlo Kardos; *Producer:* Joe Pasternak; *Screenplay:* Allen Rivkin; *Director of Photography:* Robert Surtees; *Editor:* Albert Akst; *Songs:* Dorothy Fields, Haven Gillespie, Robert MacGimsey, Jimmy McHugh, Harry Ruby, Spencer Williams, Oscar Hammerstein II, Bert Kalmar; *Musical Director:* George E. Stoll; *Orchestrators:* Leo Arnaud, Pete Rugolo; *Art Directors:* Cedric Gibbons, Leonid Vasian; *Set Decorators:* Alfred E. Spencer, Edwin B. Willis; *Costume Designer:* Helen Rose; *Makeup:* William Tuttle; *Hair Stylist:* Sidney Guilaroff; *Assistant Director:* Sid Sidman; *Sound:* Douglas Shearer; *Special Effects:* A. Arnold Gillespie, Warren Newcombe; *Montage:* Peter Ballbusch; *Choreographer:* Nick Castle.

Cast Mickey Rooney (Stanley Maxton), Sally Forrest (Jane Tafford), William Demarest (Fluff), James Craig (Delwyn ["Sonny"] Johnson), Kay Brown (Edna), Louis Armstrong (Himself), Tommy Rettig (Artie Ardrey), Tom Powers (Lieutenant Detective Bonnabel), Jonathan Cott (Behr), Tommy Farrell (Boynton), Myrna Dell (Paulette Ardrey), Jacqueline Fontaine (Frieda), Vic Damone, Monica Lewis (Themselves), Joel Allen, Carl Saxe (Boyfriends), Bette Arlen, Carmen Clifford, Ward Ellis, Betty Jane Howarth, Bert May, Jack Regas, Leo Scott, Dee Turnell (Dancers), Dolores Castle (Girl), Fred Datig, Jr., Dan Foster, Jeff Richards (G. I. Ward Patients), Bert Davidson, Tay Dunn, Sam Finn, Sig Frohlich, Larry Hudson, Donald Kerr, Roger Moore (Bookie Joint Clerks), Lester Dorr (Police Surgeon), Robert Foulk, Robert Malcolm, John McGuire, Russell Trent (Deputies), Alex Frazer (Horticulturist), Fred Graham (Detective), Don Haggerty, William Tannen (Arresting Detective), Sherry Hall, John Maxwell, Tom Quinn (V.A. Doctors), Earl "Fatha" Hines (Himself), Earle Hodgkins (Steve), Frank Hyers

(Police Sergeant), Joyce Jameson (Girl), Art Lewis (Sam), Samuel London (Fred), Jeffrey Sayre (Tenant in Hallway), Helen Spring (Elderly Secretary), Jack Teagarden (Himself), Wilson Wood (Patron).

Here Comes the Groom (September 20, 1951)

Paramount Pictures; Running Time: 113 minutes

Credits *Director and Producer:* Frank Capra; *Associate Producer:* Irving Asher; *Screenplay:* Virginia Van Upp, Liam O'Brien, Myles Connolly; *Director of Photography:* George Barnes; *Editor:* Ellsworth Hoagland; *Original Songs:* Hoagy Carmichael, Jay Livingston, Ray Evans, Johnny Mercer; *Musical Director:* Joseph J. Lilley; *Art Directors:* Earl Hedrick, Hal Pereira; *Set Decorator:* Emile Kuri; *Costume Designer:* Edith Head; *Makeup:* Wally Westmore; *Hair Stylist:* Geraldine Cole; *Assistant Director:* Arthur S. Black; *Sound:* John Cope, Harry Mills; *Special Effects:* Gordon Jennings, Paul Lerpae; *Process Photographer:* Farciot Edouart; *Choreographer:* Charles O'Curran; *Orchestrator:* Van Cleave.

Cast Bing Crosby (Pete Garvey), Jane Wyman (Emmadel Jones), Alexis Smith (Winifred Stanley), Franchot Tone (Wilbur Stanley), James Barton (Pa Jones), Robert Keith (George Degnan), Jacques Gencel (Bobby), Beverly Washburn (Suzi), Connie Gilchrist (Ma Jones), Walter Catlett (Mr. McGonigle), Alan Reed (Walter Godfrey), Minna Gombell (Mrs. Godfrey), Howard Freeman (Governor), Maidel Turner (Aunt Abby), H. B. Warner (Uncle Elihu), Nicholas Joy (Uncle Prentiss), Ian Wolfe (Uncle Adam), Ellen Corby (Mrs. McGonigle), James Burke (Policeman), Irving Bacon (Baines), Ted Thorpe (Paul Pittit), Art Baker (Radio Announcer), Anna Maria Alberghetti (Theresa), Chris Appel (Marcel), Louis Armstrong, Frank Fontaine, Phil Harris, Cass Daley, Dorothy Lamour (Themselves), John F. Bray (Bit), Adeline De Walt Reynolds (Aunt Amy), Neil Dodd (Priest), Don Dunning, Franklin Farnum, Julia Faye, Frank Hagney (Passengers on Airplane), Charles Evans (Mayor), James Finlayson (Bit),

Charles Halton (Cusick), Howard Joslin (Newsreel Cameraman), Donald Kerr (Neighbor), Charles Lane (FBI Agent Burchard), Michele Lange (French Matron), J. Farrell MacDonald (Man), Walter McGrail (Newsreel Director), Odette Myrtil (Gray Lady), Ed Randolph, Charles Sullivan (Photographers), Kasey Rogers (Maid), Almira Sessions (Passenger on Airplane), Carl "Alfalfa" Switzer (Messenger).

Glory Alley (June 6, 1952)

Metro-Goldwyn-Mayer Pictures; Running Time: 79 minutes

   Credits   *Director:* Raoul Walsh; *Producer:* Nicholas Nayfack; *Screenplay and Story:* Art Cohn; *Director of Photography:* William Daniels; *Editor:* Gene Ruggiero; *Musical Director:* George E. Stoll; *Orchestrator:* Pete Rugolo; *Art Directors:* Malcolm Brown, Cedric Gibbons; *Set Decorators:* F. Keogh Gleason, Edwin B. Willis; *Costume Designer:* Helen Rose; *Assistant Director:* Joel Freeman; *Sound:* Douglas Shearer; *Special Effects:* A. Arnold Gillespie; *Montage:* Peter Ballbusch; *Choreographer:* Charles O'Curran.

   Cast   Ralph Meeker (Socks Barbarrosa), Leslie Caron (Angela), Kurt Kasznar (the Judge), Gilbert Roland (Peppi Donnato), John McIntire (Gabe Jordan), Louis Armstrong (Shadow Johnson), Jack Teagarden (Himself), Dan Seymour (Sal Nichols), Larry Gates (Dr. Robert Ardley), Pat Goldin (Jabber), John Indrisano (Spider, the Bartender), Mickey Little (Domingo), Dick Simmons (Dan), Pat Valentino (Terry Waulker), David McMahon (Frank, the Policeman), George Garver (Newsboy Addams), King Donovan (Telephone Technician), Kit Guard, Charles Sullivan (Raffle Ticket Buyers), Court Shepard (Himself), Charles Sherlock (Bar Patron).

The Glenn Miller Story (December 10, 1953)

Universal International Pictures; Running Time: 115 minutes

   Credits   *Director:* Anthony Mann; *Producer:* Aaron Rosenberg; *Screenplay:* Valentine Davies, Oscar Brodney; *Director of Photography:* William Daniels; *Editor:* Russell

Schoengarth; *Music and Songs:* Glenn Miller, Julian Dash, Edgar De Lange, Buddy Feyne, Joe Garland, Jerry Gray, W. C. Handy, Erskine Hawkins, Henry Mancini, Andy Razaf, Carl Sigman, Spencer Williams, Enric Madriguera; *Musical Director:* Joseph Gershenson; *Music Adaptor:* Henry Mancini; *Art Directors:* Alexander Golitzen, Bernard Herzbrun; *Set Decorators:* Russell A. Gausman, Julia Heron; *Costume Desinger:* Jay Morley, Jr.; *Makeup:* Bud Westmore; *Hair Stylist:* Joan St. Oegger; *Assistant Director:* John Sherwood; *Sound:* Leslie I. Carey, Joe Lapis; *Technicolor Consultant:* William Fritzsche; *Technical Adviser:* Chummy MacGregor; *Choreographer:* Kenny Williams.

   Cast   James Stewart (Glenn Miller), June Allyson (Helen Berger/Miller), Henry Morgan (Chummy MacGregor), Charles Drake (Don Haynes), George Tobias (Si Schribman), Barton MacLane (General Hap Arnold), Sig Ruman (W. Krantz), Irving Bacon (Mr. Miller), James Bell (Mr. Burger), Kathleen Lockhart (Mrs. Miller), Katherine Warren (Mrs. Burger), Frances Langford, Louis Armstrong, Ben Pollack, Gene Krupa, Barney Bigard, Trummy Young, Marty Napoleon, Arvell Shaw, Cozy Cole, Babe Russin, Alan Copeland, Bob Hamlin, Paula Kelly, Bill Lee, Thurl Ravenscroft, Max Smith, Paul Tanner, the Modernaires (Themselves), Cicily Carter, Lisa Gaye (Bobbysoxers), William Challee (Dispatch Desk Sergeant), Kevin Corcoran (Steve Miller, age 4), Hal K. Dawson (Used Car Salesman), Bonnie Eddy (Irene Miller), Phil Garris (Joe Becker), Ruth Hampton (Young Singer), Harry Harvey (Doctor), Roland Jones (Waiter), Dayton Lummis (Colonel Spaulding), Leo Mostovoy (Dr. Schillinger), Damian O'Flynn (Colonel Baker), Steve Pendleton (Lieutenant Colonel Bassell), Davis Roberts (Steve Miller, age 2), Marion Ross (Polly Haynes), Dick Ryan (Auto Garage Repairman), Anthony Sydes (Herbert Miller), Deborah Sydes (Joanie Dee Miller), Nino Tempo (Wilber Schwartz), Carl Vernell (Musician Technician), Carleton Young (Adjutant General).

High Society (July 17, 1956)

Bing Crosby Productions/Sol C. Siegal Productions; Metro-Goldwyn-Mayer Pictures; Running Time: 107 minutes

Credits *Director:* Charles Walters; *Producer:* Sol C. Siegal; *Screenplay:* John Patrick; Based on the play *The Philadelphia Story* by Philip Barry; *Director of Photography:* Paul Vogel; *Editor:* Ralph E. Winters; *Musical Score:* Cole Porter, Saul Chaplin; *Musical Director:* Johnny Green; *Orchestrators:* Nelson Riddle, Conrad Salinger; *Art Directors:* Cedric Gibbons, Hans Peters; *Set Decorators:* Richard Pefferle, Edwin B. Willis; *Costume Designer:* Helen Rose; *Makeup:* William Tuttle; *Hair Stylist:* Sidney Guilaroff; *Production Manager:* Dave Friedman; *Assistant Directors:* Arvid Griffen, Hank Moonjean; *Sound:* Wesley C. Miller; *Special Effects:* A. Arnold Gillespie; *Technicolor Consultant:* Charles K. Hagedon; *Choreographer:* Charles Walters.

Cast Bing Crosby (C. K. Dexter-Haven), Grace Kelly (Tracy Samantha Lord), Frank Sinatra (Mike Connor), Celeste Holm (Liz Imbrie), John Lund (George Kittredge), Louis Calhern (Uncle Willie), Sidney Blackmer (Seth Lord), Louis Armstrong (Himself), Margalo Gillmore (Mrs. Seth Lord), Lydia Reed (Caroline Lord), Gordon Richards (Dexter-Haven's Butler), Richard Garrick (Edward, Lord's Butler), Hugh Boswell (the Parson), Billy Kyle, Trummy Young, Edmond Hall, Arvell Shaw, Barrett Deems (Themselves), Paul Keast (Editor), Richard Keene (Mac), Ruth Lee, Helen Spring (Jazz Festival Organizers), Reginald Simpson (Lawrence, Uncle Willie's Butler).

The Beat Generation (July 3, 1959) [aka *This Rebel Age*]

Albert Zugsmith Productions; Metro-Goldwyn-Mayer Pictures; Running Time: 95 minutes

Credits *Director:* Charles F. Haas; *Producer:* Albert Zugsmith; *Screenplay:* Lewis Meltzer; *Director of Photography:* Walter Castle; *Editor:* Ben Lewis; *Costume Designer:* Kitty Mager; *Choreographer:* Hamil Petroff.

Cast Steve Cochran (Detective Sergeant Dave Culloran), Mamie Van Doren (Georgia Altera), Ray Danton (Stan Hess), Fay Spain (Francee Culloran), Margaret Hayes (Joyce Freenfield), Jackie Coogan (Jake

Baron), Louis Armstrong (Himself), Cathy Crosby (the Singer), Ray Anthony (Harry Altera), Dick Contino (Singing Beatnik), "Slapsie" Maxie Rosenbloom (Wrestling Beatnik), Regina Gelfan (Dancer), Charles Chaplin, Jr. (Lover Boy), Billy Daniels (Dr. Elcott), Irish McCalla (Marie Baron), James Mitchum (Art Jester), Vampira (Poetess), Anne Anderson, Bobi Byrnes, Paul Cavanagh, Gerry Cohen, Phyllis Douglas, Fred Engelberg, Diane Fredrick, Melody Gale, Paul Genge, Norman Grabowski, Fred Hansen, Shirle Haven, Darlene Hendricks, Carolyn Hughes, Nancy Kay, John Melfi, Sid Melton, Gil Perkins, Hamil Petroff, Kathy Reed, William Schallert, Cole Simpson, Phyllis Standish, Guy Stockwell, Larri Thomas, Renata Vanni, William Vaughn, Camille Williams.

The Five Pennies (August 1959)

Dena Productions; Paramount Pictures; Running Time: 117 minutes

Credits *Director and Screenplay:* Melville Shavelson; *Producer:* Jack Rose; *Director of Photography:* Daniel L. Fapp; *Editor:* Frank P. Keller; *Musical Score:* Thornton W. Allen, Sylvia Fine, M. W. Sheafe, Leith Stevens; *Art Directors:* Tambi Larsen, Hal Pereira; *Set Decorators:* Sam Comer, Grace Gregory; *Costume Designer:* Edith Head; *Makeup:* Wally Westmore; *Hair Stylist:* Nellie Manley; *Assistant Director:* Richard Caffey; *Sound:* Charles Grenzbach, John Wilkinson; *Special Photographic Effects:* John P. Fulton; *Choreographer:* Earl Barton; *Process Photographer:* Farciot Edouart; *Assistant to Producer:* Sylvia Fine; *Second Unit Photographer:* W. Wallace Kelley; *Production Assistant:* Hal C. Kern; *Technicolor Consultant:* Richard Mueller; *Trumpet Solos:* "Red" Nichols; *Vocalist for Barbara Bel Geddes:* Eileen Wilson.

Cast Danny Kaye (Loring ["Red"] Nichols), Barbara Bel Geddes (Bobbie Meredith), Louis Armstrong (Himself), Harry Guardino (Tony Valani), Bob Crosby (Wil Paradise), Bobby Troup (Arthur Schutt), Susan Gordon (Dorothy Nichols, age 6 to 8), Tuesday Weld (Dorothy Nichols, age 12 to 14), Ray Anthony (Jimmy Dorsey), Shelly Manne (Dave Tough), Ray Daley (Glenn

Miller), Valerie Allen (Tommye Eden), Bob Hope (Guest), Blanche Sweet (Headmistress of School), Henry Beau.

Paris Blues (September 27, 1961)

Diane Productions; United Artists Pictures; Running Time: 98 minutes

Credits *Director:* Martin Ritt; *Producer:* Sam Shaw; *Executive Producers:* George Glass, Walter Seltzer; *Associate Producer:* Lee Katz; *Screenplay:* Walter Bernstein, Irene Kamp, Jack Sher; *Adaptation:* Lulla Rosenfeld; Based on the novel by Harold Flender; *Director of Photography:* Christian Matras; *Editor:* Roger Dwyre; *Musical Score:* Duke Ellington, Billy Strayhorn; *Songs:* Irving Mills, Mitchell Parish; *Art Director:* Alexandre Trauner; *Unit Manager:* Christian Ferry; Sound *Editor:* Jack Fitzstephens.

Cast Paul Newman (Ram Bowen), Joanne Woodward (Lillian Corning), Sidney Poitier (Eddie Cook), Louis Armstrong ("Wild Man" Moore), Diahann Carroll (Connie Lampson), Barbara Laage (Marie Seoul), Andre Luguet (Rene Bernard), Marie Versini (Nicole), Moustache (Drummer), Aaron Bridgers (Pianist), Guy Peterson (Bass Player), Serge Reggiani (Michel Duvigne), Roger Blin (Gypsy Guitarist/Junkie), Helene Dieudonne (Pusher), Niko (Ricardo), Maria Velasco (Pianist), Francoise Brion, Dominique Zardi.

When the Boys Meet the Girls (October 10, 1965)

Four-Leaf Productions; Metro-Goldwyn-Mayer Pictures; Running Time: 97 minutes

Credits *Director:* Alvin Ganzer; *Producer:* Sam Katzman; *Screenplay:* Robert E. Kent; Based on the play *Girl Crazy* by Guy Bolton, Jack McGowan; *Director of Photography:* Paul C. Vogel; *Editor:* Ben Lewis; *Songs:* George Gershwin, Ira Gershwin, Johnny Farrow, Fred Karger; *Art Directors:* George W. Davis, Eddie Imazu; *Set Decorators:* F. Keogh Gleason, Henry Grace; *Makeup:* William Tuttle; *Hair Stylist:* Sidney Guilaroff; *Unit Production Managers:* Robert Stone, Bobby Stone; *Assistant Production Manager:* Lindsley Parsons, Jr.; *Assistant Director:* Eddie

Saeta; *Sound:* Franklin Milton; *Special Visual Effects:* J. McMillan Johnson, Carroll L. Shepphird; *Choreographer:* Earl Barton; *Conductor:* Fred Karger; *Assistant to Producer:* Jerome Katzman; *Camera Operator:* James V. King; *Assistant Camera:* George Hollister.

Cast Connie Francis (Ginger Gray), Harve Presnell (Danny Churchill), Herman's Hermits (Themselves), Louis Armstrong (Himself), Sam the Sham (Himself), the Pharoahs (Themselves), Liberace (Himself), Sue Anne Langdon (Tess Rawley), Fred Clark (Bill Denning), Frank Faylen (Phin Gray), Joby Baker (Sam), Hortense Petra (Kate), Stanley Adams (Lank), Romo Vincent (Pete), Susan Holloway (Delilah), Russell Collins (Mr. Stokes), Pepper Davis (Himself), William Quinn (Dean of Colby), Tony Reese (Himself), Buster Bailey, Danny Barcelona, Buddy Catlett, Tyree Glenn, Billy Kyle (Themselves).

A Man Called Adam (August 3, 1966)

Trace-Mark Productions; Embassy Pictures Corporation; Running Time: 99 minutes

Credits *Director:* Leo Penn; *Producers:* Ike Jones, James Waters; *Executive Producer:* Joseph E. Levine; *Associate Producer:* Merrill S. Brody; *Screenplay:* Lester Pine, Tina Rome; *Director of Photography:* Jack Priestley; *Editor:* Carl Lerner; *Musical Score:* Benny Carter, Kim Gannon; *Trumpet Solos:* Nat Adderley; *Art Director:* Charles Rosen; *Set Decorator:* Sam Robert; *Production Manager:* Merrill S. Brody; *Assistant Camera:* Vinnie Gerardo.

Cast Sammy Davis, Jr. (Adam Johnson), Ossie Davis (Nelson Davis), Cicely Tyson (Claudia Ferguson), Louis Armstrong (Willie ["Sweet Daddy"] Ferguson), Frank Sinatra, Jr. (Vincent), Peter Lawford (Manny), Mel Torme (Himself), Lola Falana (Theo), Jeanette Du Bois (Martha), Johnny Brown (Les), George Rhodes (Leroy), Michael Silva (George), Michael Lipton (Bobby Gales), Benny Carter, Kai Winding (Themselves), Ted Beniades, Brunetta Bernstein, Don Crabtree, Elvera Davis, Morris D. Erby, Michael V. Gazzo, Roy Glenn, Will Hussing, George Kirby, Carl Lee, Gerald S. O'Loughlin, Matt Russo, Kenneth Tobey, Lester Wilson, Morgan Freeman.

Hello, Dolly! (December 16, 1969)
Chenault Productions, Inc.; 20th Century–Fox Pictures; Running Time: 146 minutes

Credits   *Director:* Gene Kelly; *Producer:* Ernest Lehman; *Associate Producer:* Roger Edens; *Screenplay:* Ernest Lehman, Michael Stewart; Based on the play *The Matchmaker* by Thornton Wilder; *Director of Photography:* Harry Stradling, Sr.; *Editor:* William Reynolds; *Musical Score:* Lennie Hayton, Jerry Herman, Lionel Newman; *Casting:* Alixe Gordon, Joe Scully; *Production Designer:* John DeCuir; *Art Directors:* Herman A. Blumenthal, John DeCuir, Jack Martin Smith; *Set Decorators:* Raphael Bretton, George James Hopkins, Walter M. Scott; *Costume Designer:* Irene Sharaff; *Makeup:* Daniel C. Striepeke, Edwin Butterworth, Richard Hamilton; *Hair Stylist:* Edith Lindon; *Production Manager:* Francisco Day; *Assistant Directors:* Paul Helmick, Robert J. Koster; *Music Editors:* Robert Mayer, Kenneth Wannberg; *Music Mixer:* Douglas O. Williams; *Sound:* Jack Solomon, Murray Spivack, Vinton Vernon; *Construction Foreman:* Lloyd R. Apperson; *Set Construction:* Greg C. Jensen; *Set Dresser:* Craig Binkley; *Special Photographic Effects:* L. B. Abbott, Art Cruikshank; *Stunts:* Jeannie Epper, Stephanie Epper; *Orchestrators:* Warren Barker, Frank Comstock, Don Costa, Alexander Courage, Lennie Hayton, Philip J. Lang, Joseph Lipman, Herbert W. Spencer; *Conductors:* Lennie Hayton, Lionel Newman; *Dialogue Coach:* George Eckert; *Still Photographer:* Ernest Haas; *Choreographer:* Michael Kidd; *Assistant Choreographer:* Shelah Hackett;

Dance Arranger: Marvin Laird; *Wardrobe Supervisor:* Courtney Haslam; *Wardrobe:* Barbara Westerland, Ed Wynigear; *Script Supervisor:* Mollie Kent; *Choral Arranger:* Jack Latimer; *Unit Publicist:* Patricia Newcomb; *Assistant Camera:* Dave Friedman; *Production Assistant:* Randee Lynne Jensen.

Cast   Barbara Streisand (Dolly Levi), Walter Matthau (Horace Vandergelder), Michael Crawford (Cornelius Hackl), Marianne McAndrew (Irene Malloy), Danny Lockin (Barnaby Tucker), E. J. Peaker (Minnie Fay), Joyce Ames (Emmagarde Vandergelder), Tommy Tune (Ambrose Kemper), Judy Knaiz (Gussie Granger/Ernestina Simple), David Hurst (Rudolph Reisenweber), Fritz Feld (Fritz, German Waiter), Richard Collier (Joe, Vandergelder's Barber), J. Pat O'Malley (Policeman in Park), Louis Armstrong (Louis, Orchestra Leader), John Command (Dancing Waiter), Scatman Crothers (Mr. Jones), Jim Hutchison (Stanley), Patrick O'Moore (Officer Gogarty), Eddie Quillan (Mr. Cassidy), Tucker Smith, Shep Houghton (Dancers), Cecil Lester Stout III (Drummerboy), Lisa Todd (Rhine Maiden), David Ahdar, Sam Edwards, Ken Hooker, Jerry James, Charles Lampkin, Guy Wilkerson (Laborers), William "Billy" Benedict (News Vendor), James Chandler (Sullivan, Ticket Seller), Jimmy Cross (Drunk), Morgan Farley (Workman), Jessie Garnier (Woman with groceries), Bern Hoffman (Harmonia Gardens Patron), Hubie Kerns (Keystone Kop), Russ Kimbrough (Onlooker), Michael Mark (Pushcart Man), Judith Woodbury (Dinner Guest), Allyce Beasley, Linda Dano.

Appendix C:
A Glossary of Satchmo-speak

Louis Armstrong used the following slang or "jive" terms, many of which were invented or made popular by him. They are used throughout this book.

beat the chops: play music

blow: to play a horn/wind instrument

bread: money

break: a brief improvisational solo

cat: a man; a jazz musician or admirer

chick: a girl or young woman

chippie: a prostitute

chops: mouth; lips

conk: head

cool: very good; excellent; very accepting or tolerant

crib: a person's home; a prostitute's dwelling

Daddy: respectful term for a hip male

dig: to understand; to appreciate

dipper: a person with a large mouth; short for "dippermouth"

dough: money

gage: marijuana

gasser: something terrific

Gate: proper title for a jazz musician

gig: jazz jam session or job

gut bucket: very earthy style of music

hep or **hip:** wise; cognizant; enlightened

homes: a person from the home town or neighborhood; home boy

hot: traditional New Orleans–style jazz music

jam: to play collectively improvised music

jive: jargon; deceptive slang; doubletalk

junkie: drug addict, particularly a user of opium or heroin

lick: musical phrase, usually improvised by a soloist

Mama: respectful term for a hip female

man: a respectful greeting used by African American musicians to counter the racist term "boy"

mezz: a particularly good type of marijuana, named after "Mezz" Mezzrow

muggles: marijuana

ofay: a white person; pig Latin for "foe"

pad: prostitute's place of business; residence

Pops: patriarch of jazz

riff: musical phrase or passage

scat: a form of singing using nonsense syllables

shuzzit: marijuana (literally, "shit")

solid: excellent; trustworthy

swing: a form of jazz with a pulsing beat originated by Armstrong

take it: sing or play a solo

tonk: honky-tonk

Notes

Preface

1. *Satchmo the Great* compact disc booklet (Columbia Legacy CK 62170, 2000), p. 18.
2. Robert O'Meally, "Louis Armstrong and Jazz Biography," part three of "Writing Lives: The Past and Future of Biography" (New York: Center for the Humanities, The City University of New York, 10 April 2003).
3. *Louis Armstrong: The Complete Hot Five and Hot Seven Recordings* compact disc book (Columbia Legacy C4K 63527, 2000), p. 54.
4. Ernest Morrison, Interviewed by Scott Allen Nollen (St. Paul, Minnesota, July 1988).
5. Ernest Morrison interview.
6. *Louis Armstrong: The Complete Hot Five and Hot Seven Recordings*, p. 55.

Introduction

1. David H. Ostwald, "Louis Armstrong, Civil Rights Pioneer," *New York Times* (3 August 1991).
2. Gary Giddins, *Satchmo: The Genius of Louis Armstrong* (New York: Da Capo Press, 2001), pp. 6–7.
3. Donald Bogle, *Toms, Coons, Mulattoes, Mammies and Bucks: An Interpretive History of Blacks in American Films*, Fourth Edition (New York: Continuum International Publishing Group, 2001), p. 75.
4. Donald Bogle, pp. xxi–xxii.
5. Donald Bogle, p. 75.
6. Donald Bogle, p. 41.
7. Krin Gabbard, in Joshua Berrett, ed., *The Louis Armstrong Companion* (New York: Schirmer Books, 1999), p. 204.

8. Donald Bogle, p. 179.
9. Rudi Blesch, *Shining Trumpets: A History of Jazz* (New York: DaCapo Press, 1988), pp. 257–258.
10. Dizzy Gillespie, in *The Louis Armstrong Companion*, p. 157.
11. Duke Ellington, *Music Is My Mistress* (New York: Da Capo Press, 1973), pp. 235–236.

Chapter 1

1. Mezz Mezzrow and Bernard Wolfe, *Really the Blues* (New York: Kensington Publishing Corporation, 2001), p. 125.
2. Louis Armstrong, *Satchmo: My Life in New Orleans* (New York: Da Capo Press, 1986), p. 9.
3. Louis Armstrong, *Satchmo*, p. 10.
4. Louis Armstrong, *Satchmo*, p. 14.
5. Louis Armstrong, *Louis Armstrong in His Own Words*, ed. Thomas Brothers (New York: Oxford University Press, 1999), p. 18.
6. Louis Armstrong, *Louis Armstrong in His Own Words*, pp. 16–17.
7. Louis Armstrong, in *The Louis Armstrong Companion*, p. 9.
8. Louis Armstrong, *The Louis Armstrong Companion*, p. 8.
9. Louis Armstrong, *The Louis Armstrong Companion*, p. 9.
10. Louis Armstrong, *Satchmo*, pp. 34–35.
11. Louis Armstrong, *Satchmo*, p. 40.
12. Louis Armstrong, *Satchmo*, pp. 93–94.
13. Louis Armstrong, *Satchmo*, p. 75.
14. Louis Armstrong, *Satchmo*, p. 76.
15. Louis Armstrong, *Swing That Music* (New York: Da Capo Press, 1993), p. 34.
16. Louis Armstrong, *Satchmo*, p. 150.

17. Louis Armstrong, *Satchmo*, p. 151.

18. Louis Armstrong, *Satchmo*, p. 179.

19. Louis Armstrong, *Swing That Music*, p. 36.

20. Louis Armstrong, *Satchmo*, p. 182.

21. Louis Armstrong, *Swing That Music*, p. 68.

22. Louis Armstrong, *Swing That Music*, p. 69.

23. Louis Armstrong, *Swing That Music*, p. 69.

24. Louis Armstrong, *Louis Armstrong in His Own Words*, p. 50.

25. Louis Armstrong, *Swing That Music*, p. 70.

26. Louis Armstrong, *Louis Armstrong in His Own Words*, p. 86.

27. Louis Armstrong, *Swing That Music*, p. 71.

28. Louis Armstrong, *Louis Armstrong in His Own Words*, pp. 40–41.

29. Louis Armstrong, *Swing That Music*, p. 76.

30. Louis Armstrong, *Swing That Music*, p. 77.

31. Mezz Mezzrow, p. 221.

32. Louis Armstrong, *Swing That Music*, p. 81.

33. A.H. Lawrence, *Duke Ellington and His World* (New York: Routledge, 2001), p. 253.

34. Louis Armstrong, *Swing That Music*, p. 82.

35. Louis Armstrong, *Swing That Music*, p. 85.

36. *Louis Armstrong: The Complete Hot Five and Hot Seven Recordings*, p. 55.

37. Louis Armstrong, *Louis Armstrong in His Own Words*, p. 96.

38. Laurence Bergreen, *Louis Armstrong: An Extravagant Life* (New York: Doubleday Dell Publishing Corporation, Inc., 1997), p. 278.

39. Laurence Bergreen, p. 278.

40. Louis Armstrong, *Louis Armstrong in His Own Words*, p. 114.

41. Gary Giddins, *Satchmo*, pp. 75–76.

42. Louis Armstrong, *Swing That Music*, pp. 91–92.

43. Mezz Mezzrow, p. 211.

Chapter 2

1. Ken Murray, "Louis, Bix Had Most Influence on Der Bingle," *Down Beat* (14 July 1950).

2. Donald Bogle, p. 34.

3. Gary Giddins, *Bing Crosby: A Pocketful of Dreams: The Early Years, 1903–1940* (New York: Little, Brown and Company, 2001), p. 234.

4. Gary Giddins, *Bing Crosby*, p. 234.

5. *Variety*, January 1931.

6. Mezz Mezzrow, pp. 138–139.

7. Mezz Mezzrow, pp. 234–235.

8. Gary Giddins, *Satchmo*, pp. 9–10.

9. Donald Bogle, pp. 36–37.

10. Mezz Mezzrow, p. 236.

11. Louis Armstrong, *Louis Armstrong in His Own Words*, p. 21.

12. Louis Armstrong, *Swing That Music*, pp. 99–100.

13. Louis Armstrong, *Swing That Music*, p. 100.

14. Laurence Bergreen, p. 355.

15. Laurence Bergreen, p. 365.

16. Louis Armstrong, Letter to unknown recipient, undated, regarding Bing Crosby (Louis Armstrong House and Archives, Queens College/CUNY, Letters-3, 118).

17. Krin Gabbard, in Joshua Berrett, ed., *The Louis Armstrong Companion*, p. 214.

18. *Variety*, 16 December 1936.

19. Minutes, Negro Actors Guild of America, Inc., New York, 27 September 1936 (Schomburg Center for Research in Black Culture, New York Public Library, NAG, box 3, 3/1).

20. Minutes, NAG, 27 September 1936.

21. Certificate of Incorporation, Negro Actors Guild of America, Inc., State of New York, City of New York, County of New York, 1 October 1936 (Schomburg Center for Research in Black Culture, New York Public Library, NAG, box 1, 1/1).

22. Constitution and By-Laws, Negro Actors Guild of America, Inc., New York, 1936 (Schomburg Center for Research in Black Culture, New York Public Library, NAG, box 1, 1/2).

23. Constitution and By-Laws, NAG, 1936.

24. Dan Morgenstern, in Louis Armstrong, *Swing That Music*, p. vii.

25. Rudy Valee, in Louis Armstrong, *Swing That Music*, p. xvi.

26. *Variety* (April 1937).

27. Krin Gabbard, in *The Louis Armstrong Companion*, p. 231.

28. *Variety*, 4 August 1937.

29. Laurence Bergreen, p. 383.

30. Louis Armstrong, Letter to Leonard Feather, Atlanta, Georgia, 10 October 1941 (Louis Armstrong House and Archives, Queens College/CUNY, Letters-3, 119).

31. *Variety* (22 December 1937).

32. Louis Armstrong, Interviewed by Jack Hirshberg, 20th Century–Fox Film Corporation, Transcription, May 1968 (Louis Armstrong House and Archives, Queens College/CUNY, Letters-1, 1/27).

33. *Doctor Rhythm* pressbook (Paramount Pictures Corporation, 1938).

34. Frank S. Nugent, *New York Times* (19 May 1938), p. 25.

35. *Variety*, 11 January 1939.

36. Fredi Washington, Letter to the members of the Executive Board, Negro Actors Guild of America, Inc., 7 October 1938 (Schomburg Center for Research in Black Culture, New York Public Library, NAG, box 3, 3/2).

37. Bill Robinson, Negro Actors Guild of America, Inc., Letter to Frank C. Walker (December 1938).

38. Louis Armstrong, *Louis Armstrong in His Own Words*, p.186.

39. Leonard Feather, *Down Beat* (December 1939).

40. Louis Armstrong, Letter to Madeleine Berard, San Francisco, 25 November 1946 (Louis Armstrong House and Archives, Queens College/CUNY, Letters).

41. Louis Armstrong, Letter to Leonard Feather, Atlanta, Georgia, 18 September 1941 (Louis Armstrong House and Archives, Queens College/CUNY, Letters-3, 119).

Chapter 3

1. *Satchmo the Great* compact disc booklet, p. 18.

2. Laurence Bergreen, p. 414.

3. B.B. King, with David Ritz. *Blues All Around Me: The Autobiography of B.B. King* (New York: Avon Books, 1996), pp. 65–66.

4. Brooks Atkinson, *New York Times* (26 October 1940).

5. *Cabin in the Sky* compact disc booklet (Rhino Movie Music/Turner Entertainment Company R272245, 1996), pp. 7–8.

6. *Cabin in the Sky* compact disc booklet, pp. 9–10.

7. *Cabin in the Sky* compact disc booklet, p. 11.

8. Ethel Waters, with Charles Samuels, *His Eye is on the Sparrow, An Autobiography* (New York: Doubleday and Company, Inc., 1951), p. 258.

9. *Variety* (10 February 1943).

10. *Variety* (10 February 1943).

11. *New York Times* (28 May 1943), p. 19.

12. Donald Bogle, p. 129.

13. Donald Bogle, pp. 81–82.

14. Donald Bogle, p. 118.

15. Louis Armstrong, untitled document, c. 1970 (Louis Armstrong House and Archives, Queens College/CUNY).

16. *Variety*, 1944.

17. *New York Times* (3 May 1944), p. 25.

18. *Variety* (July 1944).

19. *Variety* (July 1944).

20. *Cabin in the Sky* photograph, inscribed to Lucille Armstrong from Louis Armstrong (Louis Armstrong House and Archives, Queens College/CUNY, PHOTO-2 No. 29 818).

21. Louis Armstrong, Letter to Frances Church, Opelousas, Louisiana, 10 March 1946 (Louis Armstrong House and Archives, Queens College/CUNY, Letters).

22. Louis Armstrong, Letter to Frances Church.

23. Stuart Nicholson, *Billie Holiday* (Boston: Northeastern University Press, 1995), p. 153.

24. Louis Armstrong, *Satchmo*, p. 96.

25. Louis Armstrong, Letter to Madeleine Berard, San Francisco, 25 November 1946 (Louis Armstrong House and Archives, Queens College/CUNY, Letters).

26. Louis Armstrong, Letter to *Melody Maker*, 21 December 1946 (Louis Armstrong House and Archives, Queens College/CUNY, Letters-3, 119).

27. Billie Holiday and William Dufty, *Lady Sings the Blues* (New York: Doubleday and Company, 1956), pp. 119–120.

28. Billie Holiday, pp. 121–122.

29. *Variety* (30 April 1947).

30. *New York Times* (20 June 1947), p. 25.

31. Mezz Mezzrow.

Chapter 4

1. Louis Armstrong, Interview (May 1968).

2. Howard Hawks, in Joseph McBride, *Hawks on Hawks* (Berkeley: University of California Press, 1982), pp. 87–88.

3. Howard Hawks, p. 87.

4. Howard Hawks, pp. 85–86.

5. Gerald Mast, *Howard Hawks: Storyteller* (New York: Oxford University Press, 1982), p. 353.

6. George Hoefer, in *The Louis Armstrong Companion*, p. 160.

7. *Metronome* (March 1948).

8. *Down Beat* (15 July 1949).

9. Miles Davis and Quincy Troupe, *Miles: The Autobiography* (New York: Simon and Schuster, 1989), p. 83.

10. Negro Actors Guild of America, Inc., "Negro Actors Guild Asks for Consistency in Picketing Policy," c. 1947 (Schomburg Center for Research in Black Culture, New York Public Library, NAG, box 1, 1/7).

11. Hall Johnson, Letter to Mabel A. Roane. New York, New York, 6 June 1947 (Schomburg Center for Research in Black Culture, New York Public Library, NAG, box 3, 3/19).

12. John Lester, National Jazz Foundation, Inc., of New Orleans, 30 April 1948 (Louis Armstrong House and Archives, Queens College/CUNY, Scrapbook 10).

13. *Variety* (24 November 1948).

14. Mrs. Paul Robeson, Negro Actors Guild of America, Inc., "The Negro Contribution to Culture," 27 March 1949 (Schomburg Center for Research in Black Culture, New York Public Library, NAG, box 3, 3/24).

15. Arvell Shaw, in *The Louis Armstrong Companion*, p. 167.

16. Arvell Shaw, in *The Louis Armstrong Companion*, p. 167.

17. *New York Times* (21 September 1951), p. 19.

18. *Variety* (3 October 1951).

19. *New York Times* (30 July 1952), p. 20.

20. Ralph Meeker, *Glory Alley* photograph, inscribed to Louis Armstrong (Louis Armstrong House and Archives, Queens College/CUNY, Scrapbook 18).

21. Philip ("Monk") Friedman, *Glory Alley* photograph, inscribed to Louis Armstrong (Louis Armstrong House and Archives, Queens College/CUNY, Scrapbook 18).

22. *Variety* (24 September 1952).

23. *Louis Armstrong and His Concert Group*, All Stars tour program (1957), p. 16.

24. *Louis Armstrong and His Concert Group*, All Stars tour program, p. 17.

25. Louis Armstrong, *Louis Armstrong in His Own Words*, p. 78.

26. Gary Giddins, *Satchmo*, p. 138.

27. *Variety* (6 January 1954).

28. *New York Times* (11 February 1954), p. 33.

29. Gary Giddins, *Satchmo*, p. 140.

30. Louis Armstrong, Letter to Marili Mardon, Springfield, Massachusetts, 27 September 1953 (Louis Armstrong House and Archives, Queens College/CUNY, Letters-3, 112).

31. *Louis Armstrong Plays W. C. Handy* compact disc booklet (Columbia Legacy CK 64925, 1997), p. 5.

32. Louis Armstrong, Interview (May 1968).

33. *Variety* (23 February 1955).

34. *Variety* (18 May 1955).

35. *Variety* (18 May 1955).

36. *Variety* (18 May 1955).

37. *Louis Armstrong and His All Stars: Ambassador Satch* compact disc booklet (Columbia Legacy CK 64926, 2000), p. 7.

38. *Variety* (21 December 1955).

39. *Variety* (21 December 1955).

40. Laurence Bergreen, p. 451.

41. Louis Armstrong, Reminiscence for Hughes and Madeleine Panassie, Corona, Queens, 6 February 1956 (Louis Armstrong House and Archives, Queens College/CUNY, Cassette 8, Reel 18).

42. Louis Armstrong, Reminiscence.

43. Louis Armstrong, Reminiscence.

44. Louis Armstrong, Reminiscence.

45. Louis Armstrong, Reminiscence.

46. Louis Armstrong, Reminiscence.

47. *Variety* (18 July 1956).

48. *Louis Armstrong: The Great Chicago Concert, 1956, Complete* compact disc booklet (Columbia Legacy C2K 65119, 1997), p. 5.

Chapter 5

1. Louis Armstrong, in *The Louis Armstrong Companion*, p. xv.

2. "Louis Armstrong Quips as Bomb Rocks Concert," Los Angeles *Examiner* (20 February 1957).

3. *The Complete Ella Fitzgerald and Louis Armstrong on Verve* compact disc booklet (Verve 314 537 284-2, 1997), p. 15.

4. *Satchmo the Great* compact disc booklet, p. 7.

5. Louis Armstrong, Interview (May 1968).

6. *Variety* (September 1957).

7. *Variety* (September 1957).

8. *New York Times* (1 May 1958), p. 12.

9. Dave Brubeck, Interviewed by Scott Allen Nollen (18 July 2003).

10. *Louis Armstrong: Louis and the Good Book* compact disc booklet (Verve Master Edition 314 549 593-2, 2001), p. 10.

11. Will Friedwald, *Jazz Singing: America's Great Voices from Bessie Smith to Bebop and Beyond* (New York: Da Capo Press, 1996), p. 42.

12. *Variety* (28 May 1958).

13. Krin Gabbard, in *The Louis Armstrong Companion*, p. 221.

14. Mezz Mezzrow, pp. 151, 199.

15. Susan Gordon, Interviewed by Scott Allen Nollen (12 July 2003).

16. Susan Gordon interview.

17. Susan Gordon interview.

18. Susan Gordon interview.

19. Susan Gordon interview.

20. *New York Times* (19 June 1959), p. 30.

21. *Variety* (26 June 1959).

22. *Variety* (26 June 1959).

23. *Variety* (13 May 1959).

24. *Variety* (23 September 1959).

25. *Variety* (23 September 1959).

Chapter 6

1. Dave Brubeck interview.

2. *Variety* (4 January 1960).

3. Iola Brubeck, Interviewed by Scott Allen Nollen (18 July 2003).

4. Dave Brubeck interview.

5. Dave Brubeck interview.

6. Bert Stern interview, 10 August 1999, *A Summer's Day with Bert Stern* (New Yorker Video DVD, 2000).

7. Bert Stern interview.

8. Bert Stern interview.

9. Bert Stern interview.

10. Bert Stern interview.

11. *Variety* (30 August 1960).

12. Bert Stern interview.

13. A. H. Lawrence, p. 356.

14. *New York Times* (8 November 1961), p. 41.

15. *Louis Armstrong and Duke Ellington: The Great Summit/Complete Sessions/DeluxeEdition* compact disc booklet (Roulette Jazz/Blue Note/EMI, 7243 5 24547 2 2/3, 2000), p. 8.

16. Dave Brubeck interview.

17. Iola Brubeck interview.

18. Iola Brubeck interview.

19. Dave Brubeck interview.

20. Dave and Iola Brubeck interviews.

21. Dave Brubeck interview.

22. Dave Brubeck interview.

23. Dave Brubeck interview.

24. Dave Brubeck interview.

25. Iola Brubeck interview.

26. Dave Brubeck interview.

27. Iola Brubeck interview.

28. Iola Brubeck interview.

29. Dave Brubeck interview.

30. Dave Brubeck interview.

31. Iola Brubeck interview.

32. Dave Brubeck interview.

33. Dave Brubeck interview.

34. Dave Brubeck interview.

35. Dave Brubeck interview.

36. Dave Brubeck interview.

37. Dave Brubeck interview.

38. *New York Times* (24 September 1961).

39. *New York Times* (24 September 1961).

40. *Variety* (11 October 1961).

41. *Variety* (11 October 1961).

42. President John F. Kennedy, Letter to Louis Armstrong, the White House, Washington, D.C., 18 June 1963 (Louis Armstrong House and Archives, Queens College/CUNY, Letters-1, 1/33).

43. Gary Giddins, *Satchmo*, p. 142.

44. Jose Ferrer, Letter to Louis Armstrong, 10 March 1964 (Louis Armstrong House and Archives, Queens College/CUNY, Letters-1, 1/14).

Chapter 7

1. Louis Armstrong, Interview (May 1968).

2. Laurence Bergreen, p. 485.

3. Laurence Bergreen, p. 485.

4. *Variety* (5 May 1965).

5. *Variety* (20 October 1965).

6. Louis Armstrong, Letter to Lucille Armstrong, Los Angeles, 24 September 1965 (Louis Armstrong House and Archives, Queens College/CUNY, Letters-3, 112).

7. *Variety* (1 December 1965).

8. *New York Times* (20 January 1966), p. 29.

9. *New York Times* (20 January 1966), p. 29.

10. *A Man Called Adam* pressbook (Embassy Pictures, Inc., 1966), p. 2.

11. *A Man Called Adam* pressbook, p. 3.

12. *A Man Called Adam* pressbook, p. 4.

13. *Jazz: A Film by Ken Burns*, episode 9 (Florentine Films, 2000).

14. *Jazz: A Film by Ken Burns*, episode 9.

15. *Variety* (29 June 1966).

16. *New York Times* (4 August 1966), p. 24.

17. Donald Bogle, p. 214.

18. *New York Times* (21 August 1966).

19. *New York Times* (21 August 1966).

20. *New York Times* (21 August 1966).

21. *New York Times* (21 August 1966).

22. *Variety* (14 September 1966).

23. *Variety* (23 November 1966).

24. *Variety* (1 May 1968).

25. *Variety* (1 May 1968).

26. *Louis Armstrong: What a Wonderful World* compact disc booklet (Decca/GRP Records GRD-656, 1996), pp. 3–4.

27. *Louis Armstrong: What a Wonderful World* compact disc booklet, p. 5.

28. Louis Armstrong, Interview (May 1968).

29. Louis Armstrong, Interview (May 1968).

30. Louis Armstrong, Interview (May 1968).

31. Gary Giddins, *Satchmo*, p. 143.

32. *Variety* (August 1968).

33. Bing Crosby, Letter to Louis Armstrong, 18 December 1968 (Louis Armstrong House and Archives, Queens College/CUNY, Letters-1, 1/9).

34. Laurence Bergreen, p. 490.

35. Joseph Glaser, "Last Will and Testament of Joseph Glaser," 3 June 1968 (Louis Armstrong House and Archives, Queens College/CUNY, Papers-1, 1/11).

36. Mike Douglas Entertainments, Inc., Contract for *The Mike Douglas Show*, with Lucille Armstrong, KYW-TV, Philadelphia, 16 April 1970 (Louis Armstrong House and Archives, Queens College/CUNY, Papers-1, Contracts, 1970, 1/4).

37. Janus Adams, *Freedom Days: 365 Inspired Moments in Civil Rights History*. (New York: John Wiley and Sons, Inc., 1998), p. July 3.

38. Martin Williams, "For Louis Armstrong at 70," *Down Beat* (9 July 1970).

39. Bob Phillips, A.B. Corporation, Letters to Lucille Armstrong, Los Angeles, California, 16 July and 21 September 1970 (Louis Armstrong House and Archives, Queens College/CUNY, Papers-1, 1/5).

40. Oscar Cohen, A.B. Corporation, Letter to Lucille Armstrong, Los Angeles, California, 23 July 1970 (Louis Armstrong House and Archives, Queens College/CUNY, Papers-1, 1/5).

41. Governor Nelson Rockefeller, Letter to Louis Armstrong, 28 July 1970 (Louis Armstrong House and Archives, Queens College/CUNY, Letters-1, 1/54).

42. Frank Rio, A.B. Corporation and Clerow Productions, Inc., Contract for *The Flip Wilson Show*, with Louis Armstrong, NBC-TV, Burbank, 4 August 1970 (Louis Armstrong House and Archives, Queens College/CUNY, Papers-1, Contracts, 1970, 1/5).

43. Oscar Cohen, A.B. Corporation, Letter to Louis Armstrong, Los Angeles, California, 8 September 1970 (Louis Armstrong House and Archives, Queens College/CUNY, Papers-1, 1/5).

44. William Morris Agency, Contract for *The Pearl Bailey Show*, with Louis Armstrong/Associated Booking, Inc., 30 October 1970 (Louis Armstrong House and Archives, Queens College/CUNY, Papers-1, Contracts, 1970, 1/4).

45. Alan C. Bernard, Barnaby Productions, Contract for *The Andy Williams Show*, with Louis Armstrong/Associated Booking, Inc., NBC-TV, Burbank, 6 May 1970 (Louis Armstrong House and Archives, Queens College/CUNY, Papers-1, Contracts, 1970, 1/3).

46. President Richard M. Nixon, Letter to Louis Armstrong, the White House, Washington, D.C., 7 June 1971 (Louis Armstrong House and Archives, Queens College/CUNY, Letters-1, 1/48A).

47. Laurence Bergreen, p. 487.

48. *The Louis Armstrong Companion*, p. 238.

Chapter 8

1. Janus Adams, p. July 3.

2. *Nicholas Payton: Dear Louis* compact disc booklet (Verve 314 549 419-2, 2001), p. 3.

3. Iola Brubeck interview.

4. Dave Brubeck interview.

5. Louis Armstrong, *Louis Armstrong in His Own Words*, pp. 9–11.

Bibliography

Primary Sources

INTERVIEWS

Armstrong, Louis. In *Satchmo the Great* (1957). Interviewed by Edward R. Murrow.

_____. Interviewed by Jack Hirshberg, 20th Century–Fox Film Corporation. Transcription, May 1968. Louis Armstrong House and Archives, Queens College/CUNY, Letters-1, 1/27.

Brubeck, Dave. Interviewed by Scott Allen Nollen, 18 July 2003.

Brubeck, Iola. Interviewed by Scott Allen Nollen, 18 July 2003.

Gordon, Susan. Interviewed by Scott Allen Nollen, 12 July 2003.

Handy, W.C. Interviewed by George Avakian, 1956. *Louis Armstrong Plays W. C. Handy.* Columbia Legacy (CK 64925), 1997.

Hawks, Howard. In Joseph McBride, *Hawks on Hawks.* Berkeley: University of California Press, 1982.

Morrison, Ernest. Interviewed by Scott Allen Nollen, St. Paul, Minnesota, July 1988.

Stern, Bert. New York City, 10 August 1999. *A Summer's Day with Bert Stern.* New Yorker Video DVD, 2000.

AUDIO RECORDINGS MADE BY ARMSTRONG

Armstrong, Louis. Reminiscence for Hughes and Madeleine Panassie. Corona, Queens, 6 February 1956. Louis Armstrong House and Archives, Queens College/CUNY, Cassette 8, Reel 18.

AUTOBIOGRAPHICAL WRITINGS BY ARMSTRONG

Armstrong, Louis. Untitled document, c. 1970. Louis Armstrong House and Archives, Queens College/CUNY.

LETTERS

Armstrong, Louis. Letter to Frances Church. Opelousas, Louisiana, 10 March 1946. Louis Armstrong House and Archives, Queens College/CUNY, Letters.

_____. Letter to Ken Murray. Rock Island, Illinois, 24 May 1950.

_____. Letter to Leonard Feather. Atlanta, Georgia, 18 September 1941. Louis Armstrong House and Archives, Queens College/CUNY, Letters-3, 119.

_____. Letter to Leonard Feather. Atlanta, Georgia, 10 October 1941. Louis Armstrong House and Archives, Queens College/CUNY, Letters-3, 119.

_____. Letter to Leonard Feather. 14 December 1946. Louis Armstrong House and Archives, Queens College/CUNY, Letters-3, 119.

_____. Letter to Lucille Armstrong. Los Angeles, 24 September 1965. Louis Armstrong House and Archives, Queens College/CUNY, Letters-3, 112.

_____. Letter to Madeleine Berard. San Francisco, 25 November 1946. Louis Armstrong House and Archives, Queens College/CUNY, Letters.

_____. Letter to Marili Mardon. Springfield, Massachusetts, 27 September 1953. Louis Armstrong House and Archives, Queens College/CUNY, Letters-3, 112.

_____. Letter to *Melody Maker.* 21 December

1946. Louis Armstrong House and Archives, Queens College/CUNY, Letters-3, 119.

_____. Letter to unknown recipient, undated, regarding Bing Crosby. Louis Armstrong House and Archives, Queens College/CUNY, Letters-3, 118.

Cohen, Oscar, A.B. Corporation. Letter to Louis Armstrong. Los Angeles, California, 8 September 1970. Louis Armstrong House and Archives, Queens College/CUNY, Papers-1, 1/5.

_____. Corporation. Letter to Lucille Armstrong. Los Angeles, California, 23 July 1970. Louis Armstrong House and Archives, Queens College/CUNY, Papers-1, 1/5.

Crosby, Bing. Letter to Louis Armstrong. 18 December 1968. Louis Armstrong House and Archives, Queens College/CUNY, Letters-1, 1/9.

Englebach, Dee, National Broadcasting Corporation. Letter to Lucille Armstrong. Los Angeles, California, 9 December 1952. Louis Armstrong House and Archives, Queens College/CUNY, Papers-2, 2/17.

Ferrer, Jose. Letter to Louis Armstrong. 10 March 1964. Louis Armstrong House and Archives, Queens College/CUNY, Letters-1, 1/14.

Gold, David, A.B. Corporation. Letter to Louis Armstrong. Los Angeles, California, 11 August 1969. Louis Armstrong House and Archives, Queens College/CUNY, Papers-1, Contracts, 1969, 1/2.

Hirshberg, Jack, 20th Century–Fox Film Corporation. Letter to Louis Armstrong. Los Angeles, California, 17 February 1969. Louis Armstrong House and Archives, Queens College/CUNY, Letters-1, 1/27.

Johnson, Hall. Letter to Mabel A. Roane. New York, New York, 6 June 1947. Schomburg Center for Research in Black Culture, New York Public Library, NAG, box 3, 3/19.

Kennedy, President John F. Letter to Louis Armstrong. The White House, Washington, D.C., 18 June 1963. Louis Armstrong House and Archives, Queens College/CUNY, Letters-1, 1/33.

Moseley, Thomas W., Negro Actors Guild of America, Inc. Letter to Frederick O'Neal. New York, New York, 11 October 1962. Minutes, Negro Actors Guild of America, Inc. New York, 7 February 1938. Schomburg Center for Research in Black Culture, New York Public Library, NAG.

Nixon, President Richard M. Letter to Louis Armstrong. The White House, Washington, D.C., 7 June 1971. Louis Armstrong House

and Archives, Queens College/CUNY, Letters-1, 1/48A.

Phillips, Bob, A.B. Corporation. Letter to Lucille Armstrong. Los Angeles, California, 5 May 1970. Louis Armstrong House and Archives, Queens College/CUNY, Papers-1, 1/6.

_____. Corporation. Letter to Lucille Armstrong. Los Angeles, California, 12 May 1970. Louis Armstrong House and Archives, Queens College/CUNY, Papers-1, 1/3.

_____. Corporation. Letter to Lucille Armstrong. Los Angeles, California, 16 July 1970. Louis Armstrong House and Archives, Queens College/CUNY, Papers-1, 1/5.

_____. Corporation. Letter to Lucille Armstrong. Los Angeles, California, 21 September 1970. Louis Armstrong House and Archives, Queens College/CUNY, Papers-1, 1/5.

Robinson, Bill, Negro Actors Guild. Letter to Frank C. Walker, December 1938.

_____. Letter to Johnny Green, 10 November 1948.

Rockefeller, Governor Nelson. Letter to Louis Armstrong. 28 July 1970. Louis Armstrong House and Archives, Queens College/CUNY, Letters-1, 1/54.

Shainin, Shirley, A.B. Corporation. Letter to Lucille Armstrong. Los Angeles, California, 24 June 1970. Louis Armstrong House and Archives, Queens College/CUNY, Papers-1, 1/5.

Von Blaine, Lloyd, Von Blaine Entertainment, Inc. Letter to Louis Armstrong, 24 November 1970. Louis Armstrong House and Archives, Queens College/CUNY, Papers-1, 1/6.

Washington, Fredi. Letter to the members of the Executive Board, Negro Actors Guild of America, Inc., 7 October 1938. Schomburg Center for Research in Black Culture, New York Public Library, NAG, box 3, 3/2.

ORIGINAL DOCUMENTS

A.B. Corporation and Raritan Entertainment, Inc. Contract for _Sun City Scandals_, Johnny Carson Television Special. NBC-TV, Burbank, 3 July 1970. Louis Armstrong House and Archives, Queens College/CUNY, Papers-1, Contracts, 1970, 1/4.

American Federation of Television and Recording Artists. "Standard AFTRA Exclusive Agency Contract," 1 September 1969. Louis Armstrong House and Archives, Queens College/CUNY, Papers-1, Contracts, 1969, 1/2.

_____. "Television Motion Picture Artists'

Manager Contract," 1 September 1969. Louis Armstrong House and Archives, Queens College/CUNY, Papers-1, Contracts, 1969, 1/2.

_____. "Theatrical Motion Picture Artists' Manager Contract," 1 September 1969. Louis Armstrong House and Archives, Queens College/CUNY, Papers-1, Contracts, 1969, 1/2.

Bernard, Alan C., Barnaby Productions. Contract for *The Andy Williams Show*, with Louis Armstrong/Associated Booking, Inc. NBC-TV, Burbank, 6 May 1970, Louis Armstrong House and Archives, Queens College/CUNY, Papers-1, Contracts, 1970, 1/3.

Certificate of Incorporation, Negro Actors Guild of America, Inc. State of New York, City of New York, County of New York, 1 October 1936. Schomburg Center for Research in Black Culture, New York Public Library, NAG, box 1, 1/1.

Circuit Court of Cook County, Illinois. "Petition for Probate of Will and for Letters of Testamentary [of Joseph Glaser]," 14 August 1969. Louis Armstrong House and Archives, Queens College/CUNY, Papers-1, 1/11.

Constitution and By-Laws, Negro Actors Guild of America, Inc. New York, 1936. Schomburg Center for Research in Black Culture, New York Public Library, NAG, box 1, 1/2.

Davis, Bette. Certificate of Appreciation, Hollywood Canteen, to Louis Armstrong. Louis Armstrong House and Archives, Queens College/CUNY, Scrapbook 10.

Executive Board Minutes, Negro Actors Guild of America, Inc. New York, 6 May 1938. Schomburg Center for Research in Black Culture, New York Public Library, NAG, box 3, 3/2.

Glaser, Joseph. "Last Will and Testament of Joseph Glaser," 3 June 1968. Louis Armstrong House and Archives, Queens College/CUNY, PAPERS-1, 1/11.

Hope, Bob. Certificate of Appreciation, American Theatre Wing of the Stage Door Canteen of Cleveland. Louis Armstrong House and Archives, Queens College/CUNY, Scrapbook 10.

Midas Muffler Shops. Contract for Television and Radio Commercials, with Louis Armstrong. 5 November 1969. Louis Armstrong House and Archives, Queens College/CUNY, Papers-1, Contracts, 1969, 1/2.

Mike Douglas Entertainments, Inc. Contract for *The Mike Douglas Show*, with Lucille Armstrong. KYW-TV, Philadelphia, 16 April 1970. Louis Armstrong House and Archives,

Queens College/CUNY, Papers-1, Contracts, 1970, 1/4.

Minutes, Negro Actors Guild of America, Inc. New York, 27 September 1936. Schomburg Center for Research in Black Culture, New York Public Library, NAG, box 3, 3/1.

_____. New York, 4 December 1937. Schomburg Center for Research in Black Culture, New York Public Library, NAG, box 3, 3/1.

_____. New York, 7 February 1938. Schomburg Center for Research in Black Culture, New York Public Library, NAG, box 3, 3/2.

_____. New York, 10 June 1952. Schomburg Center for Research in Black Culture, New York Public Library, NAG.

_____, Executive Board. New York, 7 November 1962. Schomburg Center for Research in Black Culture, New York Public Library, NAG.

Negro Actors Guild of America, Inc. "Negro Actors Guild Asks for Consistency in Picketing Policy," circa 1947. Schomburg Center for Research in Black Culture, New York Public Library, NAG, box 1, 1/7.

Rio, Frank, A.B. Corporation and Clerow Productions, Inc. Contract for *The Flip Wilson Show*, with Louis Armstrong. NBC-TV, Burbank, 4 August 1970. Louis Armstrong House and Archives, Queens College/CUNY, Papers-1, Contracts, 1970, 1/5.

Robeson, Mrs. Paul, Negro Actors Guild of America, Inc. "The Negro Contribution to Culture," 27 March 1949. Schomburg Center for Research in Black Culture, New York Public Library, NAG, box 3, 3/24.

William Morris Agency. Contract for *The Pearl Bailey Show*, with Louis Armstrong/Associated Booking, Inc. 30 October 1970. Louis Armstrong House and Archives, Queens College/CUNY, Papers-1, Contracts, 1970, 1/4.

ORIGINAL SCRIPTS

All Star Revue—"Tallulah." NBC, 20 December 1952. Louis Armstrong House and Archives, Queens College/CUNY, Papers-2, 2/17.

"Christmas Cavalcade for Children of the World, 1970." International Paper/CBS/UNICEF, 22 December 1970. Louis Armstrong House and Archives, Queens College/CUNY, Papers-1, 1/5.

PRESS RELEASES

Lester, John. National Jazz Foundation, Inc., of New Orleans, 30 April 1948. Louis Armstrong

House and Archives, Queens College/CUNY, Scrapbook 10.

"'Walkin the Line' with Louie." ABC-TV, November 1970. Louis Armstrong House and Archives, Queens College/CUNY, Papers-1, 1/6.

PRESSBOOKS

The Beat Generation. Metro-Goldwyn-Mayer Pictures/Loew's Incorporated, 1959.

Doctor Rhythm. Paramount Pictures Corporation, 1938.

A Man Called Adam. Embassy Pictures, Inc., 1966.

TOUR PROGRAMS

Louis Armstrong and His Concert Group. All Stars Tour, 1957.

PHOTOGRAPHS

Armstrong, Louis. *Cabin in the Sky.* Inscribed to Lucille Armstrong. Louis Armstrong House and Archives, Queens College/CUNY, Photo-2 No. 29 818.

Friedman, Philip ("Monk"). *Glory Alley.* Inscribed to Louis Armstrong. Louis Armstrong House and Archives, Queens College/CUNY, Scrapbook 18.

Meeker, Ralph. *Glory Alley.* Inscribed to Louis Armstrong. Louis Armstrong House and Archives, Queens College/CUNY, Scrapbook 18.

Middleton, Velma. Inscribed to Louis Armstrong. Louis Armstrong House and Archives, Queens College/CUNY, Photo-4, Box 12, 12/15.

NEWSPAPERS, TRADE PAPERS, PERIODICALS AND NEWSLETTERS

Down Beat, December 1939, 7 April 1948, 15 July 1949.

"Louis Armstrong Quips as Bomb Rocks Concert," Los Angeles *Examiner*, 20 February 1957.

Metronome, March 1948.

Murray, Ken. "Louis, Bix Had Most Influence on Der Bingle," *Down Beat*, 14 July 1950.

Negro Actors Guild of America, Inc. Newsletter. Volume 1, Number 1, May 1940; No. 32, March 1958; No. 35, March 1959; July-August 1971. Schomburg Center for Research in

Black Culture, New York Public Library, NAG.

New York Times, 1938–1969.

Ostwald, David H. "Louis Armstrong, Civil Rights Pioneer," *New York Times*, 3 August 1991.

Variety, 1931–1969.

PUBLISHED AUTOBIOGRAPHIES AND MEMOIRS

Armstrong, Louis. *In His Own Words.* New York: Oxford University Press, 1999.

_____. *Satchmo: My Life in New Orleans.* New York: Da Capo Press, 1986.

_____ *Swing That Music.* New York: Da Capo Press, 1993.

Davis, Miles, and Quincy Troupe. *Miles: The Autobiography.* New York: Simon and Schuster, 1989.

Ellington, Duke. *Music Is My Mistress.* New York: Da Capo Press, 1973.

Holiday, Billie, and William Dufty. *Lady Sings the Blues.* New York: Doubleday and Company, 1956.

King, B.B., with David Ritz. *Blues All Around Me: The Autobiography of B.B. King.* New York: Avon Books, 1996.

Mezzrow, Mezz, and Bernard Wolfe. *Really the Blues.* New York: Kensington Publishing Corporation, 2001.

Waters, Ethel, with Charles Samuels. *His Eye Is on the Sparrow, An Autobiography.* New York: Doubleday and Company, 1951.

DOCUMENTARY AND PERFORMANCE FILMS

At the Jazz Band Ball: Early Hot Jazz, Song and Dance. Shanachie Entertainment Corporation, 2000.

Benny Goodman: Adventures in the Kingdom of Swing. Columbia Music Video, 2000.

Ella Fitzgerald: Something to Live For. Winstar TV and Video, 1999.

Jazz: A Film by Ken Burns. Florentine Films, 2000.

Mahalia Jackson: The Power and the Glory. Xenon Pictures, 2002.

Satchmo: Louis Armstrong ("Masters of American Music Series"). Toby Byron/Multiprises— Image Entertainment Laserdisc, 1986.

Satchmo the Great. Produced by Fred W. Friendly; hosted by Edward R. Murrow, 1957. Louis Armstrong House and Archives, Queens College/CUNY.

The Wonderful World of Louis Armstrong. Winstar Video, 1999.

Secondary Sources

Books about Louis Armstrong

Bergreen, Laurence. *Louis Armstrong: An Extravagant Life.* New York: Doubleday Dell Publishing Corporation, 1997.

Berrett, Joshua, ed. *The Louis Armstrong Companion.* New York: Schirmer Books, 1999.

Giddins, Gary. *Satchmo: The Genius of Louis Armstrong.* New York: Da Capo Press, 2001.

Stratemann, Dr. Klaus. *Louis Armstrong on the Screen.* Copenhagen: Jazz Media Aps.

Conferences about Louis Armstrong

Cogswell, Michael, and Brent Edwards, Gary Giddins and Robert O'Meally. "Louis Armstrong and Jazz Biography," part three of "Writing Lives: The Past and Future of Biography." New York: Center for the Humanities, the City University of New York, 10 April 2003.

Biographies

Dickerson, James L. *Just for a Thrill: Lil Hardin Armstrong, First Lady of Jazz.* New York: Cooper Square Press, 2002.

Giddins, Gary. *Bing Crosby: A Pocketful of Dreams: The Early Years, 1903–1940.* New York: Little, Brown and Company, 2001.

Lawrence, A.H. *Duke Ellington and His World.* New York: Routledge, 2001.

Nicholson, Stuart. *Billie Holiday.* Boston: Northeastern University Press, 1995.

Books about Jazz

Blesh, Rudi. *Shining Trumpets: A History of Jazz.* New York: DaCapo Press, 1988.

Friedwald, Will. *Jazz Singing: America's Great Voices from Bessie Smith to Bebop and Beyond.* New York: Da Capo Press, 1996.

Books about African American History

Adams, Janus. *Freedom Days: 365 Inspired Moments in Civil Rights History.* New York: John Wiley and Sons, 1998.

Franklin, John Hope, and Alfred A. Moss, Jr. *From Slavery to Freedom: A History of Negro Americans.* New York: Alfred A. Knopf, 1988.

Books about African Americans in the Cinema

Bogle, Donald. *Toms, Coons, Mulattoes, Mammies and Bucks: An Interpretive History of Blacks in American Films*, Fourth Edition. New York: Continuum International Publishing Group, 2001.

Books about the American Cinema

Mast, Gerald. *Howard Hawks: Storyteller.* New York: Oxford University Press, 1982.

Nollen, Scott Allen. *The Cinema of Sinatra: The Actor, on Screen and in Song.* Baltimore: Luminary Press, 2003.

Compact Disc Liner Notes

Bessie Smith: The Complete Recordings, Volume 2. Columbia Legacy (C2K 47471), 1991.

Cabin in the Sky. Rhino Movie Music/Turner Entertainment Company (R272245), 1996.

The Complete Ella Fitzgerald and Louis Armstrong on Verve. Verve (314 537 284-2), 1997.

Esquire All-American Jazz Concert. Jazz Archives (158262), 1994.

Louis Armstrong: I've Got the World on a String and Louis Under the Stars. Verve Master Edition (314 599 831-2), 1999.

Louis Armstrong: Louis and the Angels. Verve Master Edition (314 549 592-2), 2001.

Louis Armstrong: Louis and the Good Book. Verve Master Edition (314 549 593-2), 2001.

Louis Armstrong: Mr. President. Milan/BMG (35986-2), 2002.

Louis Armstrong: Portrait of the Artist as a Young Man, 1923–1934. Columbia Legacy (C4K 85670), 1994.

Louis Armstrong: Satchmo, A Musical Autobiography. Verve (314 543 822-2), 2001.

Louis Armstrong: Satchmo Serenades. Verve by Request (314 543 792-2), 2000.

Louis Armstrong: The California Concerts. Decca Jazz (GRD-4-613), 1992.

Louis Armstrong: The Complete Decca Studio Master Takes, 1935–1939. Definitive Records (DRCD11171), 2000.

Louis Armstrong: The Complete Hot Five and Hot Seven Recordings. Columbia Legacy (C4K 63527), 2000.

Louis Armstrong: The Complete RCA Victor Recordings. BMG Classics (09026-68682-2), 1997.

Louis Armstrong: The Great Chicago Concert, 1956, Complete. Columbia Legacy (C2K 65119), 1997.

Louis Armstrong — Volume 5: Louis in New York. Columbia Legacy (CK 46148), 1991.

Louis Armstrong — Volume 6: St. Louis Blues. Columbia Legacy (CK 46996), 1991.

Louis Armstrong — Volume 7: You're Drivin' Me Crazy. Columbia Legacy (CK 48828), 1993.

Louis Armstrong: What a Wonderful World. Decca/GRP Records (GRD-656), 1996.

Louis Armstrong and Duke Ellington: The Great Summit/Complete Sessions/Deluxe Edition. Roulette Jazz/Blue Note/EMI (7243 5 24547 2 2/3), 2000.

Louis Armstrong and His All Stars: Ambassador Satch. Columbia Legacy (CK 64926), 2000.

Louis Armstrong and His All Stars: Live at the Winter Garden, New York, and Blue Note, Chicago. Storyville (STCD 8242), 1995.

Louis Armstrong and His Band, Dave Brubeck, Lambert, Hendricks and Ross, and Carmen McRae: The Real Ambassadors. Columbia (CK 65119), 1994.

Louis Armstrong and His Friends. Bluebird First Editions (09026-63961-2), 2002.

Louis Armstrong Meets Oscar Peterson. Verve Master Edition (314 539 060-2), 1997.

Louis Armstrong Plays W. C. Handy. Columbia Legacy (CK 64925), 1997.

Louis Armstrong, with Gordon Jenkins: Satchmo in Style. Verve Master Edition (314 549 594-2), 2001.

Nicholas Payton: Dear Louis. Verve (314 549 419-2), 2001.

Satch Plays Fats: A Tribute to the Immortal Fats Waller by Louis Armstrong and His All Stars. Columbia Legacy (CK 64927), 2000.

Satchmo the Great. Columbia Legacy (CK 62170), 2000.

Index

Numbers in **bold** indicate photographs